MYTHS
OF BRITAIN

MYTHS
OF BRITAIN

Peter Wright,
20, Northgate,
Oakham   LE15 6QS.
Tel :   56153

MICHAEL SENIOR

Orbis Publishing, London

This edition first published 1979 by
Orbis Publishing Limited,
20-22 Bedfordbury,
London, WC2

Produced by Guild Publishing,
the Original Publications Department of
Book Club Associates

ISBN 0 85613 244 6

Designed by Pat Ariss
Picture research by Faith Perkins

Set in Bembo by Rowland Phototypesetting Limited,
Bury St. Edmunds, Suffolk, and printed by
Lowe & Brydone Printers Limited, Thetford, Norfolk.

Illustration on reverse of frontispiece: The crowning of Arthur
from a fourteenth-century manuscript 'La douce histoire de Merlin'
Frontispiece: Glastonbury Tor rising through the mist on the Somerset moors

Contents

To the memory of
my godfather

Colin Odling

I ask that every reader who reads this book will be indulgent with me who have dared, after so many others, to write these things like a chattering bird or a weak witness. I yield to him who knows more of these matters than I do.

Nennius, *c.* AD 800

Author's note

This is a broad review of the traditional material of Britain. Since it is a book for the interested layman, rather than for the specialist scholar, it does not intend to bring to bear on the matter anything describable as an academic approach. There are many areas within this wide subject where even the most distinguished scholars disagree. One would have liked to recognize the contending cases more explicitly, but that would have brought with it the need for an apparatus of references and footnotes which would have made this a different sort of book. Such features as the alternative spellings arising from medieval sources, and modern disagreement about many dates, could have been referred to by such means, but cannot be adequately dealt with in a book such as this. It must be said, then, that there will be points in these pages which some schools of thought would dispute, and areas where I may appear bolder in my assertions than some specialists would care to be. Within the scope of a non-academic work I have not always been able to justify in full the conclusions I have adopted. In spite of this I have always been careful to assure myself that they represent at least an academically tenable standpoint; moreover, in this minefield of scholarly controversy, I have tried wherever possible to identify the current consensus.

There exists, for instance, a long-standing debate among the experts as to whether some of this material should be classified as folk-tale or as myth. From the fact that I have not been able to discuss in any detail the arguments for either side, it should not be assumed that I have lightly or arbitrarily come down on the side of myth. Both approaches to the subject provide valuable insights, and it would be wrong, I think, to regard either as excluding the other. I have the greatest respect for the work of Professor Kenneth Jackson, who has, among much else, identified the elements which stem from the international popular tale in some of the stories dealt with in this book. It would be absurd to disagree with so eminent a scholar, and of course Professor Jackson's argument is right as far as it goes. To demonstrate that something has elements of international traditional tale in it is not, however, to show that it has no elements of myth. There are also eminent scholars who prefer to stress this other aspect, the more mythic features of the tales, and if this book tends somewhat towards their side, it is because I feel that the emphasis given by Professor Jackson and his colleagues to our traditional material's background of popular tale might obscure a possible view of the matter which is both exciting and important. In dealing with the subject of the myths of Britain at all, indeed in identifying it as a subject, this book sets out among other things to clarify that view.

M.S. March 1979.

1 Britain and its myths

I suppose we all like rigid categories. The habit of clinging to the bars of the play-pen dies hard and once out of it we surround ourselves as far as we can with a neatly structured world. One of the qualities of myth is that it is not that sort of thing. It deals with marginal areas, and their numinous character is probably connected with our inability to get a proper hold over their nature. Not only is myth not like that, but life is not quite like that either. It may not always be the case that a thing is either this or that, or than an event either did or did not occur; the correct answer to a question is sometimes – more often than is convenient, perhaps – both yes and no.

This is a book about the genesis of a country as seen through the medium of its mythology; and countries, like people, have their distortions of memory – the long fine summers which for some reason we no longer get – and their scars of the traumas of first encounters with harder facts. A mythology is a record in that sense, a record of subjective response to surrounding circumstances, not a matter of factual or exclusively external happenings. It is, as it were, the dream which the psychoanalyst has to try to disentangle, and which the individual might well be content to leave as simply a dream. Dreams indeed have their own intrinsic beauty, but not a little of their value lies in their power to express by implication and allusion the worries, interests, and aspirations of the dreamer; and in some cases the suppressed fears, shocks, and unpleasant experiences. Through them one can sometimes uncover a process in action, a process of coming to grips with unalterable realities, the assimilation of undesired facts.

Every mythology bears the marks of its coming into being and these in their turn reflect the nature of the place in which that occurred. 'Britannia insula in extremo ferme orbis limite circium occidentemque' ('The island of Britain lies almost at the edge of the world, towards the west'), writes one of our primary sources. 'It is irrigated by many clear springs, with their full waters moving snow-white gravel, and by shining rivers flowing with a soft murmur, offering to those reclining on their banks the promise of sweet sleep, and by lakes overflowing with a cool stream of living water.' Britain's insularity, and its striking and yet pleasing natural beauty, have given to its mythology a distinct and vigorous spirit of independence which, for all its European and indeed universal ancestry and its later Continental influences, marks it off as belonging, in attitude

The neolithic Penrhos-Feilw standing stones in Anglesey

and temper and intention, to this particular country.

Nothing evokes the flavour of a country as effectively as its traditional material. Read the Icelandic sagas and you cannot help smelling the sheep-grazed grass at the edges of the melting snow and the resinous wooden homesteads on the shores of cold bays. The Eddas call up stony plateaux above wolf-packed pine forests; and elsewhere Lady Gregory's Lugh rides with the Riders of the Sidhe through a land pungent with the incense of turf fires. Since the people who gave rise to the myths of Britain were not a consistent whole, the firm texture of Britishness which runs through these myths must partly be due to the effect which the land has had on the outlook of the people who have come to be there. Britain's landscape is complex and varied, but it has several overall characteristics. In particular it is not savage, and its generally temperate nature has allowed a sort of equal partnership to develop between the terrain and the inhabitants, each of them affecting the other but neither party entirely dominating. As a result, the people seem to have a strong sense of identity and of place, which is reflected in their myths.

It is of course almost impossible to disentangle a country's mythology from other elements in its make-up, and in particular a nations's early history is so closely related to its mythology that the two might be taken to be different versions of the same thing. Certainly mythology is to some extent a way of expressing a memory, a pre-written record which has become consolidated and distorted by the process of its transmission; and because one of the things mythology does is express in crystallized, symbolic, and subjective form the various stages of a country's birth, it has a valuable function in any attempt to understand the nature and identity of the country – in this case, of Britain and its population.

I have no intention of attempting to give a firm definition of myth, but one of my assumptions is that this element of proto-history is a main factor in the making of mythology. Myth, as I understand it, stems partly from this proto-historical direction and partly from the direction of religion. I hope that the scope of this book will demonstrate what I consider should be regarded as myth and what should not, and that the book itself will prove to be a sort of definition. But it may help to avoid puzzlement about the reasons for certain omissions and inclusions if I outline here the sort of features characteristic of these two contributory streams of myth – the streams from proto-history and from religion.

The aspect of myth which stems from history is not historical in the sense of being a chronological record of events. Myth sees in terms of apparently single and identifiable events things which may have taken a long and often indefinable period to occur. The opening of the book of Genesis is such a transformation; the many millions of years of the earth's development are described in what can only with extreme understatement be called summary form. This is in no way to suggest that such accounts should be rejected as simply fictional or false. They are symbolically or emblematically true. In one British myth the Roman occupation occurs as a single episode, whereas it was of course a long-drawn-out process. To criticize the story as historically incorrect would be to misunderstand its purpose. Its validity is as a symbolic representation.

Another feature of the element of proto-history in myth is very similar in effect. Events of a type which may have happened again and again in different places over a long period are told of, in story form, as having happened once. All the high-kings of Argos in the five hundred years of its dominance may perhaps be summarized as Agamemnon – 'Once upon a time there was a king.' When the story relates how Agamemnon finds it necessary to placate his brother Menelaus, this episode may be a way of recording that it was often necessary for the ruler of Argos to keep a diplomatic eye on his relationship with his powerful neighbour at Sparta. Similarly, the memories of many floods in parts of Europe and the Middle East become represented by the idea of one great flood.

The religious strand in the origin of myth has, I think, several elements too. Philosophical might be a better term than religious, except that in many cases mythology does draw elements of its development from real religious systems, from sets of organized and structured beliefs and bodies of thought of an explicitly hieratic nature. Where one stops and the other starts is something which must, in the nature of things, remain undecided. Overlap and ambiguity are very much a part of the character of the subject. This religious strand, however, operates in much the same manner as the other: it sets out to construct a sort of mythic socio-psychological approach to things which, again, in some sense happened. But these are not happenings in chronology; they are not the type of things which happen historically, whether once or many times, but rather, being built into the structure of human life, they happen always and inevitably, like birth and death.

The universal, unavoidable, and constantly repeated have always been seen, ironically, as problematic – an older generation feeling its position of authority threatened by the new generation; the tendency for a wife whose husband has become more interested in his job than in her to look for a younger lover; the certain knowledge of eventual death; the continuity of the cycles and the species and the stars. Myth sets itself the daunting task of making sense of it all. Thus we find kings who try to destroy the sons who are destined (says the prophecy) to kill them; queens who elope when the institution of marriage reveals its basic weakness; heroes who struggle, uselessly, to avoid a foretold death; and again and again a conflict between a rising hero and an older power.

These are not in themselves obviously philosophical or supernatural matters, but myth's approach to them is not a scientific one. It does not (as it might have) try to reason away their problematic nature, but rather crystallizes them in their full problem state for ever. Myth presents such fundamental human perplexities as single extraordinary facts, to be awed by, to be observed with wonder and accepted, giving them a strange element of recognition and familiarity. It is as if we are asked to look for a time at a piece of white quartz – a hard and yet surprising piece of reality, in relation to which there is no question of making an attempt to

Part of the great stone circle at Castlerigg in Cumbria

understand. The approach is rather a desire to place things, to identify them, to put them in suitably superior relationship to more trivial experiences.

There is, however, occasionally a more overtly speculative and explanation seeking side to this strand of myth. From the feeling that the very limitation of sense-experience itself indicates the existence of something not sensed, not available to our limited first-hand knowledge, arises the assumption that because this world is known there must be another world which is not, and that this other world must provide the answer to several so-far unanswered questions. The logic of the reasoning is less sound than it might be, but one sees the point. If this is the world of sense-experience, where is the other? If this is – as it undeniably is – mortality, then what is its contrast? Does not our mortality, by its reality, imply a post-mortal future, or a non-mortal present? This, clearly, is the property of religion, not of philosophy or science; myth inherits it from that source, and then puts it to its own uses.

By comparison with other more famous mythologies, British mythology is relatively new. Our civilization was late in arriving, in terms of such great world civilizations as those of the Middle East and of India. We would therefore expect our mythology to reflect this relative youth, and indeed it does. By comparison with Judaic, Mesopotamian, Hindu, and Greek mythology it shows a difference of emphasis and influence. In particular the events and social changes which contributed to its make-up are more recent and therefore of a different type. British mythology is not dealing with the movements of nomadic tribes so much as with those of armies; marks have been left not so much by the coming of new gods as of new political power. For this reason too the historical and socio-logical elements in British myth are more evident than the philosophical, the speculative, and the explanatory. In such a young mythology, myth and history actually operate at times as contemporaries, as if Herodotus and Homer had written, each in his own field, of the same material at the same period. It is remarkable that myth can compete with such powerful rivals as history and science. That it did so is, I think, due to one of its main functions and characteristics.

Whenever a new country comes into existence, regardless of its period in world history, it must experience traumas. Shocks to the susceptible spirit of national identity in its formative years have to be assimilated and made acceptable to the national consciousness. That is something that myth is useful in doing. There is no doubt, for instance, that the coming into existence of the United States of America, though it took place after the beginning of the industrial age, has given rise to what can only be described as a mythology.

In Britain the cultural traumas which had to be dealt with were quite clear-cut, the result mainly of invasions and the need to adjust to them. Since these will be considered in detail later, there is no need to specify them now, but it must be said here that the tendency to see the process exclusively from the point of view of the Celtic peoples, as the rightful and original inhabitants of the British Isles, is to overlook the fact that they themselves were invaders, displacing a previous population every bit as arbitrarily as did the Anglo-Saxons. However, the Celts have the advantage that a lot is known about them. They left the mark of their period of domination on Britain, and although since 1066 Britain's culture has been thoroughly pluralistic it still undoubtedly contains a strong Celtic component. If we wish to know anything at all about the Neolithic inhabitants of this island, other than the shapes of their skulls, their funerary rites, and religious building styles, it should be in mytho-logy that the knowledge is stored. Although unfortunately it is not possible to isolate any clearly pre-Celtic elements, there are clues that some sort of superimposition did take place.

'Celtic' is actually a rather confusing word to employ; 'Gaulish', 'Gaelic', or 'British' are less misleading terms. Celtic does not signify a people, a nation, a race, a geographical distribution, or any sort of ethnic group. Strictly speaking it refers to a group of languages, and the people who spoke those languages probably varied in appearance considerably, and certainly in some cases closely resembled people who did not speak them. If Celtic is not a particularly accurate term, the 'Celts', with its implications of homogenity and self-identification, is even more mis-leading. Caesar records that the Gauls in France did call themselves

13

Celts – 'ipsorum lingua Celtae, nostri Galli appelantur' ('called Celts in their own language, Gauls in ours') – but there is no implication either there or in any of the early writings that the Britons in Britain were called the same. It was not until the eighteenth century, in fact, that it came to be assumed that the ancient Britons were also Celts, and only at that late stage that they came to be known by that term. Because of these unsound premises it came to be considered correct academically to use Celtic only as a linguistic term. Archaeology and a better understanding of the historical sources have largely reversed this trend, so that 'Celtic' now acceptably describes a group of peoples who shared several character-istics as well as language, and even the remote posterity of the identifiable influence of that group.

It was not, to make things worse, a matter of a single language, but, by the period at which anything factual can be said about it, a group of several related ones. However, along with the people who came to speak these languages and who eventually spread out over much of Europe and Asia Minor, there emerged a recognizable and distinctive material culture. Through archaeology an art form was discovered with a clear and distinct identity in the decorating of utensils and weapons, and the identifying features of this style remain common to the nations which later spoke the various Celtic languages. In this archaeological cultural sense, it is correct and meaningful to use the terms Celtic and Celts; and since mythology is another element of this culture, these terms will continue to be used here, bearing in mind the qualifications mentioned.

There are signs, then, that there was an original Celtic-language speaking group; indeed there are similar signs that there was, before that, a basic Indo-European speaking one – though its existence must remain hypothetical and could not have occurred later than about 4000 BC. Luckily the relationships and subdivisions of the various branches which stem from this hypothetical language do not concern us here, and it will be sufficient to say that one of those branches is the common source of the Celtic group.

Groups of these Celtic-speaking, Celtic-cultured people eventually came to Britain. They came in more than one wave, and from more than one part of continental Europe. They came from northern France in the eighth century BC, bringing with them organized agriculture and the use of bronze. They came a few hundred years later, now with iron tools and weapons and in larger numbers, showing to the modern digger the tell-tale signs of their distant origin, north of the Alps, at the upper ends of the rivers Rhine and Danube. This was perhaps the main invasion, and spread throughout central Britain during the next two hundred years. By about 250 BC another wave of immigrants was on its way, this time apparently from the Rhine Valley via central France. They spread and eventually superimposed their slightly different Celtic culture on the areas already occupied. One more wave, at least, arrived before the Romans, the clearly identified people known as the Belgae, who came from the area which is now central France, people of the same name and

Antonine Wall

GODODDIN

BERNICIA
NORTHUMBRIA

•Bamburgh

RHEGED

Hadrian's Wall

•Carlisle

DEIRA

Catraeth (Catterick) ×

Deganwy

ANGLESEY

ontium (Caernarfon) • _Snowdon_
GWYNEDD
Caer Aranrhod •
•Dinas Bran
•Dinas Emrys
•Harlech

CANTREF
GWAELOD

POWYS

Offa's Dyke

R. Severn

DYFED
Preseli Hills
Maridunum
•(Carmarthen)

Isca (Caerleon) •

× Dyrham

KINGDOM
OF KENT

•Glastonbury   o_Stonehenge_
•Cadbury   •Winchester

WESSEX

Tintagel •
R. Camel
DUMNONIA

•Castle Dore

YONESSE

Pre Saxon-Invasion   Harlech RHEGED
Post Saxon-Invasion Winchester D E I R A

Land over 300ft

0   50 miles

A Pictish symbol stone in Aberlemno churchyard, Tayside, showing mounted and foot warriors in action

nation as one of those against whom Caesar later directed his campaign. It was because he found that Britain was supplying reinforcements and support, from out of his reach, to the Gauls whom he was trying to control, that the Romans took an interest in annexing this island to their empire. What is significant about all these invasions, however, is that Britain was to a very great extent a part of the central stream of European civilization. It was not until long afterwards that it began to develop separately, as an independent island with a mind and habit of its own.

For several reasons, of which this is one, it could be argued that there is no such thing as British mythology. The form of this argument is determined by which of the last two words is stressed. There is no such thing as *British* mythology, because the mythology of the island of Britain is originally Continental Celtic, later modified not just by insular but also extensively by other Continental influences. On the other hand there is no such thing as British *mythology* because the idea of Britain and its distinction from Europe came into being much too late for the traditional material to rank as true mythology, rather than as folk-culture, legend, or lore. One school of thought, while admitting that there was at one time a Celtic mythology, sees the fragments of it which found their way into British stories as being used simply for narrative and entertainment purposes by story-tellers exclusively concerned with popular tales. Others, however, while not denying the fragmented and imperfect state of the mythic residue, treat the matter as one of literary archaeology, in which by the process of disinterring and piecing together we can see what the material once looked like.

While appreciating the reasoning of both these views, I feel that their approach to the subject is too restricted. A body of material does not have to be very ancient to be mythology. It simply has to stand in a certain recognizable relationship to a national culture and a stage of national development.

Because of the way it came into being Britain has a body of traditional matter which spans a long transition. In it we see the reflection of the changes in its cultural circumstances, in its attitude and values. One process which we shall see taking place is the overlaying of one set of elements by another. More immediately significant in its effects is the historical accident that the residue of the earliest of the national attitudes became forced, rather literally, into a corner. To be precise, it survived in Wales and from there in due course it re-emerged, to form, eventually, a new and expanded version of its original self, when circumstances in the altered world had become sufficiently stable.

The fact that it was Wales in which the material survived and mainly the West Country where it re-emerged, should not mislead us into thinking that the material belongs peculiarly to Wales. Wales is only a retrospective term, and at the time at which the ideas and traditions were first formulated Britain south of the Antonine wall was a single land. The narrow waist caused by the firths of Clyde and Forth formed the boundary to what was technically Britain. North of that were the

Caledonians, known to the Romans as Picti, and hence to us as the Picts. The Scots crossed from Ireland during Roman times and had occupied large parts of Caledonia by the end of the fifth century; by the ninth the Picts had become absorbed by them and Caledonia became Scotland. The rest of the island was Britain.

The reason, then, for the almost complete absence of Scotland north of the Antonine wall from the British material is that it was inhabited and later colonized by different people. So little is known of the Picts that even their name is a nickname – 'Picti' or painted people; their language is still something of a puzzle, and what we can tell from their buildings and artefacts does not much help us to know where they came from or what they were like. Their obscurity is caused by their early disappearance under the waves of invading Scots, and it is to these that historical Scotland belongs. Because they came from Ireland their mythology is not British but Irish, and although the two have very close similarities, often indicating some period of common identity, they had, by the time that Britain's mythology becomes recognizable, separated considerably.

Britain must therefore be distinguished from Scotland and equated with all the rest of this island, on historical grounds. The name comes from that of one of the groups of invading Celtic peoples (probably among the main wave of Iron Age arrivals), the Pretani, or Pritani. To the Greeks the place was known as Albion, apparently an adaptation of a Celtic or pre-Celtic name, and it was not until the fourth century BC that the islands in general came to be called Pretanic islands. In Latin this became Britanni and Britannia, and in the native language Prydain, which is still the Welsh for Britain.

The remnants of the material from this period survived in Wales largely in oral form, and emerged from there as literature at a fairly late date. With an accumulation of material over a long period, like this, there develops a familiar pattern of periodic reappraisal, either by a group of people doing much the same thing at the same time or by an enterprising individual. It is inevitably from these sources that we get our material, the form in which it comes to us being greatly influenced by whoever it was who put it together. In the case of the primary compilers we see their work only through the transcriptions of medieval copyists, who added their own errors and occasional interpretations. Our earliest surviving manuscripts, however, are not necessarily the earliest traceable dates of the material, since very often they show clear signs of having been copied from older works, and a tentative date can often be assigned to those. For instance, though a lot of important items of early history and tradition are all collected in a document written in about 1100, we can identify the sources from which this was copied as having themselves been composed at various dates back to the seventh century. Some of the crucial historic

Opposite above: A chamber tomb at Maen-y-bardd, above the Conwy valley
Opposite below: The view from the summit of Dinas Emrys over the Gwynant valley. Here Merlin is said to have first come into being

Opposite: The eye of the White Horse at Uffington
Above: A manuscript illustration of Bede at his writing desk

poetry only exists in thirteenth-century versions, but seems to have been first written down at least as early as the ninth, and we can feel reasonably confident that some of it would have been created as oral art at the time to which its contents refer, the late sixth century.

The Welsh work known as the Mabinogion is found in its first complete form in the late-fourteenth- or early-fifteenth-century collection known as the Red Book of Hergest, but since bits of it appear in two books dating back to nearer 1300, and small fragments even appear a century before that, we can assume a much earlier original source. The Triads, similarly, though they have been collected and interfered with at much later dates, appear in some cases to record genuinely ancient British matter. Source-dating is a technical and rather controversial matter, but some things are fairly certain. The earliest documentary history comes from a British cleric called Gildas, who lived and wrote during the mid-sixth century – though again we have his work in manuscripts of the eleventh century and after. He is of limited use to us in our knowledge of the period, because of the restricted aim and interests of his book. The first of the succession of collectors was a Welsh priest called Nennius, who put together, in about the year 800, all the traditional matter available to him. In so doing he preserved for us both myth and history, and indeed seemed quite unable, himself, to distinguish between the two. Because he did not actually write the bulk of his collection himself, but copied it from unknown and various sources, we cannot precisely date all his material; we should particularly like to because his may be the first mention of Arthur. It seems possible that Nennius drew from works which may have actually been written down as early as the seventh century, which brings them close to the events to which they refer.

There is no doubt, from the point of view of mythology, that the greatest and most important of the periodic reappraisals of the material was that made by Geoffrey of Monmouth, who wrote his 'History of the Kings of Britain' in or near to 1136. He drew from Gildas, Nennius, and Bede, from many other sources both written and remembered, and also very greatly from his own imagination, or that of some unidentified immediate predecessor. We shall of course be coming across the results from time to time throughout this book.

All these chroniclers wrote in Latin, so that although their works had been derived partly from Welsh sources, their potential educated audience was more or less universal. With the occurrence, after the Norman conquest, of yet a further transformation of the nation which inhabited Britain, a new process of self-identification took place. In this redefining of the British identity the mythology, as again we shall see, played a major part. Geoffrey of Monmouth's Latin version of the British myths at this time formed the beginning of a movement which spread out in various directions. In the 1150s the subject matter of Geoffrey's 'History' was translated into verse, in French, by the Anglo-Norman poet Wace. During the succeeding decades the subject matter increased in popularity in France, largely due to the skill and success of the poet Chrétien de Troyes. And by about the end of the twelfth century it had taken its first English form in the works of Layamon.

It was from all these sources and others that Malory drew. He indeed was the last and the greatest of the succession of compilers, who put together in the second half of the fifteenth century the stories and themes which have become the paradigm of the matter of Britain, a great saga of heroic and elegiac narrative which came to be called 'Le Morte d'Arthur'. The heroic poets, the writers of the Mabinogion, Geoffrey of Monmouth and Wace, Chrétien and Layamon had each in their turn imprinted on the material both the requirements of their time and their own personal habits of mind, as no doubt Homer did on his; and Malory did so too.

The point about the course of this process is that the material had, surreptitiously and step by step, regained its rightful domain. It was, after Geoffrey, the matter of Britain. In the hands of Chrétien, Wace and Layamon, of William of Malmesbury and others, and in the metrical romances, it was treated as a proper part of the traditions of the people of mainland Britain. It was the heritage of the country in which they lived. For Malory, in fact, it clearly represented true Britishness, the summary of the elements which went to the making of the identity of the nation. Although Arthur's Cornish connections occasionally reveal themselves, he was the king of Britain as a whole. He had his court at Winchester, and his actions range throughout the country.

The chronological progression of the myths sets the form of this book. They had been forced into retreat in Wales, and we find the earliest elements of them there. They expanded to reinstate themselves in the culture of England, and in the last two-thirds of the book we follow the shift of the mythology back again into England.

The Remnants of Deities

Who the first inhabitants of Britain were, whether
natives or immigrants, remains obscure; one must
remember we are dealing with barbarians.

Tacitus, *Agricola* II, *c*. AD 97

2 Gods of the West

Nobody who has seen those vast poised capstones of the megalithic chamber-tombs could ever think that the early inhabitants of this island lacked a religion. The huge blocks perched on pointed uprights demonstrate some sort of compulsive need. To deal with the basic problems of survival, they polished their arrow-heads and hollowed their grinding stones, leaving scattered fragments as evidence of such mundane work. The problem of death evidently required the use of much more weighty stones, and in the effort and ingenuity required to heave them to their present position, we see a familiar stubbornness in the face of the blank regard of the inevitable. That is religion, if only because no drably practical purpose can possibly be served by it. It is, after all, an easy matter to dispose of the dead; but a hard one to deal with the idea to which they give rise.

It is with such emblems of a response to the inexplicable, when the first breathing-space granted by increased technology gave birth to the first failure to comprehend, that the beginnings of attention to the non-material world belong. There is the start of our abstract thinking. Pentre Ifan, Maes Howe, New Grange – and all those standing stones and circles, their near contemporaries, relating our location to the seasons and stars – form the physical evidence of the genesis of speculation. They have survived: they were supposed to, and they were made of stone. If the ideas which went with them have also survived we can only tell by inference and analogy, since ideas survive in a different way, partly by being continuously tended and fed with life from age to age, and partly by being reborn, like transmigrated souls, in form after form in world after resurrected world.

Since the physical symptoms of religion are found almost all over Europe in much the same form, we may guess that the religion which went with them was evenly diffused as well. If so it probably came in embryo form in the minds of the particular wing of the Indo-European speaking peoples which swept west as the Stone Age neared its end in Europe, when groups of farming people seem to have been on the move, sometime towards the end of the third millennium BC. Knowledge of such matters is inevitably vague, but what we can guess from early customs and forms which survived indicates that these people brought a patriarchal social system and a male-dominated pantheon into a land previously matriarchal, matrilinear, with priestesses supervising its cults

The great capstone at Lanyon Quoit in Cornwall

The entrance to the burial chamber of Bryn-Celli-Ddu in Anglesey

devoted to the earth-mother. If so, they have these factors in common
with at least two sets of linguistically-related peoples, those who swept
into the Indus valley in the middle of the second millennium BC, and the
Achaeans who brought the Mycenaean age to Greece perhaps a little
before that. And this seems likely to be important to the understanding of
the mythologies of all three, since if such an imposition of new on older
orders took place, it would have left its mark on the religious and
speculative thinking of the peoples of those countries. This would be the
first and perhaps most basic of the national cultural traumas. And because
there is residual evidence of something of the sort in the mythology the
picture is of more than fanciful theoretical interest.

Unfortunately it is not until much later that we hear anything about
the results. The Bronze Age had left the standing stones, but in western
Europe our knowledge of the habits of its people is much less full than is
the case in Mycenae or Crete. Indeed the merging of the Bronze Age into
the Iron Age, and the earlier culture into that which came to be known as
Celtic, bears nothing of the clarity of a distinct event which, for instance,
the tradition of the 'Dorian invasion' provides for us in Greece. We hear
nothing about these people and their ways until it is almost too late for
the news to be useful, because, in this relatively impoverished side of
Europe, there was nobody suitable there to tell us. We have no early-
Celtic Homer. In fact we have only Julius Caesar, viewing his enemy
with surprising objectivity and sympathy even while systematically
destroying the way of life he recorded. That was in the last decades before
this era, and by then the traditions which he noted had been evolving in
western Europe for at least two thousand years.

One thing which impressed Caesar was the strength of the oral
culture. Writing had reached the western Celts by his day, but the habit
of memorizing and reciting had, it seems, become such a characteristic of

the tradition that it could not be discarded. The Druids, he said, believed that their religion prohibited them from committing their teachings to writing, and he attributed this to the esoteric nature of the material. Caesar gives us some clues, not necessarily very reliable, as to what the Druids actually taught. Like the Aryan tribes who became eventually the Hindus they believed that the soul is immortal and subject to endless reincarnation in body after body. They were also, it seems, astronomers, perhaps even astrologers. And they dealt with the functions and characteristics of the gods.

Caesar names these gods, but in translation. As an anthropologist he was subject to the great weakness of ethnocentrism: he saw all forms of behaviour from the point of view of his own. Thus the Celts worshipped Apollo, Mars, Jupiter and Minerva, he says, in much the same way as did the Romans. Clearly they did not, or at least not as explicitly as Caesar implies. We can only identify the gods to which he gives these confident Roman names by analogy of their functions, so that, for instance, a sun-god would seem to Caesar to be Apollo, a war-god Mars, a king of the gods Jupiter, and so on. Most of all, he says (it seems with some surprise) they worshipped Mercury, the guide and companion of men in their journeys and of souls on their migration after death; Mercury the inventor of arts and the god of trade and commerce.

'In Britannia reperta atque inde in Galliam translata existimatur,' he says of the religion of the Druids. ('It was thought to have originated in Britain and to have been taken to Gaul from there.') People still, he tells us, go to Britain, if they wish to study it in depth.

It would be surprising indeed if all trace of this body of thought had disappeared. There are some clues that it has not; that instead of dying it has undergone a metempsychosis which renders it hardly recognizable as the same matter. The gods turn up again wearing new disguises. If this is so, then it is that very idiosyncrasy which Caesar noted, the strength and perpetuity of the oral tradition, which has provided the medium of survival. Writing, after all, is destructible. The long chain of memory is not.

For historical, identifiable reasons the Druids' overt, even prominent, power became suppressed. The tide on which Caesar rode through Gaul, the impetus of Empire, surged over Britain. In those hundred and thirty years or so between the first systematic contact of the invading armies with the Celts in Gaul and the last advances of the occupation forces into the wilds of western Britain, the religion beat a rear-guard action back towards its roots. In the process we focus in on the old religion's homelands, 'in Britannia reperta' – invented, or discovered, in Britain.

We shall see later how the Romans themselves contributed to the body of knowledge which the bards salvaged from the ruins of the native culture left by their onslaught. There was inevitably much that was new about the bardic tradition which emerged from the Dark Ages following the withdrawal and began to flower again in the early medieval period. But this too was an oral art, a matter of remembering and reciting, although it was now the telling of old stories rather than the teaching of ideas. There is therefore the probability that the bardic tradition represents the rebirth in a new form of the old Druid teaching, which had been suppressed for so long but not, in its essence, destroyed.

Focussing further on the Romans' military erosion of Celtic independence, we pick up the impressive sight of an army of two legions and four thousand mercenaries, together with cavalry and a supporting fleet, progressing into north-west Wales in about the year AD 60. No doubt the smell of leather and horses and the creak of gear often go ahead of great cultural changes. They were bound, Tacitus tells us, to subdue the island of Anglesey, 'which was feeding the native resistance'. An apparently eye-witness account tells of the Druids waiting on the shore of the island to curse the invading army, and we have archaeological as well as traditional support for the supposition that that was the seat of the Druid religion – so that it was the religion itself, in its heartland of north-west Wales, which was actually the force feeding the native resistance.

Suetonius Paulinus and the army cut down both the Druids and their sacred groves, and a further attack on Anglesey under Agricola later completed the job of suppression. As far as the Romans were concerned the native religion in its Druidic form had now been destroyed, as they had intended, but it is much more likely, in view of the survival of Celtic tribal life throughout the occupation, that it had been driven underground. If so we would not be surprised to find it emerging again when the danger was passed. But something radical had taken place in the meantime. Suppressed by the Romans, the gods had become disguised; the traditions of their doings and qualities had become stories. And when the bards began to tell them again in the newly-awaked Celtic kingdoms of the post-Roman, pre-Saxon times, they did so in the context and environment of the new religion of Christianity. Perhaps as a result the gods kept their disguises on, and their activities remained as tales. Had it been otherwise, we should not have received even these faint impressions of them, since the written versions of the stories were almost inevitably first made by Christian clerics.

Along with many elements which are clearly on the level of entertainment, common features of popular tales all over Europe, the mythology which resulted from those memories of earlier wisdom preserved by the bardic tradition was eventually formalized in such collections as the epigrammatic Triads, and in the great treasury of stories called the Mabinogion. Because we can discern in those stories something more archaic than the heroic events they superficially retell, it is there, if anywhere, that the remnants of the gods of the Celts are to be found.

One story in particular deals with the doings of powerfully supernatural figures in that same area into which Suetonius and Agricola drove their assaults against the old gods. 'Math, son of Mathonwy', both the most complex and the most intriguing of the Mabinogion tales, is so explicitly located in the weather-swept country of the extreme west of North Wales that it seems that it presents the memory of a cult which once flourished there.

'Math' is such a jumble that one can hardly take it seriously as art; layer on layer of tenuously related material seems to have been put together by someone who was not quite clear what he was doing. But through it runs a deep current of myth, in the form of a sort of magical appreciation of the wonder of the natural world. And over its often absurd events loom the huge misty figures of Gwydion and Aranrhod, brother and sister divinities playing here the roles of wizard and enchantress. Many of the images too which are almost accidentally thrown out are memorably intense.

The story concerns a king of Gwynedd, Math, and Gwydion, his sister's son, known to the tale as Gwydion son of Don. Both these figures are portrayed as magicians of great power, and in the opening episode Gwydion plays a complicated trick on his uncle by acquiring the sacred swine of Pryderi, king of South Wales, in exchange for a set of horses and dogs which he had made out of toadstools, and which revert to their less impressive form as soon as he and the swine have got out of range. He makes a specific and epic trek back to the North with the sacred animals, and finds on arrival that he has succeeded in his ploy, which was to cause war between North and South. The war ends with a hand-to-hand fight between the two who have caused it, Gwydion and Pryderi, the two protagonists of the North and South coming face to face in front of their armies, on that great stretch of estuarial marsh, now reclaimed and tamed, which forms the silt-plain of the river Glaslyn as it drains the Snowdon range into Tremadoc Bay. It seems that Gwydion rather unfairly resorted to his magic powers, and Pryderi (whom we shall meet again in other tales at earlier stages of his career) was killed, at a site located in the lower Ffestiniog valley, and buried there.

Math then discovers that one reason for Gwydion's intrigue was that he and his brother had wished to make use of the distraction of the war to rape the maiden who held the office of 'foot-holder' in his court – a post which unexpectedly actually existed, and in fact survived until the Middle Ages. She held the king's feet in her lap, and whatever the purpose or connotation of this it seems that it was necessary for her to preserve her virginity in order properly to carry out her function. When the brothers, the sons of Don, eventually come to court, Math inflicts on them, by his magic, a strange and rather disturbing punishment for the rape.

Gwydion is turned into a stag; Gilfaethwy, his brother, into a hind. It was their fate then to live together, to mate and produce offspring. Math instructed them to come back to him in a year's time, and sure enough, a year from that day, when the barking of the dogs under the walls of the court set off the barking of those inside, Math looked and saw a stag, a hind, and a fawn outside. He lifted his staff again, and the one who had been female before he now made into a wild boar, the one who had been male into a sow. With the same instructions as before he sent them away, taking the fawn back into the human race; and a year later the barking of the dogs again signalled their return.

Math inflicted one more round of this inhabiting of the bodies of wild animals on the unfortunate sons of Don, this time in the form of wolves, so that by the time they returned again they had each had young by the other, in one case twice. He reckoned this then to be enough punishment, and set them free.

The story now changes direction, with the entry (as a replacement foot-holder) of Gwydion's sister Aranrhod. Already we have become involved with what seems to be several different types of material – the acquisition of the otherworld animals by cunning, a theme which seems like the fragmentary remains of a heroic narrative, coupled with some special significance attributed to the pig; the battle of magicians, in the course of a war between the North and South, an episode suggesting the conflict of two tribal groups with their rival religious cults; and now this strangely compelling image of two brothers mating in the forms of wild animals and producing progeny.

In the last there are probably several residues, but we cannot help being struck by its strong overtones of the belief in transmigration. Firstly, it assumes that there is an essential individual which exists in separation from the body, and which may therefore be transferred from body to body – so that transmigration is a possible idea. Secondly, the round of rebirths in different, lowly, forms, is represented as a punishment, with Math in this case acting rather like the Hindu principle of Karma, by subjecting the sinners to repeated reincarnations until they have worked off their sin. He then, like Karma, releases them. It is not difficult to see in this little interjection into the story of Math the remains of a belief in metempsychosis, transmigration of soul, which Caesar said the Druids believed in 'and took particular care to teach'.

This theme of men being transformed into animals occurs in other mythologies, for instance in the Greek story in which the enchantress Circe changed Odysseus's sailors by a spell into swine, or the Peloponnesian legend of a man changed for a year (like Gwydion) into a wolf and freed at the end of the year if he refrained from eating human flesh – freed, that is, for good behaviour – and again the punishment inflicted on Actaeon by Artemis for his crime of seeing her undressed, when she metamorphosed him into a stag and then hunted him to death. Oddly enough, in these three Greek instances we have the same three animals, stag, swine, wolf, as in the Gwydion episode.

In this story we may also see, though rather less clearly, the possible record of the cults of various animal gods. Perhaps a carving or a memory of a ritual has been misunderstood, as can be shown to have happened occasionally in myth, and the image of a man wearing a stag's antlers or a wolf's head (its meaning as part of a cult ritual forgotten) has seemed to require explanation in the form of a narrative. For instance we see on some very ancient bronze plaques found on the island of Öland, Sweden, a human figure wearing horns, identified as Odin, accompanied by another with a wolf's head, and, in a separate tableau, two men with helmets of the heads of boars. Whatever it is that is being said by the plaques, the story of Gwydion's metamorphosis seems to be saying something equivalent.

Gwydion's triple change of shape might indicate that three sorts of animals were sacred to him, or that his name is being used as a sort of summary of separate references to three gods, all sometimes represented in animal form. Although there seems to be no evidence of the worship of a wolf-god (and indeed this third transformation may have been an addition, since the purpose of the punishment was that each brother should produce offspring by the other, which had by then been achieved) there is plenty of indication in the more basic British myths that boars were considered sacred or supernatural. But it is in the case of the first appearance of the magicians as animals, in their stag form, that the clearest case of a religious cult becomes apparent, since the horned god, known to us as Cernunnos, is familiar from archaeology, though oddly not from the early writers, as one of the main gods of the Continental Celts.

Cernunnos was not actually his name, but seems to have been a description, meaning (presumably from the Celtic and Latin root 'corn') the 'Horned One'. Although it is found only on one example, a relief carving on what was perhaps an altar, in Paris, the word 'Cernunnos' has

The fourth-century Gallo-Roman relief of Cernunnos, discovered on the site of Notre Dame in Paris

31

been applied in modern times to all the many Celtic-period representa-tions of horned gods found in France and Britain. If it is indeed one god who is being depicted in all these reliefs – and the similarity of appear-ance and posture, the stag's horns and the cross-legged position, is often remarkable – then it seems likely that his name was either so well known or so sacred that it was not written. The 'Horned One' sounds sus-piciously like a respectful title. The god seems to have been connected with animals in general, and, again linking him to the punishment of the sons of Don, with their fertility in particular. As a substantial item of sustenance the stag was of major importance among animals in pre-farming, hunting times, and the aura of this may well have been carried over into agricultural Gaul. We know that in such diverse places as Africa and Mexico hunters enacted the deer-hunt in ritual dance form before undertaking it in reality, and this probably often involved the representa-tive of the deer, like Cernunnos, wearing antlers on his head. Something of this sort seems to be referred to in the cave-paintings of Lascaux, which show men dressed as deer with antler head-dresses being chased by bowmen, and oddly enough the custom of such a mock hunt, with men wearing reindeer horns, has survived into modern times in the Staffordshire village of Abbots Bromley.

Interestingly there seems to be a close connection between the best representation of Cernunnos, that on the Gundestrup bowl (where he is shown surrounded by animals, including a deer wearing antlers just like his own) and a seal found at Mohenjo-Daro in northern India, apparently belonging to the pre-Aryan Indus culture of before 2000 BC, which shows a horned figure sitting, like Cernunnos, cross-legged, and like the Gundestrup Cernunnos surrounded by animals; this one, in common with several of the horned figures of Celtic archaeology, has three faces, one forward and one at each side. The three heads and the surrounding animals, as well as the cross-legged position, suggest that this is an early representation of the god Siva in his role as Lord of the Beasts. Both these gods appear as lords of all animals, and in relation to this we might remember Gwydion's triple transformation, stag first, other animals afterwards.

One theory holds that elements of the old religion, suppressed and sublimated, survived in the cult of witchcraft. For his part the horned god too perhaps lingered on in early medieval depictions of the devil – confused, no doubt, with his other conventional representation in bacchanalian goat-form – that antlered being still alive in the back-ground of what is left of witchcraft today. In local folk tradition he seems to reappear as well, when, under the name of Herne the Hunter, he rides out of the woods at night on his black horse with his hound pack, a figure who might not be recognizable to us as anything other than a child-scarer, were it not that the lore insists that he wears antlers. It is reason-ably supposed that the sites at which this figure is said to appear, in particular Windsor Great Park, were ancient places of worship of the horned god.

Cernunnos surrounded by animals on the Gundestrup bowl

Returning to the tale, we find Aranrhod, candidate for the post of foot-holder, failing the crucial test. She does it, as might by now be expected, in the most extraordinary way. When asked to step over Math's magician's staff she drops two children, the first a fine boy-child who leaves the story at once by running into the sea, the second described as a small object, which Gwydion takes up (as Aranrhod flees in shame) and hides in a chest.

It is a boy, who grows at a remarkable rate; and Gwydion has him reared. The story moves into its central episode when he takes the prodigious child to confront his mother at her castle, Caer Aranrhod. The sequence is imbued with an atmosphere of unexplained tension, as Aranrhod, at first humiliated by the confrontation, begins to try to assert her rights as mother. He shall not have a name until he gets one from her; he shall not bear arms unless he receives them from her; he shall not have a wife of any race then on earth. As Gwydion contrives to trick her into overcoming each curse she then utters the next, until the last one seems to present even him with a problem. Lleu Llaw Gyffes, as the boy is now called, is by then a fully-grown man, and Gwydion consults his uncle and fellow-magician Math as to how they may outwit Aranrhod and find him a wife.

The two wizards then perform a ceremony which must rank as one of the most appealing images in this generally imaginative mythology. They make for him a wife out of wild flowers, using those common and indigenous flora of the Welsh countryside in its flush of early summer – the flowers of the oak, the meadowsweet, and the broom. And out of these they made the most beautiful woman ever seen. They called her Blodeuedd, from the Welsh bloddeu, flowers.

Aranrhod now fades from the tale, and Blodeuedd becomes a central figure. In the series of events preceding her creation we can easily infer a reference to the tension between patriarchal and matriarchal conventions, as Gwydion himself brings up the boy while Aranrhod on the other hand claims the exclusive right to give him a name, arms, and a wife – each time to be outwitted by the dominant attitude of Gwydion, who in effect acts as a father to his sister's son. In the ensuing tangle which Blodeuedd creates for Lleu a different type of social theme becomes apparent, namely the old and familiar set of circumstances crystallized in Europe by the convention of courtly love, the plotting of a dominant woman and her lover against an absent husband.

Up in their court of Mur Castell, Blodeuedd takes as a lover a neighbouring lord who happens to be passing while Lleu is away visiting Math. She invites him to stay with her in the court, so that in effect he becomes, like Paris with Helen at Sparta while Menelaus was away in Crete, under the assumed obligation of a guest in the husband's house. In spite of this they plot together to dispose of Lleu on his return, a matter made more difficult by the fact that he can only be killed under certain circumstances. This too is a common mythic feature, combining both a narrative interest – we know that he will die, we know that it is apparently impossible, and wait to see how it can be done – with the deeply intriguing idea of a predestined fate always being unavoidable, just as Achilles was doomed to die in the Trojan War and could not evade it even by his almost total invulnerability: his only mortal portion, his heel, would inevitably produce his destined death. Similarly in the very elaborate case of an Irish hero, Conaire, no less then eight conditions have to be fulfilled before he can die, and one by one they come about, with the sound of the ominous steps of fate going about its business, like Birnam Wood on its incredible progress towards Dunsinane.

Lleu Llaw Gyffes can be killed neither within a house nor outside, neither on horseback nor on foot, and (it appears) neither on water nor on dry land. Blodeuedd lures him into telling how these contraries can be reconciled, and as a result we find him in due course perched with one foot on the back of a he-goat and the other on the edge of a bath-tub, under a canopy of thatch on the bank of the river Cynfal near their home. It might, as she puts it icily, have been avoided easily. But fate is not easily deterred, however ridiculous its ruses.

Lleu becomes an eagle on his death, thus returning us perhaps to the concept of transmigration of souls, and at the same time connecting him distinctly with the other gods whose sacred emblems have been eagles, particularly with the sky-god Zeus. Heracles, Zeus's son, was said in some versions of his story to have soared to heaven, on his death, in eagle form. Clearly it is a sky-connected concept, and as such is often taken to be the mark of a sun-god. Gwydion devotedly searched the forests and valleys of North Wales for Lleu in his new form, found him perching in a tree in the Nantlle valley below Snowdon, and by using his magic again returned him to human form. As for Blodeuedd, an element of absurdity attended her to the end. As Gwydion and Lleu vengefully approached the heights of Mur Castell, she set off with her maidens from the court, crossed the mountain and the Cynfal river in its upper coomb. Foolishly they all looked back in fear as they went, with the result that the maidens, walking ahead, stumbled backwards into a lake and were drowned. There at the edge of the moorland lake Gwydion caught Blodeuedd up, confronted her with terrible and rightful anger, and, by his magic, turned her into an owl.

'Blodeuedd', the tale says, is still 'owl' in our language, as it may well have been, meaning as it does 'flower-face'. What is more certain is that the lake, lying in a shallow depression of the moors high above Ffestiniog, is still called the Maidens' Lake. The story-teller shows a detailed and appreciative knowledge of the more evocative places in western Gwynedd. At Mur Castell today, known now as Tomen-y-Mur, we find the long regular rampart of a Roman camp skirting a hollow-topped conical mound of considerable size, apparently a medieval castle. Up on these exposed moors the permanent threat of rain dominates the desolate land. A rise to the north hides the Cynfal valley, site of Lleu's assassination, and a long stretch of reed, marsh, and rough land extends, rising slowly, to the east, a country which can hardly have changed in appearance since the time when some unchronicled lord in the early Middle Ages used the mound as a motte and the remains of the Roman camp as the basis for a fortress. And then it must have been much as it had been when the Romans came to this hilltop, driving their great road, Sarn Helen, across the moors. Had they perhaps found part of that mound already there? It certainly has about it the proportions, though enlarged, of a burial mound. The Romans sometimes used such artificial hills as look-out towers, so that its use in the Middle Ages might possibly have been the third phase of its career. In any case it is clear that the tale of Lleu has become associated with this spot because there was something significant there, so that either a post-Roman cult grew up there, as happened when the British reoccupied Roman sites elsewhere; or alternatively the Romans themselves used an already existing site. Their immediate surroundings, at any rate, must have been this heather-scape. So natural is the rough moorland country that it could not have been much different even when Blodeuedd and her maidens left the court and crossed the hill towards the lake.

So too the little river Cynfal runs still below Tomen-y-Mur down its hidden valley, to pass under a bridge which now carries the road up from Ffestiniog. Bordered by clumps and lines of indigenous oak, its bank broken by protruding knolls, it still offers convenient opportunities for a

Blodeuedd to station her lover out of sight while coaxing an ingenuous Lleu into his absurd position. So too, down on the coast, the fort where Gwydion housed Lleu before his marriage is still called after him, Dinas Dinlle, from Din-Lleu, Lleu's fort, though now the sea is working a slow destruction on this vast, steep, complex Iron Age ring-fort. The sea has gone one step further in the case of Caer Aranrhod, seat of the wicked goddess, since, if it ever existed, it is now submerged for ever. From Dinas Dinlle one can see at low water a line of stones at sea, the waves breaking over them, the only feature in the bland, oceanic sweep of the flat coast. Is it a drowned city or an eroded drumlin? The failure to establish the case conclusively either way leaves it in the powerful position of being, like so much about the distant past, unclassifiable, unamenable to our beloved distinctions of either/or.

We know where these figures of the myth, Gwydion, Aranrhod, Lleu, were said to have been when the events connected with them occurred, almost to a few yards being able to locate the bizarre episode on the banks of the Cynfal or the confrontation of Gwydion and Blodeuedd. Perhaps partly for this reason we feel tantalized by not knowing more about them, where they came from, who they originally were. Messy as it is the story does, however, give us some slight clue, and the rest of the tradition fills in some of the gaps.

Caer Aranrhod is, it seems, something other than a reef of stones off the Gwynedd coast. It is also a name for the Corona Borealis, the half-circle of stars adjoining the constellation of Hercules, in which case this connection relates Aranrhod to the Greek goddess Ariadne, whose circlet these stars are said to be in that mythology. From the reference to Caer Aranrhod in the riddle of Taliesin (which we shall come across again) Robert Graves argues (in *The White Goddess*) that this – the circle of stars – is regarded as the otherworld to which souls go after death, and

The remains of Dinas Dinlle hill fort, Gwynedd

before rebirth, which would make Aranrhod a sort of goddess of death.

Most significant of all, however, is the name of the parent of both Gwydion and Aranrhod, who are referred to as the children of Don, interestingly not originally a male personage but a goddess, and therefore intended at an earlier stage of the story to be understood as Math's sister. Apart from this indication of a matrilinear system of descent, the mention of the goddess Don brings the story directly into the heart of European myth.

Don is identified as the same deity as the Irish goddess Danann, or Danu, the mother of the gods, and the stories of her children, therefore, must have formed part of an equivalent branch of myth to the Irish tales of the people of the goddess Danann, mythical invaders of Ireland who no doubt correspond, in the looser time-scale of myth, to one of several major waves of colonization which we know to have taken place during the Bronze Age and Iron Age. To suggest that the people of Danann were the 'Celts' would be misleading, if only because several of the groups of invaders of Ireland and Britain might be classifiable as Celtic. But because the matter does not stop there we can guess that, whoever they were, they were people who were widespread and powerful in Europe at the end of the Bronze Age.

Indeed if it were not for this diffusion all we could say of Gwydion and Aranrhod would be that their Welsh stories seem to be related to the Irish ones. But Don and Danann are clearly not so local. To begin with, they gave their name to several rivers, not just the two or three examples in England and France but the great Russian waterway which flows to the east of the Ukraine down to Rostov, emerging into the Sea of Azov, an offshoot of the Black Sea; one of Europe's major rivers, it is still called the river Don. Two other great Black Sea rivers, the Dnieper and the Dniester, also seem to have been called after her. But most significantly of all she claims the Danube, in the basin of which came into being those cultures, known to archaeologists as the 'Urnfield' and later the 'Hallstatt' cultures, which form the roots of the recognizable Celtic style. Traditionally, the Celtic peoples spread out from the area of the Danube, and indeed our earliest reference to them, by Herodotus in the fifth century BC, mentions them in direct connection with the source of that river.

There is an Irish tradition of an ancient migration northwards from Greece, in which the people of Danann spread to Ireland by way of Denmark, to which country they gave its name. Certainly there is further evidence from the similarity of names for the Greek connection, since such was the central role of the Argive princess Danae, mother of Perseus and one of the wives of Zeus, and, in another and seemingly later tradition, the Argive king Danaus, that at one time the name 'Danaans' stood for the Greeks themselves, by extension from the ancestral title of the Argives. Nor does the goddess who is said to have given her name to the Danube and the Danes end her chain of associations at Argos, since she can be recognized too in the pre-Hindu pantheon, where, as Danu, mother and wife of major gods, she appears in that most holy and ancient of Indian scriptures, the Rig Veda, which almost certainly preserves for us the oral tradition of priests of the Aryan people who absorbed the Indus valley civilization in the second millennium BC.

If all this is correct (and of course too much can easily be made of philological connections) then Danu is a personage of some importance. We would therefore expect the other characters who fall under her auspices in the tale to be of general significance too. Lleu himself, who ends as the hero of the story of 'Math', seems to be a version of the Irish god Lug, who, by his representation in Irish stories as someone skilled, clever, and inventive, has been compared to Hermes or Mercury. Frequent references to his brightly shining face, as well as his name, which means 'bright one', make it seem that to the Irish he was, among other things, a sun-god. As the European god Lugus he seems to have given his name to places as far apart as Lyon, Leiden, and Carlisle; and his Mercury connection would gain some support by the trickery in which Lleu participates during the process of outwitting Aranrhod were it not for the fact that in this he is overshadowed by his uncle and instructor Gwydion. No equivalent to Gwydion occurs in the Irish stories, but in the Welsh one everything that might be said about Lleu as evidence for his connection with Mercury might be said more convincingly about Gwydion. Is Lleu therefore perhaps a sort of secondary version of Gwydion in Britain, fulfilling his function in Ireland, and merging with him in Gaul to make a composite god, two instances of one type, summarized by Caesar as Mercury? With their position as sons and new arrivals in the stories of the deeds of older characters, Lleu and Lug (like their equivalent in Greek myth, Heracles) bear in their various exploits and attributes all the marks of the hero–god who replaces the established order of deities, and thus of the gods of later and perhaps more secular and developed civilizations, the gods of invading cults ending or changing a native tradition.

It is Gwydion who dominates the tale – on the shores of Aber Menai taking the boy to Aranrhod's castle, imposing his patriarchal will on his rebellious sister, creating Blodeuedd, pursuing her in anger to the edge of the Maidens' Lake, searching for Lleu in his eagle form. Some ideas not fully revealed through the enchantment of the tale seem to be involved here, and from two directions we can draw slight clues as to the roots of this impressive figure.

It is his name which gives him away, since it seems to be cognate with Woden, the Teutonic god who gave his name to the day in the middle of our week, known in his Scandinavian form as Odin. Twice in the tale of 'Math' Gwydion stirs up a battle – once to embroil Math in war with the South, and once by magic in the seas around Aranrhod's castle, to trick her into giving arms to Lleu. And Woden and Odin too were concerned with battle, the former usually in a supervisory capacity, like Gwydion interfering only magically. Gwydion's constant trickery too, and his habitual use of magic, are distinctly reminiscent of the methods of

A Viking stone showing Odin on his eight-legged horse Slepnir

Woden. Trickery and magic in fact were very much the province not only of both these parties but of Mercury too; and if in the leading of Lleu to Caer Aranrhod we can justfiably see a symbolic journey to the castle of death, then a further link is provided to draw together the composite identity of this deity. The role of guide on journeys, and particularly the journey to the otherworld, was the characterizing function which Mercury inherited from his Greek prototype, Hermes. Tacitus said that Mercury was the main deity of the Germans, just as Caesar said that Mercury was the main deity of the Gauls. And it seems to have been agreed from an early period that the Mercury that Tacitus meant was really Woden, to the extent that the Germans in adopting the Latin system for naming their days translated 'Mercurii dies' as Woden's-day. It is possible then, by further inference, to see the Mercury referred to by Caesar as also the counterpart of Woden, and therefore Gwydion, his Celtic form.

Whether we should be tempted further into this speculation is doubtful, attractive though it would be to draw together Odin in his horned helmet, Gwydion with his antlers on, and the many carvings of Cernunnos, and to speculate that Caesar and Tacitus, recognizing the similarity of the functions of all these gods, were further tempted to make the identification because Mercury too was shown as having sprouting excrescences on his head, though certainly not horns but wings. It is hard not to be struck by the fact that Odin in his aspect of leader of the wild hunt, a figure which has survived in folklore in several parts of continental Europe, is represented in England by the antlered huntsman Herne. Such evidence is too slight to substantiate a theory. We do know that on the one hand archaeology shows us that Cernunnos was one of the main objects of worship of the European and British Celts, without telling us further who he was; and that on the other hand the Romans tell us that it was Mercury who was their main god, and that their images of him were common; and in the case of the Germans at least we know that Mercury meant Woden. All we can say with regard to the British myth is that Gwydion has points of contact, however tenuous, with all three.

3 Some basic themes

It is not at all clear why the idea of another world, a world running in parallel with this one, should ever have occurred. But all myth has this concept, and British myth, in its manifestation in the sources we are considering, has it as strongly as most. It may not follow from the persistent recurrence of this theme that there actually is a counter-world; but it does follow that there is a permanent need to consider what the situation would be if there were one.

Two of the stories in the Mabinogion proper, the section known as the 'four branches' which forms the central mythic block of that collection, deal with this otherworld. Annwfn, they call it, or (since it is variously spelt) Annwfyn or Annwn. It runs somehow alongside our world of woods and hills and people, and seems at times to be indistinguishable from it, the same but not the same. The clearest encounter with this otherworld comes at the beginning of the story of Pwyll, who is lord of the kingdom of Dyfed, that jutting lump of south-west Wales. It is through that rolling land above the coast of Carmarthen Bay that he rides out to hunt, from his court at Arberth, and meets unexpectedly a huntsman like himself, after the same stag, who on introduction proves to be no ordinary huntsman but Arawn, the king of Annwfn, the otherworld. There too apparently they have border wars and trouble-some neighbours, and to deal with one of these the king of Annwfn enlists Pwyll's help. They are to exchange kingdoms for a year, Pwyll changing form to look like him, he to look like Pwyll, so that nobody could tell that they had as it were become each other. Even the queens could not guess that each king was in fact the other, and the otherworld queen only noticed the change because Pwyll kept noble loyalty to his counterpart by refraining from what he alone knew would have been adultery. Pwyll rids Annwfn of the neighbouring rival who is threaten-ing it – a feat which apparently for magical reasons its own king could not have done – and at the end of the year they come back to the place where they first met hunting, and become their former selves again. The story appealingly mentions that Arawn's wife was glad (if a little puzzled) to find her husband reverting, after a year's lapse, to his previous nocturnal behaviour.

The annual nature of this exchange suggests a reference to the cycle of the natural year, a powerful theme best shown in the annual journey of Persephone to the kingdom of Hades, Demeter's mourning for her

The great white horse on the hillside above Uffington, Berkshire

bringing nature's withdrawal, her return in the spring bringing renewal of vitality. But if what we have here is the vestige of some such symbolism – Pwyll goes below, Pwyll returns – it is distorted or fragmented. Perhaps it would be better to think of the two realms constantly swinging in counterbalance, Pwyll in one place, the counterpart king weighted against him in the other, and yet each of them in some sense the other one.

That is only the beginning of the story called 'Pwyll, Prince of Dyfed', and the otherworld keeps breaking through into that gentle coastal country as the tale goes on. Pwyll sits upon a mound outside the court at Arberth, a peculiarity of which is that whenever a nobleman sits on it he experiences a fight or sees a wonder. It is the wonder in this case, and as he sits there a woman rides by on a white horse. What is wonderful is that she cannot be overtaken, and although Pwyll sends his fastest horses and riders to find out who she is she keeps easily ahead of them without changing her trotting pace. At length he goes himself, and calls to her, at which she stops. Her name, she says, is Rhiannon, and her reason for being there is her love of him.

Rhiannon is to marry a man against her will, but she and Pwyll plan to avert this. A feast is to be arranged for a year from that day, which Pwyll must attend – the reintroduction of the annual cycle hints at lost symbolism or forgotten ritual. When the feast takes place (with the ease of time's passage which the story sustains throughout) the rival suitor duly arrives at it. He tricks Pwyll – by the familiar folk-tale ruse of getting him to offer to give whatever he asks for – into parting with Rhiannon. The third episode of the story then brings back the yearly sequence for the third time, since it is at once arranged for the marriage to take place a year from that day. At the end of that third year it is Pwyll's turn to arrive as petitioner at the feast, now presided over by his rival, illustrating again the counterbalancing effect which this story constantly seems to emphasize. He works a suitably mysterious trick, and gains the lady.

Much that takes place in this story of Pwyll seems to be common popular material, folk-motifs of tricks and magic and transformations. But the presence of the figure of Rhiannon lifts the business into an altogether more important sphere. In the Gaul into which the Romans came the inhabitants made many statuettes of a lady on a horse. She is riding it side-saddle and with some confidence, going always at a sedate trotting pace. Partly because she then gained popularity with the horse-loving Romans, we know that she was known as Epona, 'the divine horse'. Her identity is secure from a large number of inscriptions, and the name recognizably comes from the Celtic word for horse 'epos', which is the equivalent of the Latin 'equus' and the Greek 'hippos', and finds a modern descendant in the Welsh word 'ebol', meaning colt. Celtic worship of a horse figure is suggested also by that lean white animal on the hill at Uffington, in Berkshire, galloping eternally towards the nearby Iron Age hillfort which at this point dominates the Ridgeway, which was then undoubtedly a central communication link of the greatest importance.

So common and widespread are the idols and altar reliefs of Epona that we know that we have here a major Celtic deity, the horse goddess of a horse-using people. The identification of Rhiannon with Epona is well-established, and we shall see further evidence for it shortly. But the name Rhiannon also sets her on a higher level than mere tale-telling, since it is agreed by the linguistic authorities to be derived from the British title Rigantona, which means 'Great Queen'. And as the tale develops we sense more and more that this powerfully portrayed figure is carrying into the mild world of Dyfed, perhaps unknown even to the story-teller, a burden of associations which the humble structure of the story can hardly support.

Rhiannon, now the wife of Pwyll, bears a child. The women who are supposed to watch her, however, fall asleep, and when they wake the new-born infant is no longer there. In their fear they make it look as if Rhiannon herself has killed and (apparently) eaten it. At the same time in the home of a neighbouring lord, Teyrnon, a mare gives birth to a foal, which is nearly stolen by the same agency as that which has abducted Rhiannon's child. When Teyrnon prevents the theft the child is discovered along with the rescued foal, as if the two are in some sense one, or two aspects of the same identity, or alternatives, substitutable in some way for each other.

This episode of the stolen child seems to relate to another in the Mabinogion collection, in which someone called Mabon son of Modron was stolen (and this is almost all we hear of him) from his mother, when only three days old. His name identifies him as the god known to us from Romanized inscriptions in north Britain as Maponus, a god of music sometimes equated with Apollo, and its meaning of 'divine Son' counterparts that of his mother, Modron, the Gaulish goddess Matrona, 'divine Mother', who gave her name to the river Marne. Are Rhiannon and Modron, Great Queen and Great Mother, two aspects of the same deity?

Meanwhile, in the story, Rhiannon is obliged to do penance, which takes the form of sitting by the horse-block outside the gate and carrying people up to the court on her back. In other words, she becomes a horse.

Teyrnon's name (although he plays a small part in the story as it now exists) seems to indicate that he must originally have been her consort, since it comes from Tigernonos, and therefore means 'Great King' to her 'Great Queen'. He brings up both the boy and the foal, so that the child-foal pair in a sense belong to Teyrnon and Rhiannon rather than to Rhiannon and Pwyll. In the end the boy and foal are returned to Rhiannon together. Her horse connections relate Rhiannon more firmly to Epona, and indeed to horse-goddesses in general. In particular it springs to mind that the Greek goddess Demeter changed herself into a horse in order to escape the attentions of Poseidon, whose behaviour then, however, rather indicates to us that the story has become distorted, since he at once changed into a stallion and mated with her. Perhaps originally they were horse-god and horse-goddess, horses being sacred to them both, and perhaps at some stage in some part of Europe this beast was of such importance that the deities associated with it were the 'Great King' and 'Great Queen' of the gods. Demeter and Poseidon are in any case very fundamental gods. It is suggested by some that their names, De-meter and Posis-Das, mean respectively Earth-mother and Earth-consort.

One wonders how figures of Rhiannon's and Teyrnon's apparent importance can have come to end up here, in the centre of the sea-surrounded land now once more known as Dyfed, the name of the old kingdom of south-west Wales. One wonders why such a humble countryside should have been thought sufficiently sacred to be the habitat of these old gods. At Narberth there is a mound with a thirteenth-

Pentre Ifan chamber-tomb, Dyfed

century ruined castle on it, from which one looks out over the character-istic rolling hilliness of Dyfed. The name connects it with Pwyll's Arberth, but in fact the magic mound on which he sat is considered to be elsewhere, either a few miles south or up in the north of the peninsula, where still an Arberth river runs towards Cardigan Bay.

Looking around there one begins to see that Pembroke's loveliness has a serious depth to it. It is an extremely anciently-inhabited land. It was the later Stone Age which saw the construction of the great cromlechs, the poised stone chambers which still stand so impressively on our hillsides. And one of the finest of all of these stands near the north coast of the Pembroke peninsula, the chamber-tomb known as Pentre Ifan, an example so striking in its confidence and stylishness that it must have represented both a feature of importance in its own right and the out-come of the development, here in south-west Wales, of skill, technique, and intelligence. These structures are so ancient that one can hardly grasp the scope of the achievement which their perfection represents. When the Celts started to emerge from the central European Bronze Age as a recognizable unit, Pentre Ifan was already there. It belongs, like the hypothetical mother-tongue of nations, Indo-European, very literally to pre-history. It signifies, if nothing else, a highly-developed mental faculty, a working-out in material terms of some complicated ideas. It is not just the ability to raise and balance that immense monolithic capstone on those elegant uprights, but the ability by doing so to encapsulate the beliefs and aspirations of a culture. That effect too is achieved by the mythology, though with more signs of struggle against the opacity of communication, since words are less eloquent than stones.

Pentre Ifan lies on the north slopes of the foothills of the Preseli Mountains, and here again, in this area where we have found Pwyll and Rhiannon and the otherworld breaking through into their rural lives, we find a direct contact with the earliest religious forms in Britain. Stone-henge sits with bland factualness, a complicated artefact, out on the airy plateau of Salisbury Plain. Its existence tempts people into probably quite unnecessary speculation, as if all apparent complexities unavoidably need explanation, but one thing in particular has been puzzling from the start of the investigations into it. Some of the stones – the outer circle, to-gether with the larger stones of the inner one – come from the immediate area. But the inner, and perhaps therefore the most sacred, of the rings was not acquired from the plentiful natural quarries of Wiltshire and the Marlborough Downs. It is reliably concluded that this inner temple was transported from Preseli. And one cannot, in this case, avoid asking why.

The conclusion comes from the fact that the only part of Britain where all the non-local stones of the monument could have originated was Preseli. The bluestones could literally not have come from anywhere else in southern Britain. How the journey of the stones took place is of enough interest in itself, but it looks quite dull beside this question of why. Only a matter of religion, one feels, would have been sufficiently

Stonehenge, showing one of the bluestones from Preseli in the centre

compelling. Since the bluestone circle was added to the greater structure in a second phase of building, it begins to seem like a capture or at least a transference of sacredness: a temple already in existence near to its source of material being removed wholesale and incorporated in another one. If that were so then the Preseli monument must have been of an unrivalled holiness, to the extent that its stones themselves were sacred and could carry with them their charisma all the way to Salisbury Plain. Evidently some memory of this great task survived through several thousand years, since Geoffrey of Monmouth describes in some detail the transportation of an existing monument to form Stonehenge, though not from Preseli but from Ireland. The operation was supervised by Merlin, who gave what seems likely to have been the true reason for the removal, when the king objected that Britain was not lacking in adequate stones: 'These stones are connected with certain religious rites and they have various properties which are medicinally important.'

In view of the very ancient connections of this area of Wales with sacredness, it is perhaps not as surprising as it might be to find a few remaining traces of ancient European deities located there. The other story in which Rhiannon occurs is (though perhaps under the influence of the first) also attributed to this same area of central Pembroke, the land of Dyfed. The story of Manawydan, son of Llŷr, shows more than any of the other Mabinogion stories a sense of being related to the surrounding material. It forms both a sequel to 'Pwyll' and to the tale of 'Branwen' which we shall encounter later. Although this might indicate a later date of composition, the themes contained in it seem by contrast to be some of the most ancient.

After the death of Pwyll, Manawydan comes to Arberth to marry Rhiannon. He and Rhiannon and her son Pryderi and his wife then form the quartet about whom the story is told. One night they go out from the court and sit on that fateful mound, and with a clap of thunder and the fall of a thick mist the whole of their habitual surroundings is removed; when the light comes back the countryside is empty of all signs of civilization, flocks, herds, houses, and all their companions. The houses of their court remain, but desolate and uninhabited, 'without man, without beast within them'. They are alone in a suddenly empty land.

Deprived of herding they turn to hunting, and are led one day by a shining white wild boar, clearly an otherworld animal, to a castle which had not been there before. Their dogs disappear into it, following the boar, and after waiting for some time for them to reappear, Pryderi rashly follows them in.

Inside he finds the castle completely empty, except for a golden bowl on a marble slab, hanging in the middle of the courtyard from four chains which disappear into the air above. The beauty of the bowl tempts him to touch it, and when he does his hands stick to it and his feet to the slab below and he becomes unable to speak. After some time waiting for him outside, Rhiannon follows him in.

She sees the bowl with Pryderi fixed fast to it, and impulsively she too clasps it. Her hands stick to the bowl, her feet to the slab, and her power of speech goes. In another explosion of thunder and another heavy mist they, and the castle in which they are imprisoned, disappear.

Manawydan and Pryderi's wife are thus left alone in an empty Dyfed. The story as we have it in the Mabinogion interposes into these events three trips to England, showing a curious and unusual recognition of the geographical relations of the setting. 'England', though, seems to be a mistranslation of the name of the place to which they go. This is called by the tale Lloegyr, which in the old traditional divisions of Britain was the area which is now England (as opposed to Wales and Scotland). Lloegr is the present Welsh word for England, but to early Welsh literature the term meant a geographical area equally applicable to pre-Roman Britain as to the Britain of the post-Saxon-invasion. It is possible that the Lloegwyr, the 'Lloegrians', as opposed to the Cymru, or Cambrians, were, as the Triads in fact claim for them, one of several Celtic tribes which colonized Britain. The Triads, which say the Lloegwyr came from Gascony, are unfortunately highly unreliable; but we do have evidence that the European Celts did have some such sub-nation or tribal branch, since at least one river and one region, apart from Lloegyr, seems to have been called after them. The old name for the river Loire was Liger, and the Celtic area of northern Italy is still known as Liguria.

The interjections, in the story, of the references to Lloegyr, and particularly the two large repetitive sequences in which the characters travel in Lloegyr as craftsmen, seem to infer that some of the material came from that direction. Perhaps we have two sets of elements, the Lloegyr-craftsmen stories and the Dyfed-enchantment stories, which have been put together through connection with, for instance, the figure of Manawydan. At any rate when Manawydan comes back from his second stay in Lloegyr he brings into Dyfed the seed of its rejuvenation, and sets the story moving into its final phase. He brings wheat and with it the practice of agriculture into a country where previously it had been necessary to live by hunting.

The wheat does well; but as the time for harvest comes the stalks are stripped and the ears carried away by some mysterious agency under cover of night. This happens field by field as Manawydan prepares to harvest, until he decides to watch the last remaining field throughout the night.

The corn, he finds, is being carried off by an enormous army of mice. And when he tries to catch them they all scatter − except for one which, because it is heavy and slow, he manages to grab. He then threatens to hang this representative culprit as a thief, and as he does so several attempts to dissuade him are made by passing characters, who seemingly turn up specially for the purpose. He has the gallows erected ready on the mound at Arberth and the mouse in the noose before this figure who has come to him in several guises is forced to reveal his identity. He is the one who has put the enchantment on Dyfed, captured Pryderi and Rhiannon, and systematically destroyed Manawydan's corn by changing his army into mice. The mouse which Manawydan has caught is, by good chance, this personage's wife, slower than the others because pregnant, and consequently he is willing to agree to anything to ransom her.

Manawydan makes his terms: the return of Rhiannon and Pryderi, the lifting of the spell of desolation, the promise that such things will never take place again. Wisely he adds the condition that the enchanter shall not take revenge on him or the others for this victory, and with that security, and the return of Pryderi and Rhiannon, he sets the mouse free. The houses and the herds and homesteads return, as he looks around at Dyfed.

It is added as a sort of postscript that Rhiannon's suffering while imprisoned in the otherworld had involved having an ass's collar hung around her head, a detail unconnected with the plot which seems likely to be an interjected explanation of the occasional depiction of Epona, the Romano-Celtic horse-goddess, wearing a horse's trappings – or perhaps, again, of a ritual in which a priestess personified Epona. In the portrayal of Rhiannon as a whole, we can see a very probable case of a statue or relief of a mother-goddess in horse-form, perhaps with a horse-child, its meaning largely lost, being reinterpreted in the light of hazy memories of old gods and cults, before being transformed again at some later stage (by someone ignorant even of such sources) into a feature of a narrative sequence designed to entertain.

There are three themes, contained in this simple sequence connected with the names of Manawydan and Rhiannon, which relate the story to the central stream of European mythology and indeed to much else. The theme of the waste land; that of the journey to or imprisonment in the otherworld; and the introduction of agriculture. We have seen already that Rhiannon, through her connection with horses, appears to be related to the eastern European goddess Demeter. Demeter too was a mother-figure – indeed her name is based on the Indo-European root word for mother, meter – and Rhiannon, having lost her child once in the earlier story, now loses Pryderi again in the mysterious castle. In the Demeter myth she would have searched for him, perhaps following him to the otherworld rather than going with him, and the desolation of the land would have been connected directly with this. If we have the same sort of myth here it has become confused, but the elements of something recognizable as an earth-mother, barren-land, renewal-of-vitality sequence remain quite clear.

In the Greek myth, which appears to have come into Europe from the Middle East, the sudden barrenness of the land is caused by Demeter's mourning for the loss of her daughter, abducted by the king of the underworld and imprisoned in his kingdom. When the daughter is eventually freed, through the intervention of Zeus, the trees sprout again and the flowers bloom; but since Persephone, the daughter, is now obliged to spend a period of the year below, this sequence becomes a regular event. The theme of the waste land as it appears in Celtic myth is related but slightly less explicit. It bears rather more a psychological air than an agricultural one, and indeed seems to be more abstract and mysterious than Demeter's simple seasonal mourning.

The symbolism of the waste land is on several levels; we shall come across it again in its fullest form in connection with the search for the grail. The Rhiannon-Demeter version, with its close connections with descent into the otherworld, seems almost a simplified form of the image. It occurs too at the end of another Welsh mythic tale, 'Branwen, daughter of Llŷr', in the form of the desolation of the land of Ireland following the wounding of Bran; and this, the idea of the maimed king's disability causing the infertility of the country over which he rules, is its true grail form. Jung and the Jungians have much to make of this series of ideas, for instance in Jung's book *Psychology and Alchemy* and the expansion of his ideas by his widow in *The Grail Legend*. The lameness of the king causes the barrenness of the land through the magical relation of kings to their kingdoms, his cure bringing about its revitalization; and this symbolically reflects the need for the debilitated psyche to undergo renewal or symbolic rebirth. That sort of mental waste land is familiar enough to most people, often occurring after illness and on Monday mornings. It is variously termed, for instance by sociologists, anomie or accidie, or, by some psychologists, regression or loss of libido. Everything seems futile, the meaning of life is suddenly missing, nothing seems worth the effort. For that state Demeter's arid Attica, the maimed king's infertile kingdom, and Manawydan's bewitched Dyfed, empty of its population, herds, and flocks, all seem adequate expressions.

There is also the view that the theme of the failure of vegetation reflects the memory of great droughts and consequent crop failures or loss of pasture, which is strongly borne out by the frequent incidence of this element in the myths of lands where such disasters happen more often, such as western Asia. In such matters there is always a tendency to take up combative positions; but we are not, in mythology, in the land of either/or. Many contributory factors from different directions go to make up a cohesive whole. An image can be at the same time the collective memory of bad years and failed crops and, with no contradiction, the expression of the withdrawal of the spirit, which occurs to everyone at times – especially, as with Demeter, at times of mourning.

The connection of the waste land with the grail highlights another aspect of this story of Rhiannon, since, although as so often in myth the elements of the sequence have got into a different order, the same set of events seems to happen here as in the grail stories. Myth is kaleidoscopic. Elements continually re-sort themselves into new patterns. Here, however, the ingredients seem to be in remarkably pure (and therefore perhaps progenitive) form.

The sacred bowl in the mysterious castle will concern us again, when we come to consider the origins of the holy grail. The adventure of Pryderi and Rhiannon belongs to this group of themes, the mysteries of grail castle; and so to a certain extent does what happens to them then, the transportation to another world. Several times in the grail group of stories a leading character enters a trance-like state, being, like Pryderi when Rhiannon finds him, rendered unable to speak by, in some of these cases, the presence of the mystic bowl. Sometimes there is a more definite journey involved; particularly the crossing of a dark ocean in a mysterious boat. This otherworld trip occurs independently in almost all mythology, and seems therefore to be the bearer of significance in its own right.

We have already seen how Pwyll, Rhiannon's husband and Pryderi's father, exchanged his kingdom with the king of the otherworld, thus spending a period of time below. The earliest known version of the Persephone theme is probably that of Ishtar, the Babylonian character, whose disappearance also caused the earth to become unfruitful. In Greek

*The Sagrani stone in the National Museum of Wales, an example of the Irish
'ogam' script*

myth we know that Orpheus and Odysseus both visited Hades and
returned, as did the Attic hero Theseus. There is little doubt that it is
through the strength and continuity of this descent theme that the idea
eventually got into Christianity. There is no evidence in the Gospels
which would justify the inclusion of the phrase 'He descended into Hell'
in the Apostles' Creed.

Many characters in Celtic myth also made this trip into and back from
the counterpart realm. There is a long early Welsh poem, 'The Spoils of
Annwn', about a sort of raiding expedition made on it, in which Pwyll
and Pryderi, and also Arthur, are mentioned. On that occasion too a
magic bowl is involved, the property of the Chief of Annwn, which
Arthur and company have apparently gone there to steal. In the Irish
stories the journey usually takes the form of a voyage, the best example
of which is that of Bran, who sets out on a timeless trip which takes him
to islands of Odyssean strangeness. In mainland Britain the otherworld is
not so specifically located across water, but rather, as these examples of
the transference of Pwyll, Pryderi, and Rhiannon illustrate, it seems to be
right here amongst us, but in a different dimensional system.

As in the grail stories the land becomes fertile again when the lame king
is cured, so in the Demeter-Rhiannon one the restoration of life to the
countryside is closely connected with the return of the missing characters. But here too we have a further linking theme, since what has
happened in the meantime is that Manawydan has introduced the
practice of agriculture to Dyfed. Similarly before she left Elevsis to
return to Olympus Demeter taught the royal family there how to culti-
vate, sow, and harvest, and told them to travel the world teaching this
craft; consequently the origin of the cultivation of grain in Attica became
a Greek tradition. In both the Greek and the British stories the idea of
agriculture being invented occurs in connection with the unusual destitu-
tion of the land, as if it is a precaution which can in future be taken against
droughts and bad seasons.

That Manawydan should be entrusted with these rather large ideas
makes him a person of some importance. Named in the Welsh version as
the son of Llŷr, he is clearly the same person, or much the same, as the
great Irish god Manannan mac Lir, the god of the sea (with also slight
connections with horses) who is therefore a sort of Celtic Poseidon. In
Irish myth he rides across the waves – to his wonderful horse the sea is

the same as the dry land – from his off-shore palace, very much in the manner of Poseidon as he appears in Homer's *Iliad*. Since there is a clue in the stallion and mare transformations of Poseidon and Demeter that they were at an early stage thought of as consorts, Great King and Great Queen, Manannan's equivalent function might in itself be enough to explain Manawydan's otherwise rather unexpected appearance as the husband of Rhiannon. W. J. Gruffydd, in his great work of literary detection *Rhiannon,* traces the possible course of the name itself, from Manannan to Manawydan, via early forms of orthography and copyists' errors, and in spite of the complete absence, in 'Manawydan, son of Llŷr', of any of Manannan's sea-riding super-heroism, the connection is secure between this rather humble figure in the countryside of Dyfed and the great Irish sea-god.

Manannan among other things gave his name to the Isle of Man, the only piece of land in his domain, which by its midway position between Wales and Ireland well suits his apparently overlapping scope. At several points in the Mabinogion material we can infer Irish influence – just as we know from the place names and from the ogam inscriptions and intertwined carvings found in the area where the story is set that there were early Christian contacts between Ireland and Dyfed, which we can reasonably guess would be only the historical end of a long tradition of either invasion or communication. We know that in the fifth and sixth centuries the Irish occupation of south-west Wales amounted to a colonization. Probably Manawydan and some of the ideas came into this area by this route, but if they did they must have come as graftings onto a native stock, since much of the material does not find any correspondence in the rich and extensive body of myth across the Irish Sea.

In Irish Manannan's patronym 'mac Lir' means 'son of the sea'. The name Llŷr is always treated in the British versions as the name of the person, though he never occurs in his own right but only as the father of various important characters. We shall see in the grail sequence how Bran and his sister Branwen were said to be, like Manawydan, the children of Llŷr. The suggestion seems to be that Llŷr, like Don or Danann, was the identifying deity of a tribal group, the children of Llŷr thus being the representatives of one branch, though probably a minor one, of the Celtic peoples.

Once into mythology Llŷr took root, retaining his father-figure character, and through a confusion with the much more firmly-established figure Lludd (whom we shall meet in a later chapter) acquired a daughter named Creiddylad. He did so through Geoffrey of Monmouth's transformation of the original Llŷr, father of some minor divinities, into Leir, an early king of Britain, and of Lludd's daughter Creiddylad into Leir's daughter Cordelia, with the addition of two other daughters and a story of flattery and tragedy. This concoction of Geoffrey's then passed into the Chronicles from which Shakespeare drew, with the result that it has become one of our best known but least authentic national myths.

On the Borders of History

Whatever I write in this book (in a crude style indeed,
but well-meant) is rather for lamentation than display;
let no one think that it comes from contempt for others
or from self-esteem, (for indeed I weep with bitter
tears the loss of all good things and the piling up of
evils) but from my sympathy with my country in her
heavy miseries, and a desire to see the remedy of them.

Gildas, *c.* AD 546

The Iron Age fortress of the Ordovices at Pen-y-Gaer in Gwynedd

4 The Romans leave

A few of the great events and periods in the early life of a country will stick in its memory for ever. We have, for instance, never forgotten that for some four hundred years of our childhood as a nation we were subject to the pedagogic authority of Rome. Perhaps what was so incisive about the Roman occupation was that it was clearly bounded. They came and they went. The seeing and the conquering were an interim between those fixed limits. The other invaders of this island, the Celts, the Saxons, and the Normans, came and then were absorbed and assimilated by their predecessors. The Romans went away again. They never became Britons, nor, completely, did Britons become Romans. And yet it could hardly be the case that the people of Britain do not include in their attitudes and outlook the influences of those four centuries of occupation.

Rome is consequently in the background of much of the mythology. Geoffrey of Monmouth has Arthur refusing to pay tribute to the Emperor and instead marching against Rome to defeat the imperial army; and Malory devotes a long section of 'Le Morte d'Arthur' to repeating and expanding this (in terms which show that the Crusades had taken place in between), ending with the crowning of Arthur as Emperor of Rome. This was the high peak of his career, and of our wish-fulfilling daydream, in which we put the bullies in their place and emerge as universal hero. No doubt the high fantasies of such heroic achievements always come from the weaker side, and myth owes a lot to such compensations. 'Mankind as a whole had a like dream once,' says Yeats. But the facts were different.

We can easily see from archaeology that the centre of the occupation was the area which probably always was and will be the population base of Britain, the south and east. This is a result of the form of the land, since Britain is somehow heaped up towards the north and west, as if an attempt to sweep away its rough surface had been abandoned once enough smooth land was cleared. The Romans were essentially urbanized, and the fullest expression of their domination was in the building of a town; by contrast with the fortified enclosures which the native tribes lived in, these towns were square, planned and mortared, and mostly on low-lying sites. The best evidence that the Romans did not completely control Wales, even at the height of their occupation of Britain, is the lack of Roman towns there. We know that they hardly penetrated Scotland at all, and had to be content with fencing it off.

What the Romans had in mind for the British is exemplified in Wales solely by Caerwent, its very exception making the point that the subjection of the tribes was never a complete reality. The great South Wales tribe, the Silures, were evidently moved out of their hillfort and settled in the purpose-built town of Caerwent, to continue their lives in a more orderly fashion on the plain, under Roman supervision. The nearby fortress of Caerleon forms the material evidence of that watchful eye. Such control did not exist elsewhere in Wales, nor did those villa homesteads spring up which are common in the pacified lands, so that during the whole occupation there was this lingering westerly tension keeping the Romans attentive.

One should not think in terms of Italians living in these square, carefully-mortared outposts, although no doubt there were some who came from as far away as Rome. The widespread use of Latin must have been achieved by the climax of the occupation, enabling troops of many varied nations to work together effectively. In Britain there were Germans and Gauls, as well as British Roman troops, and, as we shall see, the man through whom the myths remember the ending of the period was born in Spain. Europe was unified by Roman central administration as it has never been unified since, and Britain was, from that point of view, only an outlying bit of Empire. There was intermarriage at several levels, and we shall see how the leaders of the late and post-Roman period are remembered as a sort of Romano-British elite. But what kept Britain identifiable, and allowed it to emerge eventually as something other than just a part of early-medieval Europe, was this ragged edge to the Empire, the mountainous terrain of the west and the north, which favoured loosely-organized guerrilla action and the sort of tribal resilience which survives best when on the defensive, thriving on those easily-defended hill tops, the same terrain which most obstructs the cumbersome machinery of highly-equipped imperialist expansion.

Perhaps because the Romans penetrated even into this heartland, myth finds it necessary to deal with them here, to assimilate them in the wish-revised memory and subordinate them by absorbing them into the national culture. The story which encapsulated the whole period, from arrival to departure, in a single simple image, is called 'The Dream of Lord Maxen', and it starts off, with great courage and imagination, in the countryside around Rome.

The Emperor Maxen has gone out hunting with his retinue of subject kings, and because of the great heat in the middle of the day he had a canopy raised over him, and fell asleep. As he slept, in that Italian river valley, he dreamt that he was travelling across another country, then on a sea voyage which took him to an island, 'the loveliest in the world', which he then crossed to its further shore. Here he came to a rough and mountainous land full of steep slopes and crags. From the heights of that land he could see another island near the shore, and at the mouth of a river flowing towards the sea he saw a great castle. He went down and entered it, and found it to be richly furnished. It was the daughter of the house who greeted him, and in his dream he sat down with her in her golden chair. And at that moment of the dream, with his arms around her and their cheeks together, the story says, 'What with the dogs straining at their leashes, and the edges of the shields banging against each other, and the spear shafts hitting together, and the stamping and neighing of the horses, the Emperor woke.' The poor man found that he was so in love with the girl he had dreamt of that no part of him, down to the tips of his fingernails, was free of that love. In great depression he rode back to Rome; and during the next week his lack of appetite and spirit began to worry his attendants. All he wanted to do was sleep, so that he could dream of the woman.

Eventually he reveals his dream and sends out messengers to find the place of it, and after an initial year of failure they at last find the route he dreamt he took. They cross the sea in the ship he used in his dream, and come to the island of Britain. After travelling across the island they reach the mountains of the west, and having penetrated these they see ahead of them the island of Anglesey, and the land of Arfon in between. They see the river Seint, with a castle at its mouth, and find within it everything exactly as the Emperor had described. Falling on their knees before the woman they had come to find, they proclaim her Empress of Rome. When given the choice of going to Rome or awaiting the Emperor in Arfon, the lady very reasonably expressed slight scepticism about the whole thing, and suggested that if the Emperor really loved her he had better come to Wales.

The messengers went back, and repeated the journey as guides to their lord. The Emperor then, the tale says, conquered the island of Britain from Beli, its current king, and drove him and his people into the sea. Without pausing he then went on to Arfon. He recognized the land as soon as he saw it, and the castle at the mouth of the river Seint, and went straight in to marry his Empress. As a wedding present she asked, among other things, for three strongholds to be made for her, one here in Arfon, the other two at Caer Fyrddin and Caer Llion. In these latter we recognize the two chief Roman forts of Wales, at Carmarthen and Caerleon.

After her marriage, the story says, Elen, the new Empress, set about making great roads from one fortress to another across the whole country. The Emperor, we are told, stayed in Britain for seven years, as a result of which a new Emperor was proclaimed in Rome. When Maxen heard of this he gathered an army and set out to restore his rule, conquering France, Burgundy, and Italy, and laying siege to Rome. It was eventually the British troops who followed him ('Better fighters were in that small host than twice their number of Romans') that won the city, by making skilful use of a culture difference between the two forces. All the Romans of both sides used to take their main meal at midday, when fighting would stop, but the Britons favoured a large breakfast, after which they drank. Not too much, apparently, to handle scaling-ladders, and one noontime while both Emperors were eating they went over the ramparts. It was thus the British who took Rome, and only as an act of generosity did they give it back to the rightful Emperor, and his British wife. Some of the Britons went home, after further European conquests, while some stayed on, and founded the colony in Brittany.

Part of the charm of this story is its innocent simplicity, which can represent the invasion, the occupation, and the departure all in terms of a tale of love, and an absurdly simple one, even for a tale of love. You dream of a woman in a castle, and when you go there, there she is. Falling in love in dreams is of course a common predicament in folk tales – the Irish 'Dream of Oengus' is a good example – but it is seldom so easily resolved. But behind this characteristically pleasing and direct interpretation lies a great wealth of historical material, much of it indeed quite grand and heroic, though located in an altogether less satisfactorily ordered world, the real one.

What the tale summarizes is a long and multiple process, representing the several phases and waves of Roman invasion and also, very probably, the various British actions in continental Europe. Nevertheless there are several elements in it which can be clearly identified. We have on one level occasional references to deeply-rooted mythic material, such as the statement that Beli (who occurs also as the father of Lludd, whom we shall meet in the next chapter) was king of Britain when the Romans came. As we shall see, this Beli is a recognizable Celtic god, so that perhaps what is being said is that the pre-Roman island was still subject to the traditional religion. The story shows an understanding of the effects of the imposition of Roman systems onto an already firmly established native order, the partial absorption of the one by the other. And it reveals an inevitable awareness of the solid relics of Roman buildings themselves, which, since they are still so clearly visible today, must have been remarkable reminders of the significance of the long visit paid by Rome.

The one with which the story of Maxen deals in particular, the castle at the mouth of the river Seint, in Arfon, lies now a little way away from the river, which has moved, and a little way inland from its mouth, which has silted. From it you look down today onto the water of the Menai Strait, on the town of Caernarfon beside the shore, and indeed (since the Roman site is slightly raised in relation to the shore-level) over the tops of the towers of King Edward's impressive and famous castle. The Romans called it Segontium, Latinizing, as was their habit, the name of the nearby river Seint. The place is mentioned also in the tale of 'Branwen', and occurs in the early British history compiled by Nennius as Caer Segeint, one of the twenty-eight cities of the island.

That Segontium should have been chosen as a representative Roman site by the mythology perhaps reflects its distinction in being so far west, deep in the heartland where the myths accumulated. In fact, despite the claim of Nennius's 'History', it was never really a town, let alone a city. Rather it was an auxiliary fort, one of many outposts of the regional fortress at Chester, although in its final phases it seems large enough to have been a centre of local administration in its own right. It was also surrounded by the haphazard accretion of the dwellings of traders and their families, rather as a shanty town inevitably grows up around the

The outline of the Roman camp at Segontium in modern Caernarfon

intentionally planned town in so many parts of the modern world.

The fort represents the Roman awareness of the strength of resistance on this frontier of their control, taking its place very precisely in the sequence of events described by Tacitus, which occurred in the mid and late summer of the year AD 78. The Silures had just been subdued in the rather easier fighting country of South Wales. The Ordovices, however, the tribe which occupied North Wales, had succeeded in decimating a cavalry troop, an achievement which must have meant much to morale on both sides. As autumn approached it seemed that this state of play would be the governing one for the rest of that year. But the new governor, Agricola, decided on a spearhead thrust into the heart of the land which was harbouring the resistance. The Ordovices wisely stayed in the mountains, but he was sufficiently determined not to be daunted by their natural advantage there. Tacitus says that Agricola himself led his men into the hills; but Tacitus was his son-in-law. He also says that the assault succeeded in destroying almost the whole fighting force of the Ordovices. How much of this is Roman self-congratulation we do not know for certain. We do know that the building of forts along the strategic routes through North Wales was the immediate result, and that Segontium was among them.

So it was not through love that the Emperor came, nor out of a blissful marriage with the new country that he remained. The original wooden field-fort at Segontium was greatly strengthened during the next hundred years, indicating increased rather than reduced danger and need for control. This new stone-built fort, with its excellent access by sea, turned out to be a crucial link in the network which remained as at least a constant threat to overt insurrection throughout Wales until the fourth century AD. The story summarizes the arrival and the staying, but it is to its final emptying that it relates most closely.

At that early time history tends to take a simple form, and our view of it is blurred by the interests and intentions of those who relayed it, to the extent of often leaving us unsure of the difference between history and tale. But Maxen in the story undeniably represents a person in the real world of Roman Britain, to be precise a certain Magnus Maximus, a soldier under Count Theodosius who found himself serving in the British forces during the second half of the fourth century. He had been born in Spain, and his presence here in itself seems to proclaim him to be something of an adventurer, one of those willing to undertake other people's wars in places in which they have no natural interest. We know that he did well, rising to commanding rank and probably leading the successful assaults against the Picts which immediately preceded his entry into history. Bede says that he was able and energetic, though one wonders how Bede would have known, except the way that we do. He needed to be able and energetic to achieve what he then did.

It seems that the island had become rather remote from central attention, and dissatisfaction with the rule of the Emperor Gratian exploded into a rebellion in which Maximus's troops proclaimed him Emperor, early in the year 383. Whatever his own part in this sudden elevation may have been, he was quick to put it into action. At once he invaded Gaul, taking with him not only his own legion but whatever auxiliary troops he could get. By the end of the summer he had killed the Emperor and established his own court. This largely British force then held Gaul for the next four years, after which, reinforced from Britain, it moved into Italy. In the meantime the Empire had come to recognize his de facto imperiality; apart from him the nearest person to an overall leader which it then had was Theodosius, son of the 'Count' Theodosius who had led the anti-invasion campaigns in Britain in the 360s and 70s. He, as Gratian's co-Emperor in charge of the eastern Empire, had stayed conveniently out of the way while Gratian was removed. Theodosius at first accepted Maximus's victory, content to let him rule in Gaul. But his advance into Italy must have been more of a threat. By the early part of the next year, 388, the British rebels were in Rome.

For Britain the real significance of this was not that achievement but the fact that the Romans had, in the process of invading Europe, left the island. As an effective occupying force, they had gone. This, which might have seemed a long-awaited blessing, in fact filled the remaining islanders with dismay. A great deal had changed during the last period of occupation, as is quite clear from the massive strength of the forts of the

The Romano-Celtic temple inside the Iron Age fort of Maiden Castle, Dorset

Saxon Shore, built during the hundred years preceding Maximus's revolt. The wholesale removal of the island's fighting forces must have given the civilian inhabitants adequate cause for terror. The presence of the legion had no longer been a threat, but a symbol of security which was becoming more and more necessary. Certainly Gildas, two hundred years later, records an impression of treachery to Britain by Maximus, resulting in permanent and irreversible damage. 'Putting out a shoot of its own planting,' Britain sends Maximus to the two Gauls,

> accompanied by a great crowd of followers, with an emperor's tokens (*insignibus*) in addition, which he never bore worthily nor legitimately, but as one elected after the manner of a tyrant (*ritu tyrranico*) and amid a turbulent soldiery. . . . After this, Britain is robbed of all her armed soldiery, of her military supplies, of her rulers, cruel though they were, and of her vigorous youth who followed the footsteps of the above-mentioned tyrant and never returned. Completely ignorant of the practice of war she is for the first time open to be trampled upon by two foreign tribes of extreme cruelty, the Scots from the north-west, the Picts from the north; and for many years continues stunned and groaning.

Such then was the reality, as opposed to the myth, of Britain's ironic turning of the tables against Rome. It was into such a situation that the Saxons then launched their increasingly strong invasions. There is no doubt that Maximus's withdrawal was critical for the country's future, so that he is remembered both by Gildas and by the mythicized story as being of central significance, and with good reason. Both the story and the history imply that one of the results was that most of the Britons who went with Maximus stayed in Europe, founding British colonies there, and never came back. The colonization of Brittany by British refugees in fact took place as part of the immediate sequel, as Gildas recognized.

A coin found at Segontium showing Magnus Maximus

They fled there from Britain when the Saxons swept the country in the mid-fifth century. It was for this reason that Brittany became, and still is, a British-speaking country, the language there being not a separate subdivision of the Celtic group but a dialect form of the island British which, along with Latin, was spoken everywhere in Britain south of Scotland until the domination of the Saxons.

There is no doubt that colonies of Britons would have been formed when that notorious and heroic expedition finally disbanded. They would have found plentiful Celtic colonies still in existence, indeed have felt comparatively at home throughout Roman Gaul, so that it would be hard to identify any direct results of Maximus's movements. Traces of Celtic influence in such places as Gallicia and Liguria might owe something both to pre-Roman residues and post-Roman migrations. Maximus himself did not last long, once he had had the audacity to take Rome. The eastern Emperor Theodosius arrived, defeated him, and beheaded him at Aquila, in central Italy, in July 388, five years after the death of Gratian.

It is perhaps not totally without foundation that these events should have become associated, in the tradition, with Caernarfon. At Segontium we find considerable restoration shortly before the time of Maximus's rise to power, then almost complete evacuation in the year of his invasion of Gaul, in 383. The dates are fairly accurately identifiable from the finds of coins, and the presence of a small garrison there up to the year 390 is attested in this way. Remarkably there was sufficient confidence in the reality of this new British Emperor and enough time and organization for the British rebels to mint their own coins, by which no doubt the soldiers left stranded at Segontium were paid. As a result we can see the face of the Emperor Magnus Maximus on a coin found there, a long-headed, high-browed, quite un-Roman face, with a small snubbed nose and a strong, thrusting chin. Not at all an unpleasant face or a proud or aggressive one, but rather that of a youngish, open-natured man.

Emperor-making was not a new occupation for the troops in Britain, since it had been achieved with great success in 306, when the legions garrisoned at York proclaimed as Emperor the man who was to become significant to history for his establishment of Christianity as the official religion of the Empire – Constantine the Great, the son of the Emperor Constantius, who was at the time serving in Britain. And it is perhaps this local hero's mother, Helena, who is remembered by the story as Maxen's bride, the British princess Elen. Elen of the Legions, Elen of the Hosts, a heroine of the vague British memories of the Roman period, is traditionally associated with the building of the great Roman roads, as indeed she is in the story of Maxen. Probably this tradition records that it was under Constantius, her husband, and his son Constantine that the roads became fully established – though as campaigning routes they had obviously been in existence since the time of Agricola, and even then frequently followed ancient trackways.

Constantine's mother Helena was not in fact British, but probably of Asian origin. She seems to have become a well-known figure in her own right, to the extent of having coins minted in her name, and the discovery of twelve of these at Segontium testifies at least to a knowledge of her existence in these parts. Geoffrey of Monmouth, however, though he correctly relates her as wife to the Emperor Constantius and mother of Constantine, gives her as the daughter of the British king Coel (famous possessor of the cheerful temperament and the violin-trio), who he says was king of Britain when Constantius arrived, so that the Roman Emperor in effect married into the kingship. Was there a British princess somewhere in the background of the tradition, remembered both by Geoffrey's version and by the Maxen story (in both of which a Roman leader marries into the native aristocracy), who became confused with Constantius's wife, Constantine's mother, the Empress Helena, at some later date?

The most remarkable feature of the connection of the British Roman roads with Helena or Elen is that some of them still bear her name – Sarn Elen, Elen's causeway: a title which you may find still on the map and in common use. There is more than one Sarn Elen in Wales, but the great north-south road which runs through the territory of the Elen of the story still carries that name. It leaves the fort on the Conwy river to link with a southern route from Segontium, which it meets at a point we have already been to, the camp up on the moorland at Tomen-y-Mur, where Lleu Llaw Gyffes had his court in the tale of 'Math', from which Blodeuedd's maidens fled to their deaths in the lake and she to her final meeting with Gwydion and her transformation. Across the hills and heather-land of that rough country it runs straight and determinedly, a track wide enough to take a vehicle, probably there for ever. Elen as permanent representative of the wife of a British Emperor has found these strange memorials.

The tale in fact converts history. It takes some fragments of real events and transforms them, mythicizing the matter until it becomes symbolic. In doing so it provides us with a useful and instructive example. The process which happened to Magnus Maximus might have happened to the original of Arthur, or, come to that, of Agamemnon, or Moses, or even Christ. The crystallization of a whole succession of events – the coming of the Romans, their liaison with the island's natives, connections of Emperors with Britain, the withdrawal and the role in it played by Maximus – into a single story also provides a paradigm for the understanding of what is often being done in myth. History enters myth through the medium of symbolization. There were, for instance, several depletions of Britain's fighting force during the breakdown of the western Empire, but they may conveniently be represented by the one caused by Maximus.

The conclusive withdrawal of Roman power did not in fact take place until the 420s, after the death of the Emperor Honorius, when the army was apparently needed in the increasing chaos of the Continental Empire. The Britons had rebelled in 410, and though they nominally remained loyal to Honorius (the insurrection being against a usurping Emperor called Constantine) they expelled all the Roman officers in Britain, effectively ending imperial administration and proclaiming their independence. It is this act which perhaps marks the formal ending of imperial rule over this island. Between that event and the withdrawal instigated by Maximus there had even been a partial return, when the Roman general Stilicho brought troops to protect the desperately beleaguered country, in about 399. In 446, changing their minds about autonomy, the ruling citizens of Britain appealed for help again, but their plea was ignored. Britain, for military and political purposes, was by then, and from then, on its own.

Whatever the oversimplifications of the story may be, there is no doubt that the Empire removed its fighting forces from Britain to deal with trouble elsewhere. With the rebellion of Maximus we enter the post-Roman period, and although the remains of the administration in Britain continued to communicate with Rome, and even received some further help during the early fifth century, when Rome finally refused to recognize Britain as being any more its responsibility, in the year 446, the next phase of the nation's painful growth became inevitable. It is one of the more poignant ironies that the withdrawal of Rome, which cleared the way for a revival of independence, at the same time cleared the way for the forces which were ultimately to prevent that.

The 'Roman Steps' near Sarn Elen in Gwynedd

5 The Saxons arrive

The early history of this island is a catalogue of invasions. Indeed the history of islands usually is, and all that is remarkable about our island's history is that the invasions stopped. In remembering that we have not been invaded since 1066, we easily forget that what was invaded then was an amalgam of several thousand years of successive invasions. The Normans added a veneer to a lamination which included equivalent layers of pre-Celtic cairn-builders and pre-Bronze-Age cromlech-builders.

It is odd that the island is now generally thought of as England, since Angle-land must always have been something of a misnomer for the country occupied by the West Saxons, the Mercians, the Middle and South Saxons, the Jutes, and, among others, the East Angles. So late was the invention of the idea of Angle-land, so unstable its foundation in reality, and so brief its applicability, that one wonders how it could have come about. There is no doubt that at a certain point something cataclysmic took place, sufficient to make a definite break with the long sequence of events up to that time. It was not, of course, the simple set of occurrences by which myth remembers it, but once again myth gives an easily-grasped simplification of something more diffuse. We find the historical sources of the story in Gildas and in the work known as the 'Historia Brittonum', written, or rather collected from much older material, by a North Wales priest called Nennius, in about AD 800. From there the material passed through a familiar expansion in the imagination of Geoffrey of Monmouth; and a related but apparently independent Welsh tale gives another aspect of the subject.

In Geoffrey's version we have a complicated story of intrigue and treachery, but he took from Nennius the simple but compelling episode in which the Saxons and the Britons come to a meeting to discuss the terms of a truce, the former however bringing with them daggers concealed in their boots, the latter attending unarmed. The British high-king Vortigern alone survived that archetypal event, known as the Night of the Long Knives. Moving further from history into myth, Nennius takes us straight from that slaughter to Snowdonia.

The retreating king made for the fastnesses of North Wales, that bulk of scrub and crag which was to be the last-stand refuge for later independent princes too, and there, under Snowdon, he tried to build a castle. But as much as he built during the day disappeared during the night. The

A symbol of Saxon power: the superb helmet from the Sutton Hoo ship

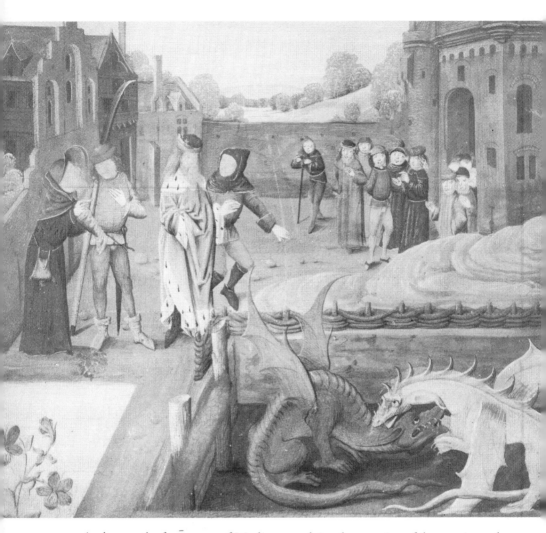

Ambros – the forerunner of Merlin – explains the meaning of the warring red and white dragons to Vortigern

king consulted his wise men – an implication, perhaps, of the heathen, perhaps Druidical surroundings of the story – who directed him to sacrifice on the spot a boy without a father. Suddenly we are into myth. The world in which one negotiates with invaders has rolled away, and that in which the mystery of supernatural conception and the ritual of child-sacrifice are dominant themes replaces it.

Messengers, the Nennius story continues, were sent out. In the south of Wales they found a boy who claimed to have no father, and they brought him north to Snowdon. Confronted on the hilltop with his imminent death, he demanded to question the wise men. What was it, he asked, that was hidden under the paving on the hill's summit? They did not know, but he did. There was a pool there. They opened the paving, and found the pool. And what was in the pool? he asked. To their ignorance he replied that there were two containers; on separating the containers they would find a wrapping – literally a 'tent' between two 'vases'; and in the wrapping two serpents, one of them white, the other red. All this was discovered as predicted, and when they then unfolded the cloth and released the serpents he told them also what would happen next. The serpents began to fight each other, the white one at first winning, and then, after the third near defeat, the red one recovering and finally driving out the white. The king and his magicians stood astonished as the prophetic boy explained all this to them. The pool, he told them, was the world, the tent Vortigern's kingdom. The two serpents were the dragons of two nations, the red one that of the natives of Britain, the white one the invading Saxons. In the end, he said, our people will drive out the Saxons and send them back to where they came from. But as far as Vortigern was concerned, there was no future for him on this hill. It was he, the boy, who should have control of the castle to be built there. He gave his name then: Ambros.

There can be little doubt that the name refers to somebody who actually existed. In the early Welsh literature he appears as Emrys, and this, it is clear, is the name given in these versions to the most notable and respected of the British leaders of the early post-Roman period, Ambrosius Aurelianus. A likely date for the rise to power of this figure would be the mid-fifth century, and this, we shall see, tallies with the archaeological remains on a hill which bears his name, Dinas Emrys. To root him thus in history, however, only makes more prominent his transformation in myth into the prodigious fatherless child, the prophetic magician, ultimately – so it turned out – into the wizard Merlin.

It is to Gildas's credit that he saw very clearly, if with the sharpened vision of bigotry, the historical causes of the turmoil of his time. Ambrosius emerges as the hero partly because of Gildas's angled concerns, since Gildas was focussing on Vortigern's blunder and its consequences. As a cleric he was perhaps more naturally inclined to the Romanized, the civilized and ordered world which Ambrosius, with his Roman name, seemed to him to stand for. We detect in the myth, at any rate, vestiges of pagan influences shadowing the character of Vortigern. He, it seems, was representative of the fragmentation, the decay of political administration, which for a time replaced all that Gildas admired.

'Tunc omnes consiliarii una cum superbo tyranno caecantur adinvenientes tale praesidium. . . .' ('All the counsellors and the high and mighty king were blinded then, such defence did they devise. . . .') He tells the story with the vigour of anger, in his dog Latin, the anger in his voice still clear to us more than fourteen centuries later. But those events which brought Ambrosius and Vortigern to this hilltop, so real to him, have results for us too, even at this distance, since, if he was right about their causal nature, they have spawned a very long descent of disordering effects.

Firstly, then, (before we see what images and ideas the myth has synthesized from the episode), we may gain from Gildas a view, partial, in two senses, but significant, of the historical background to the Nennius story. Britain was weakened by the withdrawal of her soldiery, symptomized, as we have seen, by the story of Maxen. It was misruled by petty tyrants such as the one who likewise entered myth (and the following chapter) at Deganwy. Later we shall see how the figure of Arthur grew to command the outcome of these periods. Here we are in the transitional phase, when the confusion of the time is just beginning to become shaped in the imagination of those who recorded it, expressed through figures such as Vortigern and Emrys, and located at focal spots such as the Welsh hilltop.

Vortigern, it seems, was having trouble controlling the extremities of his kingdom. He engaged Saxon troops to act as mercenaries, to combat what Gildas describes as the northern nations, presumably the Picts and the Scots. Britain apparently still suffered from a lack of fighting forces, though if we follow the dating which Bede drew from Gildas and place Vortigern's problem at around AD 446, some sixty years have elapsed since the mass exodus in the time of Maxen. The Saxons were supposed, then, to control the plundering raids from the north, and at first it seems as if they did their job well. But Gildas, with the advantage of hindsight, pinpoints the error as allowing them into the island at all, 'like wolves into folds'. Nothing, he says, more damaging and tragic happened to the island than this. What hopeless stupidity, what dullness of intelligence! 'The men who, when absent, they feared more than death, were now invited by them of their own accord. . . .'

The Saxons prophesied that they would take the country and occupy it for three hundred years – a modest aim, as it turned out, since their hold over it lasted for twice as long, until they in turn relinquished it to the Normans. Evidently they liked the look of the country which they found, and recognized its potential. The immigrants soon sent for their families and friends, and their numbers quickly became larger than Vortigern and his advisers had bargained for. They then broke the treaty on the pretext that the supplies with which they were being paid were insufficient, allied themselves to the Picts whom they had been fighting, and laid waste the land 'from sea to sea'.

Behind this heavily biased story lies a history which we can only fragmentarily verify. Bede added some detail and plausibility to Gildas's account, though this does not necessarily mean that he was working from additional sources rather than making intuitive inferences. He it was who named as Vortigern Gildas's 'superbus tyrannus', and went on too to name the leaders of the Saxons as the brothers Hengist and Horsa. To him the 'adventus Saxonum' was an important turning point, the beginning of an era, and he made much of it. However, as Leslie Alcock has pointed out in his book *Arthur's Britain,* archaeology does not tend to support either Bede's mid-fifth-century dating of the first colonial settle-ments, or the supposition that there was one main arrival at that or some

A fourteenth-century manuscript showing Vortigern being burnt in his castle

other date. It indicates rather that by 450 there had been settled groups of Saxons in Britain for some time. Germanic troops in fact fought in the Roman army, for instance defending the Wall against the Picts, fore-shadowing Vortigern's use of their compatriots for the same purpose. The Anglo-Saxon Chronicle is itself hardly an independent source, showing as it does the influence of Bede and the resulting liability to transmit errors originally received from Gildas; but for what it is worth it does corroborate the supposition that Hengist and Horsa rebelled against Vortigern in the mid-fifth century.

Vortigern turns up again in an early-ninth-century inscription on a pillar at Valle Crucis Abbey, near Llangollen, where he is said to be the son-in-law of Maximus himself, the Maxen of the last chapter; but since this represents the genealogical claims of a prince of Powys it is rather an indication of who was thought to be historically important in the ninth century than any evidence of Vortigern's actual position in British history. Indeed the name itself is said by one school of thought to be a title meaning 'high king', and this, if correct, would imply that Gildas simply translated it into Latin as 'superbus tyrannus', and Bede translated it back again.

The characters and the story go forward from there, forward from Gildas through Bede into history, forward from Nennius through

Geoffrey of Monmouth into myth. Glancing backwards we find Ambrose recorded by Gildas as leading back the terrified Britons from their places of refuge, which sound remarkably like the Snowdonia hilltops associated with the myth, 'duce Ambrosio Aureliano, viro modesto' – 'led by Ambrosius Aurelianus, a modest man, who alone of the Roman people succeeded in surviving the shock of such a tempest'. Perhaps the use of the unexpected adjective, modest, unassuming, implies that some tradition as to the man's character had reached Gildas, indicating that he was perhaps, in reality as well as in the approving eyes of the historian, a decent person. His parents, Gildas implies, were high-born Romans; questioned by Vortigern in the Nennius story on his parentage, Ambrose said that his father was a Roman consul – perhaps implying that it was for diplomatic reasons that his mother had said that he had none. Backwards, then, we have a glimpse of a late Roman-Briton who took over from the crumbling power of Vortigern, after the rebellion of the Saxon troops, and led, perhaps from Snowdonia, a heroic bout of native resistance. Looking forwards the view is very different – that way we see Merlin.

Geoffrey of Monmouth lifted, almost intact, the Ambrose-Emrys story from Nennius. His purpose, however, was to pull together the various strands of authentic British mythical material which had survived down to his time. One set of these concerned a character called Myrddin, whose origins and background we shall be dealing with in later chapters on Merlin. Geoffrey's long and rambling book has several prominent heroes, the greatest among them being Arthur. But as the expression of a less militaristic, less political aspect of British identity he needed a figure of mystery and power, representative of that undercurrent of magic and buried religion which seems always to have been part of Britishness.

The Myrddin of the tradition current in his time was (as again we shall see later) just such a figure. He came out of the depths of ancient British thought as if out of a dark forest. The hilltop confrontation of Emrys with Vortigern provided the setting for the proclamation of a national prophecy, and Geoffrey, by placing the seer Myrddin in the position of the prophetic boy Emrys, brought into being a new amalgam which, although it was his own invention, had such strong dual roots in British myth that Merlin has survived as perhaps the best-known and the most impressive native mythic figure after Arthur.

Merlin had several strands of origin, but this combination of Geoffrey's and the location in North Wales of the Nennius story pinpoint the Snowdonia hilltop still called Dinas Emrys as the place at which he came into being. Why, one wonders, should it have been here? What was it about Dinas Emrys which picked it out for this important role in myth?

Dinas Emrys stands in mountain country, so close under the shoulder of Snowdon itself that the bulk of the mountain is hidden from there by its own expanding lower slopes. Snowdon is a presence above, indicated by the jut of the boulders and the rearing horizons of heather. The valley

The summit of Dinas Emrys

curves towards Dinas Emrys under Snowdon's broader extremities, and over it stands this small, round hill, its natural cragginess blurred by its clothing of brown scrub oak, like ivy on a castle ruin.

The joining-points of any diverse elements have an intrinsic fascination, as if one can still not quite believe that it can be at one and the same time day and night. Myth often occurs in such a half-light, and perhaps not a little of its appeal lies in its ill-defined, ambiguous relationship to history. All the more intriguing is it when the overlap occurs at an identifiable place, as we shall see it do again in later chapters. Here on the round, flat summit of Dinas Emrys, overlooking the Gwynant valley and Llyn Dinas, the clustering of ideas and themes from these different, and distant, regions is almost overwhelming.

'Dinas', though it means 'city' in Welsh, is a word often given to ancient fortified settlements, and so might best be translated 'fortress'. Defensive structures have indeed been found there, in the course of excavations carried out in the mid-1950s. A castle was built on the top of the hill as late as the twelfth century, and the square base of this medieval tower is still clearly visible (though nothing further is known of it than its date and its existence), providing evidence that somebody was here during the century in which Geoffrey of Monmouth was writing. But that old ruin is simply the last period of the place's inhabitation. As early

73

as the Roman age, perhaps before, the hill was occupied. The finds – sherds, amphorae, and ornaments – indicate a court of some luxury there towards the end of the fifth century, the time, that is, of Ambrosius, immediately after the traditional date of Vortigern and the Saxon invasion. An even more remarkable connection, however, between archaeology and myth, was the opening up of a concealed pool, just as that described by the myth in which the two serpents were, it says, buried.

In the centre of the summit plateau of Dinas Emrys is a deep hollow, almost a glade, boggy and tangled with clumps of reed. During the excavations, a square depression in this miniature marshy valley was found to be a man-made pool, a cistern, probably cut during the early-Roman period of the hill's occupation; pre-Ambrosius, pre-Vortigern, and certainly long pre-Nennius and Gildas. On the banks of this pool and over an area of the pool where it had silted, a paved stone platform was discovered, thought, this time, to belong to the Dark Age period. Under the circumstances one can hardly resist the speculation that paving would have covered the whole pool and the rest of it had been removed by Vortigern's magicians in their earlier excavations carried out under the direction of Emrys-Merlin.

But they, though not the last to dig there, were, the myth tells, not the first. A story in the Mabinogion, 'Lludd and Llefelys', tells, among other events, how the dragon-serpents came to be there, and in doing so it curiously anticipates the early-Roman dating of the cistern. Though, in the form in which we have it, the story dates from the fourteenth century, and might therefore be nothing more than a conscious addition to the Geoffrey of Monmouth story, it is generally agreed that, like much of the Mabinogion, it was very probably based on much older original material – though the age of the source material is debated, and probably undiscoverable. Since episodes of the Welsh story occur in Welsh translations of Geoffrey but not, unlike the start of the story, in the original Latin version, it seems probable that both Geoffrey and the compiler of the Mabinogion tale were working from some old traditional source. If so, the later story seems to imply that the Merlin figure knew the earlier story of the burial of the dragons and used it, perhaps, to tap the spirit of nationalism by evoking traditional myth. That is, Emrys-Merlin knew from 'Lludd and Llefelys' not only what was buried on Dinas Emrys, but the significance of it. Certainly the story of Lludd and Llefelys, with its world of magic and enchantment and its primitive imagery, feels the older of the two. Certainly too it seems to have deeper roots in British myth.

Lludd's otherwise fortunate rule over Britain was disturbed by three plagues. The first was an invading nation with supernatural gifts, who could hear anything that was said, no matter how quietly it was spoken; and by this talent they avoided attack. The second plague was a scream which happened everywhere in the country every May-eve, terrifying the population and causing barrenness. The third plague was the disappearance of all the food prepared in the king's court which was not consumed on the first night.

Lludd sought the advice of his brother, Llefelys, by then king of France. The first plague was dealt with, after some set-backs, by sprinkling a magic potion over all the people, which poisoned the foreigners but left one's own folk unharmed. The third plague was revealed to be a giant, who carried away the food and drink, and this was solved by lying in wait and overcoming him. These are easy enough solutions, but it is the way the remaining plague, the second one, is dealt with which concerns us here.

Llefelys explained it to Lludd. What is causing the omnipresent scream is the battling of two dragons. The dragon of a foreign nation is struggling to overcome the national dragon, which, on the point of defeat, utters the scream. In the centre of the country Lludd was to place a tub of mead, in a pit, covered over with a silk cloth. The dragons would come to rest on the cloth, sink into the mead, drink it, and fall asleep. They were then to be wrapped up in the covering, sealed in a stone chest, and buried in the ground in the strongest place the king could find in his dominions. 'And as long as they stay in that secure place, no plague will come to Britain from elsewhere.' In other words, as in the case which we shall later encounter of Bran's severed head, they were to be a safeguard against invasion. Is the imagery making a reference, perhaps forgotten or no longer understood, to a decision to stop resisting the Romans and instead allow them to take up the role of protectors? Like all true symbolism, these dragons are suggestive but obscure.

Lludd did as he was instructed, and in due course the dragons came, fought, fell asleep, were wrapped and enclosed in their stone jar. 'And in the safest place he found in Snowdonia he hid them. And after that the place was called Dinas Emrys.'

Lludd, in the story, was one of the sons of Beli the Great – and that, the opening statement, connects him at once with Britain at the time of the Roman invasion. It was Beli from whom Maxen took the island of Britain, when he came as Emperor of Rome with his followers in search of his dream-love. The Triads, however, record a slightly different version, perhaps in recognition that the Romans came more than once; according to that source it was Lludd's son, not his father, who was king at the time of the invasion. We may therefore safely regard Lludd as a figure connected with the coming of the Romans, and thought of as ruling Britain either before or during the early-Roman period.

Both the Mabinogion story and the Triads name him as the son of Beli, and with Beli we reach the ultimate bedrock of a recognizable Celtic god, best known by his Latinized name, Belenus. Tertullian cites him as the principal deity of a Celtic state in the Alps, but he crops up in various other parts of Europe too, chiefly in Gaul. Robert Graves, in *The White Goddess,* traces a possible connection with the Babylonian god Bel. The fact that the Romans identified him with Apollo may indicate that he has connections with flocks and sunlight, and if it is correct that his name is related to that of the ancient Celtic fire-festival, Beltane, the eve of the first of May, then this too would make him a god of light and springtime. Beli occurs elsewhere in Celtic myth as a figure equivalent to that of Bran in the grail saga, and in Geoffrey of Monmouth's work he and Bran are warring rivals, suggesting that they may originally have been gods of competing cults.

His son Lludd is, we know, another Celtic deity, being the same person as Nudd, or in Irish Nuadha (nicknamed from one of the episodes in his story 'the Silver-handed'), and known to the Romanized Celts as Nodens. It was to Nodens that the fourth-century temple at Lydney in Gloucestershire was dedicated, and though the date of this makes it more an instance of a late revival of the Romano Celtic merging of religions than an authentic piece of evidence – and is thought, anyway, to indicate

The statues of Lud and his sons which stood on the Elizabethan Ludgate

rather an Irish colonization than an indigenous cult – it does at least imply that Nodens, or Nudd, or Lludd, was a highly respected deity.

From the evidence at Lydney, Nodens was a god of healing, like Apollo, as well as of other activities, such as fishing, and his shrine there was a place of pilgrimage, where the worshippers, or patients, left offerings. Some of these, as at healing shrines elsewhere, showed the parts of their bodies in need of cure; it is interesting that other offerings at Lydney bore the representations of dogs, since this connects the cult with that of Asclepius, Apollo's son, the healer-god of Epidavros in Greece, whose mascot was the dog.

None of this, unfortunately, is apparent in the story of Lludd. There we see rather a historicized being, a king of Britain who built cities. As such, however, he has a rich enough set of offshoots and effects in the

A late-seventeenth-century playing card showing Ludgate

mythology, since in the confusion of the pedigrees in another Mabinogion story he is given a daughter called Creiddylad, who, as the origin of Cordelia, makes him one of the origins of King Lear. We have already seen how Geoffrey of Monmouth derives a more direct line to the story of the king with daughter trouble through an alternative king called Leir, whose prototype is the Llŷr of a previous chapter. But even deprived of this distinction Lludd has a notable achievement to his credit, since both Geoffrey and the Mabinogion, in an identical passage, attribute to him the establishing of the city of London.

Formerly, according to Geoffrey, it was called Trinovantum. Lludd rebuilt its walls and, in both versions, 'girded it round with innumerable towers'; in making it his capital he encouraged the building there of houses of a splendour never before seen. So great was his effect on it that it was renamed after him, Caer Ludd, or, as it became, Caer Lundein. Lludd-din, perhaps, Lludd's city? Hence, in Roman times, Londinium, and from there to the name we have today? This is perhaps no place to enter such a debate, but the Romans did habitually name their settlements by Latinizing the existing name of a local place or feature, rather than making up a new one. In later ages, in any case, Lludd was not forgotten there, and indeed, as King Lud, is still remembered; one of the gates, as Geoffrey puts it, 'in the British tongue is still called Porthlud after him, although in Saxon it bears the name Ludgate'. Perhaps the gate got its name originally by its proximity to a temple dedicated to Lud's original, the god from whom he has become historicized. Interestingly Geoffrey of Monmouth says that the city has another gate which is called Billingsgate after Beli, whom he calls Belinus, thus bringing together again the father and son of this British myth.

Geoffrey of Monmouth certainly regards Lludd as being pre-Roman, so that it would not be unreasonable to see him as the patron-god of a settlement on the Thames when the Romans reached it. That is speculation without evidence. But it is, in any case, a figure of some depth and antiquity around whom this branch of the myth is centred.

Since the Lludd story specifies that the country was to be safe from invasion as long as the dragons were still buried, it seems that by instructing Vortigern's magicians to unearth them Ambrose was (by a sort of inversion of cause and effect) accepting that the Saxon invasion had taken place. Perhaps the story implies that he, unlike Vortigern, saw that it was necessary to fight, rather than run away: letting loose the dragons certainly had the effect of setting them warring again. After the easy acceptance of life under Roman protection it was perhaps a significant change; and although the invading dragon appeared to be winning, the prophet's message was that the spirit of national resistance would in the end dominate. Similarly the Ambrosius of Gildas's history (in contrast to Vortigern) stirred and drew together the remnants of British independence. Perhaps the myth recognizes in this some permanent achievement. Perhaps by refusing to take the Saxon invasion in a spirit of retreat Ambrosius made possible not only Arthur and the partial reversal of Mount Badon, but even the continuing existence of identifiable Celtic regions today. Wales and Cornwall, at least, did survive.

The symbolism too remains with us. There was a sense in which the red dragon did literally make its come-back. Probably the original story drew its imagery from an early British custom of going into battle under the standard of a dragon of an identifying colour, and if so it was simply in continuation of this tradition that Henry Tudor bore that emblem on one of his banners at the Battle of Bosworth. The figure of the red dragon on a green and white background went back to the seventh-century king Cadwaladr, from whom the Anglesey family of Tudor claimed descent, so that it was, in effect, one of Henry's family devices. It had long before been recognized as representing Wales; the Welsh troops of the Black Prince, for instance, threw such a banner over him, as Prince of Wales, when he fell from his horse at the battle of Crecy.

Henry Tudor's flying of the Red Dragon on the field of Bosworth, may well have indicated a knowledge of the Merlin story, and certainly showed a recognition of the latent power of British nationalism, even at that relatively late date. He presented himself to the people as Welsh, landed in Wales, and marched through South Wales to the border, collecting on the way the valuable support of the troops of Rhys ap Thomas, lord of Deheubarth. A bardic prophecy of the time actually referred to him as a dragon, of the blood of the old British lineage, 'the hope of our race'. Dinas Emrys had not been forgotten, and in a sense Merlin's prophecy did come true, in part, in the August of 1485.

For one hilltop to be associated with so potent a symbol as the red dragon and, at the same time, so impressive a figure as Merlin, is in itself remarkable. That it should also be the spot connected in myth with the first stage of the Saxon invasion of Britain, and thus form a junction of the streams of myth, history, and archaeology, is perhaps a little too much to assimilate. It is, after all, an unassuming hill, looking out onto the soft peace of Llyn Dinas. What the myth says and the hill embodies is that the most ancient aspects of British identity survived intact through great cultural changes by being protected from change by the hard terrain of the hills. Anywhere so clearly characterized as wild and inaccessible had a role to play both in history and in the national thinking. It is because of that that the myth which summarizes the first disruptions caused by the arrival of the Saxons sees Vortigern, as high-king, scurrying to safety, and Emrys rallying the spirit of resistance, out on that crag under the side of Snowdon.

From the top of Snowdon on a winter evening one still sees a raw country, formed of a spread of rock-ridges and spurs, the pale icing of frost and hail whitening their tops, their sides black with wet cliffs. It expands in a sweep of ranges northwards, which rear and roll in much the same conformation as they did a few million years ago when the ice slid off them.

6 The collapse of the Celtic kingdoms

Alongside the external effects of the Romans leaving and the Saxons arriving, the myths hint at an internal dissolution taking place. To some extent they echo Gildas's idea that a valuable opportunity had been wasted, in a new and Christian world, for a rebirth of the Celtic values and identity which had flourished before the Romans came.

The reason was that the Romans had been too thorough. They had not left room for the nation to fight its own wars or administer its own policy. The burial of the warring dragons perhaps expresses the idea that it was easier to live under Roman protection than to resist it; and we saw how Gildas implied that the only Briton to offer any hope of national recovery was the highly Romanized general Ambrosius Aurelianus, who, in the myth, set the dragons fighting again.

The Romans had heavily fortified the Saxon Shore, but with the withdrawal of the garrisons in the course of Maximus's rebellion, and of other imperial troubles, these thick-walled, round-towered forts must have been almost useless. It was manpower that was needed, and we saw the story presenting this as Vortigern's problem: unable to conduct a war on two fronts, he was obliged to employ one set of enemies to control the other. We also saw that the result was that he had to retreat; he left the area of the Saxon Shore, as the Saxons now swept inland, and went further west. That was in the mid-fifth century. It was perhaps a little before that that another great movement, remembered by the tradition and very probably factual, took place. Somewhere around the year 400 there was a significant withdrawal of part of a British tribe from the area of the Wall. It is represented as the coming of Cunedda and his sons to North Wales – from a territory just to the north of the Wall which bordered off the Picts – his purpose, according to Nennius's 'History', which records his movement, being to clear North Wales of Scots, who had invaded. Several points about this require some explanation.

Firstly, the Scots were, paradoxically, the Irish. Both Ireland and Scotland came to be inhabited by people known to the Romans as Scotti, a perfectly correct equation since the area now known as Scotland, previously inhabited by the Picts, was colonized from Ireland at a fairly late period. It seems that during the late-fourth century this group of Celtic tribes began to cross the Irish Sea at several more southern points too, and had completely swamped North Wales by about 400. Perhaps it was felt, by whoever moved Cunedda, that the Wall was an altogether

Hadrian's Wall with Housesteads fort in the centre

A horseman drinking on a Pictish stone from Invergowrig near Dundee

safer, and more distant, situation than that tract of land so close to the legionary fortress of Chester. There are signs that by Cunedda's probable time the Picts in his area had been considerably tamed, and probably were themselves being effectively used by the Romans to defend their land against the advance of the Scots, thus taking the pressure off the pro-Roman tribe of the Gododdin, who had been serving that purpose before.

At the time the decision may well have represented a sound assessment, since the Romans seem originally to have had more to fear from the Scots than from the Saxons, and their western edge was evidently very poorly defended; a hundred years later things were rather different, but this change in itself may have been to some extent the result of the policy which involved Cunedda's presence on the North Wales coast. The point is that his transfer had two notable effects, both due to its great success. It focussed military and political attention away from the east and north, thus getting everybody, as it were, looking towards Ireland. And it established (in the comparative safety which followed the victories of Cunedda and his sons and grandsons) a powerful and wealthy dynasty which traced its lineage from Cunedda; and which, because it legitimized the descent of the Princes of Wales and the House of Tudor, became one strand of ancestry of our present royal family, and indeed of other monarchies.

If we wish to understand this period we are obliged to turn to mythology. Archaeology for the sub-Roman period is a great deal better than it was, but archaeologists with their strictly material resources do not pretend to be able to dig and sieve in the minds of their subjects. Our only documentation is the diatribe of Gildas, which later historians such as Nennius and Bede were obliged to rely on. The mythology demonstrates again the better powers of survival of oral as against written material; the earliest form in which we have the stories discussed here is a sixteenth-century version, and it is clear that this combined the oral tradition with some fragmentary texts, so that some of the material at least (though it displays recognizably ancient features) was not written down until then.

Oddly enough the downfall of Cunedda's posterity and the independent post-Roman kingdoms of western Britain, is represented in the myths not in terms of invasions but of the combination of personalities and natural disasters. This surprising element (as when the Romans were shown coming to Britain because of the love of the Emperor for a native princess) is one of the endearing features of such stories, a feature which has no doubt contributed to their superior powers of survival. We are thus shown a scene in which, quite oblivious to the dangers from the undefended east and north, drunken and bad-tempered tyrants ruled in circumstances of great luxury and self-indulgence, until two of the most powerful of them were successively impoverished by a flood and a plague.

Unfortunately, since the stories do not occur in the two great books

Pevensey Castle: the outer walls are those of the great Roman fort built as a protection against the Saxons

which have preserved the Mabinogion collection, they have lacked the attention of the master who transcribed those and have suffered from their passage through the hands of someone less able. This and the late date of their transcription make it necessary to be selective, but through comparison with other material it is probably possible to pick out the genuine tradition from the fanciful additions made by comparatively modern collectors.

The story starts off a very long way from history, deep in a world of characteristic Celtic mystery. We find a witch called Ceridwen brewing a magic concoction with the aim of making her son omniscient, in compensation for his extreme ugliness. The cauldron containing the mixture has to be kept on the boil for a year and a day – a frequent specified period in Celtic material, which perhaps indicates a seasonal or astrological cycle. She sets a blind man and a boy to kindle the fire and stir the cauldron, and it is in the end the boy, Gwion, instead of her own son, who accidentally receives the essential drops of the potion of inspiration. At once he knows everything, not least that Ceridwen will try to destroy him. A shape-shifting sequence follows, in which he turns into a hare, she into a greyhound, he into a fish, she into an otter, he into a bird, she into a hawk, and finally, finding a barn, he hides himself as a grain in a heap of wheat. And she, as a black hen, picks him out and swallows him.

We have come across this transformation process several times before, and may therefore recognize it as a favourite Celtic theme. Gwydion, Blodeuedd, and Lleu, in animal or bird form, and the mice who attacked Manawydan's corn, seem to be examples of a similar type of thought. A set of shape-changes very reminiscent of those of Ceridwen and Gwion is undergone by two contending swineherds in an Irish story, Tain Bo Cuailnge, who change themselves by magic into birds and water animals, and are finally eaten in the form of water-worms and reborn as bulls. In another instance, which seems to parallel the chase by Ceridwen, the father of the hero Lugh turns himself into a pig and runs amongst a herd to escape his enemies, who transform themselves into hounds and rout him out. Whether all this is related to either the zoomorphic representation of gods in Celtic iconography, or to the belief in metempsychosis which Caesar records, or both, is a matter of speculation. Here it does seem to be involved with an idea of rebirth, since Ceridwen becomes pregnant with the seed she has swallowed, and in due course Gwion is born again.

Ceridwen as goddess of inspiration and knowledge plays only a background role in the mythology. It is perhaps her possession of the magic cauldron which picks her out as someone of importance, since this, as we shall see, is one of several such vessels which together went to the making of the notion of the holy grail. Her part in this story, however, is only as a sort of footnote, explaining how the prophet Taliesin came by his wonderful and all-inclusive knowledge.

Many heroes have to undergo an apparent death and rebirth before they can take up their proper occupation. When Gwion was born again he was subjected to a further trial, since Ceridwen, unwilling to destroy him, set him to sea in a sewn-up basket, just as Perseus was set adrift in Greek myth, Moses in Judaic, Mordred elsewhere in the British material. Paris and Oedipus too survived almost certain death, and like the latter

Gwion was found and fostered by a prince. No doubt the passage through water has a ritual element, the symbolization of a spiritual cleansing, as is implied in the service of baptism, which the Prayer Book compares to the crossings of the river Jordan and the Red Sea as well as to Noah's voyage. When Gwion came ashore, moreover, he acquired a new name, from the exclamation of the prince who found him: Tal-iesin, 'radiant-brow'.

He was found washed up in a weir, the property of a king called Gwyddno, and fished by his son Elffin, a prince remarkable for his ill fortune. Though the weir was normally abundant with salmon, when Elffin fished it there was nothing there except the leather-wrapped basket. Finding Taliesin inside it, however, represented a reversal of his habitual bad luck.

Tradition, and one of the Triads, interjects into the story of Elffin son of Gwyddno an element which does not occur in the main written versions. Gwyddno's territory was low lying and coastal, and therefore protected from the sea by an embankment. The Triad blames the drunkenness of Seithenin (who evidently was in charge of the sea-defences) for letting the land become submerged. The whole country, which it says contained sixteen fortified towns, was lost, and the inhabitants who escaped retreated to live in the uplands.

Clearly this episode has elements in it which are more than mere folk-tale, related as it is to the universal myths of floods and inundations, the Atlantis complex. The one recorded by Plato is only the best developed of these, and every mythology seems to have its own example. Later in this book we shall come across the other main British instance of the Atlantis myth, that of the drowned land of Lyonesse. Golden and idyllic, these places lie with their great civilized cities, their rich lands, and lovely palaces lost for ever below the unrevealing sea. The theme perhaps reflects that such things do happen, as one can see from the drowned forests of our low-tide beaches and the engulfed churchyards of our shores; partly no doubt it also expresses an idea of a past of richness and security, when a kinder climate fostered the growth of peace, all of which, the myth implies, has irretrievably gone.

Like many such notions the tradition claims a factual as well as a symbolic truth for this lost land. Gwyddno's kingdom is believed still to obtrude above the surface of the lowest tides of Cardigan Bay, in the form of a long, dark line of stones, running at right angles to the coastline out to sea, where it continues for some fourteen miles. The local strength of the story has proved resilient to the lack of evidence that this line of stones is artificial. Undeniably it is unusually straight for a natural object, and the idea will not die that this is all that is left of one of the embankments which once protected that lost land.

With the discovery of Taliesin in the weir the story moves into another phase. Elffin, it says, was the nephew of the king of Gwynedd, whose court was further north. Both the king and the court were the descendants of the settlement of North Wales founded by Cunedda, who had made his base there in his campaigns against the Irish. By the time the story occupies, his tribal offshoot of the northern nation had successfully resisted the colonization of Wales by the Irish, and thus, incidentally, had prevented Wales from becoming another branch of Scotland. In doing so Cunedda had saved from extinction the essential elements of British identity, such as its culture and language, which were to disappear in almost every other part of the island. And he had in the process established the kingdom of Gwynedd, over which (as the myth returns to the edge of history) his great-grandson Maelgwn, the uncle to whom Elffin came on a visit, ruled from the citadel-court at Deganwy.

Maelgwn appears in the story as quick-tempered and high-handed, throwing his nephew into prison at the slightest provocation. He is surrounded by flattering courtiers and bards whose job it is to recite his praise. It is partly this desperate need for eulogy that gets Elffin locked up, since he has the audacity to claim that his wife is as faithful as Maelgwn's and his bard as skilful. A strong folk-tale element enters in the next sequence with the testing of the fidelity of his wife, but immediately after that the tale gets on with its main subject, and strikes a more symbolic note again with the entry of Taliesin.

Like other heroes – like the boy Emrys of a previous chapter, and like CuChulainn in Irish myth – the child Taliesin shows a startlingly precocious talent. Other figures in other mythologies enter their careers by discountenancing their elders; one thinks of Apollo and of Hermes, of the boy David killing the giant Goliath, and indeed of Jesus confounding the elders in the temple. Taliesin, it appears, has taken skill as a bard to its ultimate length; with him poetry has become spell, and he uses it to work magic.

Two figures of myth are combined in the character of Taliesin: the wizard, and the prophet. First he spellbinds Maelgwn's flattering bards, so that all they can do is make a bubbling noise with their fingers on their lips, which the text rather attractively represents as 'blerwm blerwm'. When asked by Maelgwn who he is, he launches into a long and awe-inspiring riddle. Clearly it was a silly question.

> I was with my lord in the heavens
> When Lucifer fell into the depth of hell.
> I carried a banner in front of Alexander. . . .
> I brought seed down to the vale of Hebron;
> I was in the court of Don before the birth of Gwydion;
> I was patriarch to Elijah and Enoch. . . .

A long list of Old Testament and British references, intermingled, follows, until it is clear that what he is saying is that he is the timeless world-spirit, present everywhere on all occasions, no less at the birth of Christ than in the prison of Aranrhod. He also mentions his present incarnation and its immediate prelude: 'I obtained inspiration from the cauldron of Ceridwen'; and he ends by answering the question in the sense in which it was asked:

> Then for nine months I was
> In the womb of the witch Ceridwen;
> I was formerly little Gwion;
> And now I am Taliesin.

He then sang other verses, the effect of which was to raise such a storm over that hilltop castle that the king was afraid that the perilously perched towers would fall around them; he fetched Elffin from prison, and Taliesin broke his fetters off with another spell.

It is at that stage in the story that the texts introduce the prophecies, very much in the manner in which Geoffrey of Monmouth attributes prophecies to the wizard Merlin, who stood as a precocious child on another hilltop in front of another king. Taliesin presents to the apparently ignorant king the same situation which Emrys/Merlin had previously shown to Vortigern, but now it is changed in spirit, moved towards a pessimistic acceptance of an unfavourable outcome:

> A coiling serpent,
> Proud and merciless,
> With golden wings,
>   Out of Germany.

It is, it seems, the same yellow (or, in earlier versions, white) dragon. But now the theme is not the promise of the native dragon's eventual success.

> It shall overrun
> Lloegyr and Scotland,
> From the Scandinavian Sea,
>   To the river Severn.

> Then will the Britons be
> Like prisoners,
> Exiled from their rights
> By Saxony.

Then follows the verse which has given us, through George Borrow's fortunate use of its last line, a phrase which now comes naturally to describe the land left to these new exiles.

> Eu Ner a volant
> A'u hiaith a gadwant
> Eu tir a gollant
>   Ond gwyllt Walia.

('They shall praise their lord, and they shall keep their language; their land they shall lose, except wild Wales.')

It expresses the state of affairs which, at this point, the British nation is about to reach. We can see that it must have puzzled Maelgwn, safe in his western citadel and surrounded by his yes-men. No doubt the confrontation of the king with the prophet who could see that future is composed with hindsight, which is why it seems to us so accurate. That too is part of the function of myth, to look back and express what the people who participated should have seen, but failed to, what they could have avoided had they understood properly.

Taliesin did however go on to offer (like Emrys) eventual retrieval, after a long servitude, with the Britons in the end regaining the land and the crown, and the foreigners disappearing. To some extent this too came true, though the repatriation which it implies was not, after a certain stage, a realistic possibility. The poem, unlike much of the story, occurs in the Red Book of Hergest, a manuscript of the late-fourteenth or early-fifteenth century, and so, if it refers to the coming of the Tudor monarchy, it was indeed a prophecy.

Other prophecies too are attributed to Taliesin at this juncture, but these occur only in later versions, as does the story of the various exploits of Maelgwn and his death. In spite of the slight doubt as to their antiquity, some of these do seem to refer to authentically traditional material. The prophesied death of Maelgwn, which Taliesin said would be caused by a yellow monster from the plain of Rhiannedd, is a particularly deserving case, since it echoes the prophecies made of the death of kings in other mythologies, particularly in the Irish tales. Once foretold, such a death is unavoidable, and although Maelgwn flees from the monster to hide in a church it tracks him down, and the sight of it as he peers fearfully through the keyhole is enough to kill him.

The yellow monster of the prophecy seems to bear several references, since it cannot but be reminiscent of the yellow dragon mentioned by both Emrys and Taliesin. It is however historically equated with the Yellow Plague, and the Annales Cambriae (which may date originally from the tenth century) provide some corroboration for this. They give, for the year 547, the summary: 'an. mortalitas magna in qua pausat Mailcun rex Guenedotiae' ('a year of great death in which Maelgwn king of Gwynedd died'). We know from other sources that the Yellow Plague had spread across Europe from the Middle East during the previous five years, and swept through Britain towards the end of the 540s. We also gather from the Welsh poems 'The Stanzas of the Graves' (which occur in a twelfth-century manuscript but again are clearly a medium for remembering events of very early history as well as various heroic traditions) that the plain of Rhiannedd was a place of burials, and one of the Triads gives as the origin of the plague in Gwynedd the corpses left there after a battle. Ironically it is on that long flat spit of land between two majestic limestone headlands, the place from which that fearful monster came, that the harmonious Victorian seaside resort of Llandudno now stands.

If then the two combined tales show us a nation falling to pieces, they do so with very little immediate allocation of blame. Gwyddno suffered the disaster of the flooding of the best part of his land; Maelgwn, taunted with his failure by Taliesin, lost his people, his kingdom, and his life through the coming of a monster, or a plague. In the awful words of Taliesin we hear a mention of the real trouble, but otherwise it is ignored in the recounting of the deeds and character of the kings; and presumably this quite accurately reflects the fact that they too had turned their minds away from it. They were preoccupied with their own trivial matters. Two factors bring these mythicized versions down to earth, placing them in the real and unromantic context of the mid-sixth century in Britain. One is Gildas, a rare, written historical source. The other is the patience and skill of the modern sub-Roman-period archaeologist.

If the myth does not point out directly the damage, by neglect, which Maelgwn was doing to Britain's cause, the omission is made up for amply by the contemporary work of Gildas. We have his diatribe only in eleventh-century manuscript form, but internal evidence makes it indisputably early, and there is every reason to accept the date which he himself implies for it, towards the end of the first half of the sixth century. One confirmation of its early date is that Bede clearly had a copy of it (and evidently a rather better one than we have) since he transcribed whole sections of it verbatim. This fact also tells us that it was the only source for the period which he had, so that our appreciation of its rarity is all the more justified. Unfortunately that too has another consequence: Gildas cannot be checked.

His railing against Maelgwn bears the tone of personal animosity, and as they were probably contemporaries they might indeed have met. Certainly Gildas shows what seems like first-hand knowledge of his subject, or victim, mentioning his height and his wilfulness, and always addressing him directly, as if delivering a dressing-down. It appears from other material that they may have gone to school together, which would explain everything. The section of his book devoted to Maelgwn is considerably longer than his attacks on other princes, and this together with the urgent tone of voice marks it as being of special importance to the writer.

It is not clear why Gildas hated him so, if it was not simply a consequence of his love of Britain and his anguish at the squandering of its last chance of independence. The book is, he says, a 'tearful and complaining story of the evils of this age'. The kings wasted their energy and opportunity fighting each other; unstable and temperamental, Maelgwn's life was one of constant internal quarrelling, with his family, with the church, with the other kings. Besides less dreadful crimes he had his wife removed and married the wife of his nephew, whom he first killed in order to make her marriageable as a widow – the basis, perhaps, of his quarrel with Elffin in the story. Gildas is quite specific: 'When it is possible to catch your attention it is not hymns you want to hear, the praises of God, but your own praises, uttered by that set of lying rascals.' 'Primo in malo, maior multis potentia simulque malitia . . ' – ('First in wickedness, as in power so in malice greater than most.')

It is a long and specific charge exemplifying the general message ('made more in tears than in denunciation') of his book: that Britain has kings, but they are tyrants; the wars they engage in are civil wars, and unjust. In the forty years since the battle of Mount Badon, he says, during which there had been no outside trouble, the great cities of Britain had not been restored or reinhabited. 'Deserted and dismantled, they lie neglected until now, because, although wars with foreigners have ceased, domestic wars continue.' Instead of using the temporary respite after the victory of Badon to build a new spirit of national expansion and resistance, such was the low quality of the island's leadership that the rulers compounded the Saxons' damage by fighting each other. And Maelgwn was the worst of them.

Gildas by implication gives the battle of Mount Badon as the cause of the political vacillation of mid-sixth-century Britain; and the significance of that event forms the main subject of a later chapter of this book, since it concerns the role of Arthur. After Badon there was peace, and one of the effects of that was to enable the rulers to indulge in considerable luxury, promoting their own power and greed rather than combining to advance the cause of the island as a whole. This lack of nationhood and tendency to quarrel among each other were, moreover, characteristics which had served the British badly once before. Tacitus remarked in explanation of the ease of the Roman conquest: 'Once they owed obedience to kings; now they are distracted between the jarring factions of rival chiefs. Indeed, nothing has helped us more in war with their strongest nations than their inability to co-operate. It is but seldom that two or three states unite to repel a common danger.' The number and size of the courts of the sub-Roman period rather indicates such a disunity. Whatever Maelgwn may have thought of himself, it seems that after Vortigern there was no real high-king. The archaeology also confirms that the time of the post-Badonic decline was a time of wealth.

We have already come across one of the North Wales Dark Age sites, on the hill of Dinas Emrys, where a civilization of some luxury seems to have flourished during the late-fifth century. When we move to Arthur and the Celtic-Saxon border we shall consider the greatest and most famous of them all, at Cadbury. That the castle at Deganwy was occupied by a similar community about the same time and a little later was demonstrated by Alcock's excavations in the 1960s, in confirmation (once again) of the tradition presented by the myths. The crucial evidence of its status consists of some pieces of Mediterranean pottery wine-jars, and, although the quantity is insufficient to suggest a well-stocked cellar, the conclusion does seem to follow that a king who could afford imported wines, however little of them, was in the elite class of his time. This seat occupied at that date by Maelgwn – since we might as well call him that, whoever he was – was also much favoured by those who filled his role both before and after.

We cannot say for certain that his ancestor Cunedda built his castle there, but in view of his purpose in being in that area it seems quite likely. The high, cliff-surrounded knoll looks down onto the river mouth and the bay, out towards Ireland. Roman coins of the third and fourth centuries found there imply that somebody was guarding the shore against the Irish when Cunedda came. That the hill was defended even before that is hinted at by the discovery of a very early dry-stone wall, dating back perhaps to the second century. Unfortunately none of this can be seen now, and the present crumbled ruins belong to the long subsequent period of Deganwy's occupation, which ran right through the early Middle Ages and was only ended by a very determined destruction of what must have been a massive Norman castle, the immediate forerunner of King Edward's fortress at Conwy. Then in the possession of Edward himself, built by his father, Deganwy was toppled very thoroughly by the Welsh Prince Llewelyn (Maelgwn's descendant) when it fell after a seven-year siege, in 1263. It was ironically the immediate result of that – namely the decision by Edward to build his replacement fort to control the river access and the crossing not there but on the western bank – which effectively confirmed the Norman invasion of Wales. Edward at Conwy and Caernarfon repeated Agricola's strategy of bracketing the native heartland of Snowdonia by means of two great forts on its two main rivers, which both these commanders were able to supply from their campaign stronghold at Chester.

From the top of the fortified hill above Deganwy one can see the significance of this historic geography, looking down at the river which was both a barrier and a lifeline, and out across it to the mountains, the sanctuary of the tribes in their hillforts and of their mountain-loving descendants. While Maelgwn represents, as the myth portrays him, not so much a rear-guard stance as a turning inwards and away, the figure which confronted him, the legendary bard and magician Taliesin, brings us more in touch with the idea of Britain as a whole which was so easily neglected at Deganwy.

That some such person as Taliesin actually existed seems from the literature to be very probable. He is recorded from perhaps as early as AD 1000, in what seems to be an addition to the 'History' of Nennius, as being one of the poets famous in the last phase of independent Britain, the mid-sixth century. We know the name of another poet of this period, Aneirin, and although none of their works is extant in any version earlier than the twelfth century, the poems appear in some cases to have been written down for the first time some centuries before. Since they were intended for recital and not for written use, the absence of early transcriptions should in no way surprise us; the strength of the oral tradition, which certainly survived into the Middle Ages, would in fact discourage any written records of them.

Some of the poems under Taliesin's name do appear to be by that original sixth-century figure; they are addressed in the traditional heroic style to Urien, prince of Rheged, who occurs in a sufficient number of other sources to be historically identifiable. Rheged is thought to have occupied the western portion of North Britain, the territory to the north of the Wall, adjoining the area of the Gododdin from which Cunedda was said to have come; and one poem attributed to Aneirin, who also seems to have been a North Briton, is in commemoration of a battle fought by the Gododdin, a battle apparently fought in North Yorkshire towards the end of the sixth century. In view of these memorials of troubled times in the north-east, it is particularly easy to see Taliesin's accusatory presence at Deganwy as a justified reminder of what, while Maelgwn was occupied in throwing his relatives into prison, was going on elsewhere in Britain.

The ruins of the Norman castle at Deganwy

This poem of Aneirin's, 'The Gododdin', expresses better than most of the British material the simple nobility of a heroic time. Curbing the pain of defeat with a celebration of the courage of those who died, it tells of a battle fought at Catraeth, the Roman town of Cataractonium which is now called Catterick, a battle which probably took place between the Gododdin and the Angles in the neighbourhood of Richmond Castle during the 590s. I use Gwyn Williams's famous translation, from his collection *The Burning Tree*:

The men who went to Catraeth were famous,
wine and mead from gold was their drink
for a year according to honoured custom,
three hundred and sixty-three gold-collared men.

93

Of those who met over flowing drink
only three escaped from the fury of battle,
Aeron's two wardogs and Cynon came back,
and I from my bleeding for my song's sake.

So the poet, it seems, was also a warrior, or at least attended the army and
got embroiled in the fight. He sings verse after verse of heroism, naming
the young men who fell. 'Not one ever saw his father again.'

The men who attacked had lived together,
in their brief lives were drunk on distilled mead;
Mynyddawg's army, famed in battle,
their lives paid for their feast of mead.
Caradawg and Madawg, Pyll and Ieuan,
Gwgan and Gwiawn, Gwyn and Cynvan,
Peredur of steel weapons, Gwawrddur and Aeddan,
attackers in battle, they had their shields broken;
and though they were killed; they killed.
Not one came back to his belongings.

They died, he says, before they could grow old. 'Short their lives, long
the yearning for them by their loved ones.' Taliesin too, in one of the
poems in his name which appears to be of this early period, tells of death
in battle, and struggles to invoke the morale which must have been
desperately needed to keep this bitter and sad contest continuing.

Before the battle of Llwyfain Wood
many a corpse was made;
the crows grew red before the warriors.
Those who attacked, with their chieftain,
for a year I'll prepare the song of their victory.
When I'm old and decline to death's stubborn need
I'll not be content unless praising Urien.

Whatever may have been the fate of Taliesin, Urien and the freedom he
fought for were not destined to survive. An anonymous poem of the
same period speaks of him having been killed; and the two kingdoms
against which he and the Gododdin fought had, by the end of the sixth
century, merged. That is, in the north the kingdom of Bernicia formed
by Ida on the Northumbrian coast around Lindisfarne and Bamburgh –
that wind-dominated shoreline looking out over long lines of breakers to
a stone-grey ocean, beyond which lies Denmark. And, to the south of
the Tees, the neighbouring kingdom of Deira established by Aelle in
what is now coastal Yorkshire. Both these, ironically, came into being
towards the end of the probable lifetime of Maelgwn king of Gwynedd.

Bernicia and Deira came together under Aethelfrith, Ida's grandson,
who thus brought into being the new and mighty kingdom of Northumbria. This amalgamation would presumably have been prevented had the
fatal battle of Catraeth gone the other way, since that attack seems

The castle at Bamburgh, one of the major centres of the kingdom of Bernicia

directed like a wedge into the joining point. The Gododdin seem to have set out with some confidence, or at least with the incentive of despair, to attack such a distant point as Catraeth, and perhaps Urien's previous campaigns had given them hope. The very fact that they would have had to go past the kingdom of Bernicia to get there, from their homeland around Edinburgh, indicates that Bernicia had already been weakened by previous attacks. To take Catraeth (which was in the extreme north of Deira) would have been to surround Bernicia, preventing its expansion, and cutting off any support from its neighbour, as well as beginning a direct attack on Deira.

However Catraeth was not taken and Northumbria came into existence. This proved to be the biggest single factor in the dissolution of Celtic British nationality, since it easily spread westward to control the southern Cumbrian coast, and as it did so it cut off the northern British from the Welsh.

Since Taliesin in what appears to be history belongs to the north British area, and since Elffin's father Gwyddno also turns up in a northern genealogy, we may guess that elements of the story have come together from a more general homeland than their eventual location at Deganwy would suggest. The universal prophetic figure has become attached to the famous British bard, and allocated to the court of the Welsh king, no doubt as a consequence of the survival of the traditional material in the land of that king's descendants, and nowhere else. And this too stems from the expansion of Northumbria, which Taliesin and Maelgwn, in history, failed to stop.

One more factor then, after the death of Maelgwn and the rise of Aethelfrith, completed the blockade of the remaining groups of British peoples. Just as it was the rise and spread of the kingdom of Northumbria which cut off the Britons in Wales from their compatriots in the north, so the equivalent expansion of the kingdom of Mercia, which spread to cover the whole of the midlands during the seventh and eighth centuries, eventually separated Wales from the Celtic south-west. That Mercia did not achieve this earlier could perhaps be due to the British victory at Badon. Just as the defeat at Catraeth enabled the formation of Northumbria, so Badon seems to have checked the advance of the Mercians. If that was a real rather than a symbolic battle it would have taken place early in the sixth century; and the Anglo-Saxon Chronicle (which, on this score, is as impartial a witness as one could require) shows that there were no further advances between 514 and 547, the time of the reign of Maelgwn. A series of defeats in the south began to reverse this situation shortly after his death. The impetus of Badon was not sustained, and the borders of the territory of the Mercians crept towards those of the West Saxons, until the older nation with its heritage of culture, language, and tradition was constricted to a fragmentary survival in the west. On that disputed frontier we find Arthur, and just as Maelgwn represents the failure of the natives to revive, so Arthur stands for their attempt to do so.

Arthur as Warrior and Hero

And ich wulle varen to Avalun,
to vairest alre maidene,
to Argante there quene,
alven swithe sceone,
& heo scal mine wunden
makien alle isunde,
al hal me makien
mid haleweie drenchen
and seothe ich cumen wulle
to mine kineriche
and wunien mid Brutten
mid muchelere wunne.

Arthur, in Layamon's 'Brut', *c.* 1190

ti sunt usq; ad decũ & ualenanũ. anni
sunt sexaginta noue.

an̄	an̄ . gxc .	an̄
an̄	an̄	an̄
an̄	an̄	an̄
an̄	an̄	an̄
an̄	an̄	an̄
an̄	an̄	an̄ . lxx .
an̄	an̄	an̄
an̄	an̄	an̄ Bellũ badonis in q̄
an̄ . Pasca cō	an̄	arthur portauit crucē
mutatur sup di	an̄	dm̄ nr̄i ihu xp̄i . trib;
em̄ diuci cum	an̄ . xl .	dieb; & trib; noctib;
papa leone ep̄s	an̄	in humeros suos &
rome.	an̄	brittones uictores fuer̄.
an̄ . x . Brigida	an̄	an̄
scā nascetur.	an̄	an̄
an̄	an̄	an̄
an̄	an̄	an̄
an̄ Scs̄ patricius	an̄ .	an̄ Scs̄ coluiceille nasc̄.
ad dm̄ migra	an̄	Qui est scē brigide.
tur.	an̄ . l .	an̄
an̄	an̄	an̄
an̄	an̄	an̄ . lxxx .
an̄	an̄	an̄
an̄	an̄	an̄
an̄	an̄	an̄
an̄	an̄	an̄
an̄ . xc .	an̄ Episc ebur pau	an̄
an̄	lus mxp̄o	an̄
an̄	no . cccl . etatis	an̄
an̄	sue.	an̄
an̄ quies benigni	an̄	an̄
ep̄i.	an̄	an̄ . xc .
an̄	an̄ . lx .	an̄
an̄	an̄	an̄
an̄	an̄	an̄ Gueith cā lan̄ in q̄
an̄	an̄	arthur & medrau
an̄	an̄	corruer̄. & mortalitas

7 The battle of Mount Badon

Sometimes facts are not as important as they seem. The lack of historical certainty about the life of Jesus Christ, for instance, has made no difference to the spread of a religion based on the supposition that his life was a reality. Similarly, the lack of evidence has proved to be unimportant in the case of Arthur, even though from an early stage much of his popularity appeared to depend on his having existed.

There even seems to be a circular argument involved in this. He must have existed because his popularity implies that he did. Perhaps because of the underlying logical weakness in this reasoning, there have recently been increasingly strenuous attempts to prove the argument; yet to a large extent the more the evidence is deployed and redeployed to yield all possible support, the more obvious it becomes that a mass of theory is being erected on a perilously sparse foundation. What some of those who now protest Arthur's historicity (at length) are doing, is unwittingly engaging in their own form of myth-making. Their work has the dressings of academic orthodoxy, but on inspection it often reveals the tell-tale signs of tendentiousness, particularly in its surreptitious question–begging, and its use of such phrases as 'the Arthurian period', 'the time of Arthur', 'in Arthur's day', before, rather than after, producing the argument from the evidence. Fortunately for us, however, it makes no difference to myth whether Arthur was a fact or an invention.

The next few chapters plot the lines of derivation of the figure of Arthur in British myth. In this one we trace the possible strands which come from history. History is, after all, a part of the origin of our myths. But what we have already seen of the treatment of history by myth should be enough to make it clear that the outcome is by no means closely determined by the facts. A fallacy might well have produced as effective a result.

One historic element in the cluster of ideas epitomized by the figure of Arthur is the constantly recurring motive of nostalgia. Nostalgia is at work in the making of much myth, the regret for an ideal age in theory lost to us by past misfortune – but in practice an age never available because it is largely the result of selection and distortion of memory, and based on the hypothesis that the contrast with experienced reality must, somewhere, sometime, have existed. At the times at which myths come into being there is always ample scope for the supposition that this, at any

The page from the eleventh-century Easter Annals which may have the only factual evidence for the existence of Arthur

rate, is not as golden an age as it might be, which in this case led to a view of an ideal and highly-defined Britain which must, by elimination, be located in the past – and since, as we shall see, the Arthurian idea is strongly Messianic, in the future too.

The people who first used the idea of Arthur were looking back from the immediate end of the Saxon influx to what they imagined to be or could discover of the civilization existing at the time of the invasion. The second wave of interest in the idea came from the similar situation shortly after the Norman conquest. In some cases the two combine, the post-Norman writers resurrecting the post-Saxon ones. This view of Arthur as a figure on a frontier, the last of the independent Britons, either – according to your standpoint – explains his appeal to the people in those situations, or else arises from their special interests. Arthur either had a role in British myth because he fought the Saxons; or else he was said to have fought the Saxons because that was his role in British myth.

The battle of Mount Badon seems to summarize these historical roots. It appears to belong much more to history than to myth; and Arthur's connection with it is tenuous, and restricted to a few brief but very early references. One more-developed story does place the mythic king and the mythic battle in what seems to be their correct historical light, by looking back from a post-Norman viewpoint to a golden pre-Saxon age; by locating the whole matter on the Mercian border; and by showing a primitive and rather unromantic image of Arthur. Called 'The Dream of Rhonabwy', it occurs in the fourteenth-century manuscript known as the Red Book of Hergest, may have been written first at the fairly late date of 1200, and deals with events which clearly belong to about the year 1150. In spite of these late dates, which have distanced the Arthurian matter in so many other cases, it shows an acute sense of the historical relevance of Arthur.

We are in the kingdom of Powys, which bordered what was once Mercia, in the time of a prince whose father had resisted the Normans, but who, himself, had come to accept their advances as inevitable. Rhonabwy is a soldier engaged in some minor border trouble, and he and his companions billet themselves in a run-down and infested farm, which is described with scatalogical detail as a contrast to what is to come. As soon as Rhonabwy has fallen asleep in that unpropitious place he dreams.

He is still in Powys, on the English border, travelling with his troop down the Severn valley from a little to the north of where Welshpool now is, towards Montgomery. A rider approaches them, evidently a man of great size, since Rhonabwy and his companions flee at the sight of him. But the rider overtakes and reassures them, and together they travel towards a fording point on the Severn, at the bottom of a great valley plain. It is the land between Oswestry and Welshpool, a landscape now totally tamed, which forms the surroundings of the Shropshire Union Canal. It is a broad, flat valley at this point, correctly identified in the story as a plain, becoming more complex and wooded around the ford towards which they are heading.

There they can see from a distance the tents and pavilions of a large army; the silk and ivory and accoutrements are detailed with envious relish. When they come to the ford they find Arthur, apart, with attendants, on an island in the river, and the knight who has brought them there is asked where he found 'those little fellows'. He smiles sadly, and when asked why he replies, 'I feel sad that this island should be in the care of men as insignificant as these, after the sort of men who held it once.'

They are gathered, it is revealed, before the start of the battle of 'Baddon'. The tale says it is to be fought against Osla Big-knife, a character who occurs elsewhere in Arthurian stories, whose epithet may indicate that he is a representative Saxon from the tradition that the Saxons carried long knives. Possibly – though the identification can only be tentative – he might be intended to be Octha, the son of Hengist, whose succession to his father's kingdom is mentioned in the Nennius 'History' immediately before the passage which refers to Arthur.

The troops turn from the island towards the ford, a little upstream, to go out to the battle, at or near a place which the story calls 'Baddon Castle', indicating some fort or defensive compound. We do not hear of the battle itself, however, since the story changes direction abruptly, and a truce with the Saxons eventually allows Arthur to return to Cornwall.

The river Severn near Montgomery where the dream of Rhonabwy is said to have taken place

Rhonabwy wakes up again, and finds himself back in the squalor of twelfth-century Powys.

No doubt that spot on the Severn near Montgomery, where the river thins in the long reaches above Garthmyl, must have been an anciently and repeatedly contested junction. River crossings are the scenes of combats both in myth and in history, and here we are at the fording point of a major river on an old-established boundary. Islands tend to form in the stream in summer, and the cattle wander across the current, drinking. A nameless earthwork on the bank seems designed to defend a likely crossing, and between Garthmyl and Montgomery is the site of a Roman fort. A little to the south of that is a massive tumulus, and a Roman road comes down from the direction of Wroxeter to run parallel to the river towards the fort near the ford. Along the slope down which this road comes runs Offa's Dyke, reminding us of the later history of the kingdom of Mercia, definitively marking the Severn valley at this point as a border between the colonized and the independent lands.

The battle of Mount Badon in the early literature is significant as a great victory for the British against the Saxons. In the timetable which the sources set it fits into a gap between the campaigns of Ambrosius and the rise of Cerdic's dynasty in Wessex. Dates for those events must be speculative, but the Anglo-Saxon Chronicle indicates that Cerdic's son Cynric had expanded his hold over the south into a significant kingdom by the 550s. Badon belongs to a period some time before that, if it represents a definite reversal of Anglo-Saxon expansion. From Gildas we hear that it gave rise to a period of peace, and the best independent evidence for its reality is that the Anglo-Saxon Chronicle describes no further English advances between the years 514 and 547. There are indications from two other sources that Angles were returning to the Continent during the 530s. As far as the historicity of Badon goes, this is all we have. The Anglo-Saxon Chronicle does not mention it, and Bede's reference to it is lifted straight out of Gildas, who is therefore our only direct source: 'From that time, sometimes the citizens were victorious, sometimes the enemy. . . . This continued up to the year of the siege of Badon Hill, and of almost the last great slaughter inflicted upon the rascally crew. And this commences, a fact I know, as the forty-fourth year, with one month now elapsed; it is also the year of my birth.'

Somebody who mentions being born in the year of a great battle might be thought to be relating fact rather than hearsay, and Gildas is normally believed on this point. By internal evidence we can put his Badon at about the year 500. Our next oldest source, however, the Welsh Annals, gives the date as 516, and allowing for a deviation of a year or so this is likely to be reliable. These Annals were put together from compilations intended for religious calendar purposes, and made therefore at or about the time to which they applied, so that though the manuscript of the Annales Cambriae dates from about 1100, the material is in each case (as Leslie Alcock points out in his book *Arthur's Britain*) as old as its date. The set which was copied in 1100 was completed in the mid-tenth

Badbury Rings, one of the traditional sites of the battle of Mount Badon

century, and so is in any case quite old. The Annals are significant because they include the first mention of Arthur; in Nennius's 'History', put together in about 800 from old British sources, Arthur takes a fuller form and sets out from the battle towards his glorious future.

Gildas does not mention Arthur at all. In his report Badon is not connected with any leader, although he clearly names Ambrosius as leading the Britons to victory shortly before. It is this, together with the parallel lack of any reference to Arthur in the Anglo-Saxon Chronicle, with the result that Arthur was absent from Bede's account and consequently not included in official British history, that throws some doubt on his historical reality. This is important to the myth in several ways, and we shall have to consider the implications shortly.

Gildas gives no clue to the whereabouts of his 'Mons Badonicus', but his reference to a siege implies a defensive site, perhaps a hillfort or a Roman camp. There has been a great deal of speculation as to where it would have been and its traditional location varies from the east coast to the south-west. Alcock favours a hill near Bath; local lore tends to one or other of the many Badburys – Badbury Rings, an Iron-Age fort in Dorset; Badbury Hill, in Berkshire; or Badbury near Swindon, in Wiltshire. If, as seems almost certain, the battle was a move to prevent the spread of the newly-forming Saxon kingdoms, the site should be on the

The battle of Camlan from a fourteenth-century manuscript. Arthur, fatally injured, is being taken away in a cart on the right

borders of one of them. It may therefore have been, like Catraeth, in the north, although if so it is surprising that it was not recorded in the poetry which has come down to us from there. My own feeling is that the likely pressure in the early-sixth century must have been felt particularly in the less inhospitable stretches of the western terrain, where the Romanized lands of the midlands met the more easily defended tribal zone. The settlement under Hengist in Kent had been in existence then for about sixty years, and other settlements of which we know less for a similar period; so that the westerly creep of the invasion would be most feared in the likely period of Badon. If the historic battle was sited in the west midlands, it also helps to explain the significance of Arthur's re-emergence, in tales like 'Rhonabwy', in places such as the Severn valley.

The references to Arthur in the Annals are brief and occur in the simple records of two battles, that of Badon, and the one in which Arthur and 'Medraut' died, the battle of Camlan. In the former there is a much-debated statement that Arthur carried the cross of Christ on his shoulders for three days and nights, which presumably means that he wore a Christian emblem in some form, rather like the soldiers of Constantine the Great at the battle of Milvian Bridge. Since the Annals say that the Britons were the victors, we must assume that the enemies were pagan

Saxons. But in the case of Camlan, where all we are told is that Arthur and Medraut died, we cannot even make that assumption. In view of the tradition that Camlan was fought between rival factions of Britons, represented by Arthur and his nephew Mordred, we may well assume otherwise, and see in this bleak statement the first germ of the earliest of the themes in the great body of Arthurian romance: the theme of internal war.

The entry about Arthur in Nennius's document is a little more explicit. It comes immediately after a passage in which he has said that the Saxons have been increasing in Britain, that Hengist (who had founded the kingdom of Kent in perhaps 450) had died and been succeeded by his son. When he opens with the words, 'Tunc Arthur pugnabat contra illos in illis diebus. . . .' ('Arthur fought against them in those days'), we may well feel justified in seeing this as the first definite statement that Arthur was fighting the Saxons. A list of twelve battles is given, some of which may be tentatively traced to places as far apart as Scotland and Chester. Four of the battles, it states, took place on a river – a reminder of the importance of river-crossings, both as territorial limits and as lines of communication, in early warfare. The twelfth is Badon, 'in which in one day nine hundred and sixty men were killed by one assault of Arthur's; and nobody felled them except himself alone; and in all the battles he stood out as victor.'

Here distinctly we have the makings of a mythic hero, but coupled with this fanciful extolling of Arthur's prowess is a phrase which has provided the basis for one of the theories of the historical-Arthur school, a theory which, it must be said, has only this one phrase from either the early or the subsequent literature to support it. Arthur fought 'cum regibus Brittonum, sed ipse dux erat bellorum' ('with the kings of the Britons, but he himself was *dux bellorum*'). It is the 'dux bellorum' which is the basis of what has come to be known as the Rhys–Collingwood theory, from the names of its two main proponents.

This theory sees 'dux bellorum' as a title, comparable with 'Dux Britanniarum', which was the title of the Roman commander responsible for the northern defences. It is assumed to mean that Arthur was not one of the kings of the Britons himself, but employed by them in an official capacity to carry on their warfare: commander of the combined British forces. This was the position held in Roman times by someone known by the similar title of 'Comes Britanniarum', Count of Britain, who led the mobile forces. It accords well with the view of Arthur as a cavalry commander which is suggested by the wide spread of the traditional locations of his battles. There is, however, no need to see the word 'dux' as a title. The document is not Roman, and that it is written in Latin does not necessarily mean that the writer would have been familiar with Roman military titles. 'Dux' means simply 'leader', and all that we can read from this is that Arthur, rather than any of the others, led the battles. He might therefore have been a king or simply a soldier. In two further references in an appendix to Nennius's 'History', a list of 'Marvels', he is called 'the soldier Arthur', and it is not for a considerable time that we get any epithets suggesting rank or royalty.

Perhaps the closest we come to historical evidence for Arthur are the signs of the early popularity surrounding his name. The name itself is often put forward for the supposition that Arthur was a British leader of the first half of the sixth century, since although not known in Britain before that time, it was given to the sons of three prominent people during the 550s. However, might it not equally have been one of them, or all three together, who influenced the popular imagination to the extent of the name becoming associated with great events in the later literature? A major question, in any case, is how we know about them and not about him, if he was so well known that they were called after him. The more information we have about other people in British affairs of that time – and before, during, and immediately after the supposed period of Arthur we do know a reasonable amount (from the histories and genealogies) about a number of other figures – the more difficult it becomes to explain the elusiveness of the historical Arthur himself.

His popularity in early times is, however, well attested. There is a passing reference to him in 'The Gododdin', Aneirin's poem, parts of which do seem to be of authentic sixth-century date. But since this is a thirteenth-century manuscript apparently copied from a ninth-century original, the phrase – it is said of a warrior that 'he was not Arthur', presumably meaning that he did not rise quite to that status – might well be an interpolation. In any case it would only indicate an image of Arthur as a supreme fighter; and this is just as compatible with a purely mythic figure as with an actual man. As we have seen, Arthur (and at least one of the episodes which were later to become a part of his great story) occurs in the collection of "Marvels' attached to the 'History' of Nennius, indicating that folk traditions had become as much a part of his associations, at that early time, as battles. And from the early-twelfth century onwards he crops up, though usually in a far from heroic light, in the 'Lives' of saints. Surprisingly, and therefore I think significantly, he is described in such terms as 'quidam tyrannus', a certain upstart ruler, and 'rex rebellus', a rebel king. William of Malmesbury, in about 1125, makes it clear that popular stories about Arthur were widely in circulation by then. And at about the beginning of the 1130s Carado of Llancarvan, in his life of Gildas, features Arthur quite extensively, and tells a story (which we shall come across again in relation to Glastonbury) about him and Gildas, in which they appear to become firm friends.

This relation of Arthur to Gildas has proved the greatest stumbling-block of all to the dating of Arthur to the mid-sixth century. Why, if Gildas knew of Arthur, should he mention Badon and not say anything whatsoever about Arthur? We can understand the omission of his name from the Anglo-Saxon Chronicle, since that concerned itself more with Saxon victories than with Saxon defeats, and is not generally interested in British figures. But Gildas mentions by name Ambrosius, as well as Maelgwn and other living people. Much effort has gone into explaining why he did not mention Arthur, if Arthur was leading the Britons just before his time.

I think that Gildas himself provides the answer to this problem, and that his silence on the subject is quite compatible with Arthur having been his earlier contemporary. Gildas's purpose was not to relate the facts of his time for posterity, but to argue a theme, using, as he made clear, selected items from the past to illustrate it. In his introduction he states this purpose explicitly: 'It is not of the dangers of the massacres of war undergone by brave soldiers that it is my intention to tell, but of the idle.' If that was the purpose of the book, Arthur would not have served it.

Gildas has other equally striking omissions, which might lead us to think of this reticence as a quirk of style. Vortigern, for instance, is not identified by name; perhaps it is assumed that everyone would know to whom 'superbus tyrannus' refers. The mention of Ambrosius sticks out as an exception, and it is that which needs to be explained. Ambrosius moreover is notable as a person both named and praised; apart from Tiberius, St Alban, and a passing reference to two other saints, the only men addressed by name are those lined up to be censured. Ambrosius is cited as being the last of the Romans, a point which is relevant to Gildas's theme; and perhaps he felt that during the post-Roman reaction Ambrosius's achievements had been popularly neglected. In this light, a mention of Arthur would have been out of place since, unlike Ambrosius, Arthur's nearness in time (if the sixth-century date is right) would make his inclusion unnecessary. Also, if we are to draw any conclusions from the disapproving descriptions in the early saints' 'Lives' then it would seem likely that Arthur, if he was a warrior of Gildas's time, would have lacked Ambrosius's high-born blood and his character of 'vir modestus' which so well suited Gildas's message, offering itself as a contrast to the petty tyrants of the Britain of his time.

If, then, Arthur was indeed a military leader of the early-sixth century, who fought and won battles against the Saxons, holding together the forces and power of the various kings of Britain, he failed, because of Gildas's silence, to get into history as such, and it was not as such that he entered myth. Indeed if he had been a character in recorded history, known to us in the same way as the kings of Mercia or the later Romans, he would not have acquired the aura of the super-normal which has made him a figure of such importance in our culture. It is interesting that he attracted these super-normal aspects very early, and the same texts which provide us with what little hints we have of his historicity also contain the seeds of his later numinosity.

The battle of Camlan, we saw, was mentioned in the Annals – though not in the 'History' – and proves to be one of the most enduring of Arthur's exploits. The later tradition, as exemplified in early form by the Triads, states explicitly that Arthur and Mordred were fighting each other. One of the themes which also occurs early (and had obviously been in circulation in folklore for some time before it first became recorded) is that of the promised and prophesied return. It was common in Brittany and Wales by the twelfth century, and has survived as a folk-tale into modern times in such widely diverse places as Yorkshire, Cheshire, North and South Wales, Northumberland, and even Scotland; a cave is said to exist in which Arthur and his knights are sleeping, awaiting the summons to awake and return to save Britain. As we have said, the Arthurian matter is distinctly Messianic, and this is one of the near-religious aspects which became attached to the central character. At the same time (and with some importance during the early-twelfth century) it contained obvious nationalistic overtones. Arthur was to achieve, with his second coming, what he had left undone on the occasion of the first: the ousting of the invaders and the return of the country to its rightful owners.

These themes are of basic importance in the myths, and are clearly relevant to the essential role of Arthur. Britain's identity began to crumble seriously at the time with which he is connected, and his resurrection in the early Middle Ages aided its restoration. Assuming that he lived from about the 470s to the 530s, and that the battle of Mount Badon took place in the first quarter of that century, then for some fifty years during the peak of his career and after his death the country was in a crucial situation. A series of defeats in the south then began to establish the reality of Saxon advances. We have noted that the Anglian kingdom of Mercia did not come into existence until later, in the 630s, but in the meantime Wessex was established.

The Anglo-Saxon Chronicle tells that Cerdic arrived to start the dynasty of Wessex in 495, and with reinforcements from his homeland he and his heirs expanded their territory for the next three decades. His son Cynric had reached Salisbury by 552, and pressed on into Wiltshire. Evidently the British kingdom of Dumnonia, covering the Cornish peninsula, was able to resist their western movement; and to their east Kent was already well established, following Hengist's arrival and confiscation of land (summarized by myth in the story of Vortigern) a hundred years earlier. Probably because of this, the new Saxon kingdom at first expanded northwards until it eventually almost reached the shores of the Severn. And it was perhaps the battle of Dyrham in that area (by which the Saxons managed to capture the three old Roman cities of Bath, Gloucester, and Cirencester, and to kill three kings), in the year 577, which finally established the spread of Wessex and cut Wales off from the west country. Dyrham is now a country house and tiny village lying just off the Cirencester to Bath road a little to the south of the M4, some few miles east of Bristol. Although it has been argued that sixth-century warfare was not motivated by strategic planning, Dyrham's location at such a focal spot must have meant that a British defeat there would be critical to the balance of power between the Saxon and the Celtic kingdoms, and would reverse the effects of Badon. We have already seen how a forlorn attempt to prevent a similar outcome in the north took place at Catterick in Yorkshire in perhaps the next decade. Both battles were heavy British defeats, and signalled the failure of what has come to be viewed as the Arthurian mission.

One should not underestimate in this rather sad progression the role played by the battle of Camlan itself, which the mythology, supported by the nearest we have to early history, sees as Arthur's real downfall. Gildas says that after Badon 'although wars with foreigners have ceased, domestic wars continue'. Was it therefore perhaps this which really contradicted Badon? Was it internal quarrellings, symbolized in the stories by the quarrel of Arthur and Mordred, which led to the failure of the British forces to continue their success? Perhaps the mythology once again correctly identifies, and summarizes, an essential element of the facts.

This overlap between chronicle and tale shows us again the need to avoid taking any exclusive stand. To claim that Arthur was 'really' this or 'just' that, is to miss the main point about the function and effect of myth. We have seen from comparable cases such as Maxen that what myth does to history is to epitomize a plurality, a complexity of things. It synthesizes. Arthur is made of many components, including the historical. His importance lies in the expression, through these combinations and interplays, of an idea. If any aspect of him, including the historical one, has any interest for us today, it is because of the appeal and meaningfulness of the idea.

8 Primitive associations

Whatever the ultimate reason for the emergence of the figure of Arthur, there is no doubt that from a very early stage he exerted a sort of gravitational pull which attracted elements to him which had previously belonged elsewhere. So close is this feature to his origins, that it is itself one of the roots of Arthur, a part of what he basically is.

It is the figure to which these elements became attached that concerns us in this chapter. By the time we first see this figure, he had already been affected by this process, but at the heart of the amalgam, in the earliest stories and in the slightly later ones, a figure of extreme antiquity and universality can be identified, riding out at the head of his troop through a land of monsters, giants, and magic. It is the king of a mysterious kingdom, the lord of the otherworld, the Odin-figure, leader of the wild hunt.

One early story shows him very clearly in this light, and by doing so draws our attention to these aspects of him when he occurs elsewhere. 'Culhwch and Olwen' is ostensibly a tale of the winning of a bride, but is actually a catalogue of folk-themes and oddments gathered from a wide field of story-telling and set in a mythic framework. In its present form it was probably first written as early as 1100, but based even then on an older version. And the antiquity of its main theme, the hunting of a supernatural boar, gains striking confirmation from its being among the list of 'Marvels' appended to the ninth-century 'History' compiled by Nennius. There Arthur is reported to have hunted the pig Troit, with his dog Cabal, which left a footprint on a stone in the Brecon hills. If the battle of Camlan is the first element to enter the corpus from the direction of history, this must be the first to come from fantasy.

Among the common folk-tale elements in the story, the image of Arthur as the supernatural leader of a hunting troop stands out as being of more than narrative importance. One of the main strands of the tale, a sequence which finds its way into the myths of several countries, is the setting and completion of a list of apparently impossible tasks. Another, as we shall see, is the pursuit of the abnormal animal itself.

Culhwch, the hero of the story, sets off for the court of Arthur to seek help. His stepmother has put a curse on him – another common theme in myth and story – that he can marry no woman other than the daughter of the giant Ysbaddaden, a lady whose name is Olwen. And so effective was the prophecy that he had at once fallen in love with her, even without

One representation of an archetypal figure in British myth: the Cerne Abbas giant

having seen her. He goes to Arthur in the optimistic conviction that the latter will be able to achieve the winning of the giant's daughter. Arthur, apparently, can do anything.

Arthur at once promises, almost defiantly, that whatever Culhwch asks for he will get for him; and he is not specially put out when Culhwch asks him to get him Olwen. Messengers are sent to seek her, and at first fail, after a year's unsuccessful search, like that at first undertaken for the Emperor Maxen. Finally a small team of picked men from Arthur's close followers, all of whom possess magical abilities, sets out along with Culhwch; and at last they track her down. They come into the land of giants, and to the chief giant's castle, and they learn on their approach to the castle that no-one who came to request the hand of Olwen had ever left the castle alive. In spite of the repeated warnings which they receive

A thirteenth-century illustration of Arthur meeting the giant roasting a pig

they proceed, and eventually find themselves in the presence of the giant's daughter.

The reason all her suitors are killed, she reveals, is that her father is destined to live only until she finds a husband. She tells them, however, that there is a way to obtain his permission, and that is to offer to do for him anything he demands, as a form of payment.

The giant himself, when they go in to confront him, is clearly a formidable creature. His eyelids are so heavy they have to be lifted by his servants by means of forks; once this is done and he can see them he tells them to come back the next day for an answer, but as they leave he throws after them a poisoned stone spear. One of Arthur's men catches it and throws it back, wounding the giant in the knee. The next day he makes a further excuse, and throws a second spear, which is similarly returned and hits him in the chest; and on the third occasion they persuade him, for his own safety, to discuss the matter with them.

His daughter is obtainable (as she had told them) in exchange for their undertaking certain tasks for him. There are nearly forty of these, and the achievement of several depends on the prior achievement of others. Not all of them get done, but by that time we have forgotten what many of them were, and the attempt to do them carries the narrative along with some force and with many incidental adventures and images. It is clear from the start that they are intended to be impossible. They include such things as turning a forest into cultivated land; obtaining special animals and possessions from people who will not, and could not normally be compelled to, release them; obtaining the services, requisite for the quest, of certain notable people; collecting the super-normal hounds and horse and huntsmen necessary for the hunting of Twrch Trwyth, the magic boar; and finally hunting down that animal itself for the treasure which it carried between its ears, a comb and shears with which the giant could cut his hair.

Culhwch remains undaunted. Arthur and his men will achieve all this on his behalf. The story then embarks on a saga of wonders and exploits, in a world thick with the supernatural. But even before the hunt which forms the story's central sequence, several familiar and basic themes have established the tale as the vehicle of more than fanciful matters.

Firstly it seems significant that the king can live only until his daughter marries. There is something similar in the contest which surrounded the wooing of the daughter of the king of Elis, in Greek myth, by Pelops: one by one his predecessors had lost a chariot race against the king, by winning which she could be gained, and had been killed; when Pelops beats the king, it is the king who dies. A system of matrilinear succession would explain this, the throne going to whoever marries the daughter, as it seems happened at Sparta in the case of the wooing of Helen.

What is most striking about the opening of this story is the theme of the setting of impossible tasks, since it is this which associates this folk-tale world with several important mythologies. We have seen already that in the cases of some kings with prophesied deaths the completion of an apparently impossible set of conditions must take place before the king can die. It is certain that Ysbaddaden will die as a result of someone marrying Olwen, and all his attempts to prevent this will prove to be in vain. Two ideas are combined here: that the new generation is ineluctably arriving, signalling the departure of the old; and that death is unavoidable, dodge and dance how one may.

Impossible tasks are set elsewhere in such circumstances. Jason cannot have his kingdom until he retrieves the apparently unobtainable Golden Fleece; Perseus is sent to kill Medusa on the assumption that this will dispose of him. And in Irish myth Finn is sent out by Grainne, whom he is wooing, to collect two of every wild animal in Ireland and bring them to Tara, an episode which is very reminiscent of Arthur's pursuit of marvellous animals on behalf on Culhwch; and in another Irish story which tells of the wooing of Etain, the king of Ulster's daughter, the hero is set to clear wooded plains and divert rivers. Several of these features, which occur at the beginning of Culhwch's tasks, remind us forcibly of the labours of Heracles, who could not return to Tiryns until he had completed a series of fantastic tasks, among them the collecting of a number of supernatural animals. Perhaps the best example of this common and distinctive theme is in the punishment which the Irish god Lugh imposed on his enemies, the sons of Tuireann. Instead of killing them he gets them to agree to do whatever he asks, and the exercise, which is supposed to result in their deaths, includes the obtaining of various animals and objects which are, like those which Arthur gets for Culhwch, closely and jealously guarded.

It is at this point in the story, as it starts to become active, that Arthur begins to dominate it. His intrusion develops in stages, first as an organizing figure in the background, then, as the tasks become more demanding, as the leader of the questing band. The progress of the story is clearly towards the great boar-hunt. The hunt itself then ranges widely through western Britain and Ireland, the boar swimming the Irish Sea and the host sailing after it to the mainland. When questioned by his companions Arthur explains the history of Twrch Trwyth in a few significant words: he was at one time a king, and had been transformed into a swine because of his misdeeds.

We are clearly not dealing with any normal hunt. Firstly it is a human boar they are after: it can speak. We are reminded of the metamorphosis of Gwydion and his brother, also as a punishment for crimes, which may perhaps, like this one, be connected with a belief in the soul's future progress through lower animal forms as a result of sin committed in human form. We have seen enough instances of people being turned to animal shape already to know that we are dealing here with a theme of some importance. Secondly, the boar was once a king, and so might be connected with the particular animal form taken by the embodied god, in the rituals of Attis and Osiris; the pig which represented them became the god's enemy in more developed myth, such as that in which the Greek god Adonis is mortally wounded by a wild boar. There is plenty of

A Celtic bronze boar which may have been the crest of a helmet

evidence – such as the story in which Gwydion steals the swine of Pryderi and causes a war, and the Irish story of Diarmaid who like Adonis is mortally wounded by a boar – that pigs were considered of sacred significance by the early Celts. And some evidence for this occurs too in the iconography; we find both in France and Ireland small bronze statuettes of boars, and in one case a tableau of a charioteer pursuing one. It is of particular interest that in Gaul the god Mercury was given, among other names, the suffix Moccus, which is a Romano-Celtic word for pig, indicating that he had become equated with an earlier pig-god. We also find there a stone statue, which could perhaps have been of this god, holding in front of its body a boar, rather as if it were a baby.

In his role as huntsman, and in particular in this sequence of the hunting of the bewitched king-boar, Arthur is most closely related to Irish mythology, and therefore perhaps to the original Continental Celtic religion. His special relationship to the traditional material of Ireland lies in his similarity to the huntsman-hero Finn. Finn and his troop protected Ireland, for (as the story goes in Lady Gregory's collection, *Gods and Fighting Men*) 'they had to hinder the strangers and robbers from beyond the seas, and every bad thing, from coming into Ireland'. Arthur fulfils much the same function in his role as national defender, and at one point the two protectors and embodiments of nationalistic ideas actually meet. In the mainland British story, Arthur voyages to Ireland to acquire several of the items required by the giant Ysbaddaden; and in the Irish group of tales, on the other hand, he appears in Finn's surroundings and steals three dogs, for which he is pursued. Finn takes Arthur prisoner and forms a treaty with him, under which Arthur becomes his loyal follower. In 'Culhwch and Olwen', however, the Irish ask him for protection and offer him tributes of food.

In many ways these two great heroes are close counterparts, both leaders of remarkable troops and miraculous hounds, both invincible in the pursuit of their quarries. Finn undertakes one major boar-hunt, in which his opponent is the son, in pig form, of his rival Angus; and he is found hunting a mysterious boar again in the story which leads to the death of Diarmaid. We are reminded of Heracles once more, tracking and capturing the enormous boar on the mountain of Erymanthus.

It is in the overcoming of fearful monsters and supernatural opponents that Finn and Arthur reveal their affinity with the timeless and universal figure of the primitive mythic hero. A correspondence can be seen too with that other riding, fighting figure, the leader of the wild hunt, in which guise Odin occurs in northern myths and Herne, the hunter, in our native folklore. The rider in the night sky with his dark horses and his baying hounds, the god of storms: he overlaps with yet another aspect of the hunter-leader, the impersonation of winter, a dark figure who conducts a seasonal campaign against his rival, the representative of summer. A reference is made to such a tradition in an interjection into the story of 'Culhwch and Olwen', in which an otherwise minor character called Gwyn son of Nudd is destined to fight against his rival every May Day until doomsday, for the hand of Creiddylad, daughter of Lludd. As mentioned before, she was destined to become Cordelia. He, from his annual combat and the date of it, at the start of summer, is evidently connected with a seasonal cycle.

Arthur presides over another of these annual combats in a story which in many ways shows the transition from primitive roots to the world of romance. In the late-fourteenth-century poem from north-west England, 'Sir Gawain and the Green Knight', these two aspects of Arthurian matter co-exist: the deep roots of pagan ritual and the high ideals of Christian medieval courtliness. Some have suggested that the Green Knight himself, a mysterious opponent who appears at Arthur's court, is none other than the ritualistic figure of winter. This suggestion is partly based on the supposition that the English poet or his predecessor has mis-translated the original Welsh word for blue or grey, 'glas', as 'green' – which it can also mean, spanning as it does that range of colours. The grey knight then, carrying (as the green one does in the poem) an emblematic branch of holly, encounters the defender of summer once a year – an explanation of why the contests in the poem are divided by an otherwise puzzling span of a year.

Several of the images and episodes in this heroic English poem have undeniable Celtic roots, and illustrate the way in which the Arthurian material came together. The Green Knight challenges the hero, Gawain, to a beheading contest, a condition of which is that the Knight (who is in fact immortal) can return a year later to deal an undefended blow; Gawain's second confrontation with the Knight, the central episode of the poem, is directly related to an encounter undergone by the Irish hero CuChulainn. In 'Sir Gawain' there also appears to be some ancient Celtic

The ruins of Deganwy Castle

ammue is unkid on þᵉ Vit me ñegt ameud
Sum tÿne ẏ as tixke as ton ꝛ þꝛo þiaiue coupe hirdfe

symbolism involved in a sequence of three separate hunts: first of a stag, then a boar, then a fox, which remind us of the three transformations of Gwydion, into stag, boar, and wolf. What is so impressive and indeed almost magical about this firmly-structured poem is the way these primitive ingredients are combined to produce a high-medieval master-piece.

Arthur in 'Sir Gawain' appears as much the same figure as in the early Welsh tales, a figure symbolic of kingship, of leadership, and, at the same time, with the aura of the wonderful surrounding his mystic court and castle. It is relevant too (considering him now as being related to a deep vein of ritual and lore) that what he presides over in this poem is an encounter with a monstrous opponent, and the survival of it. There are many such episodes in myth with similar features to this one, and they are essentially quite independent of Arthur. In 'Sir Gawain' we have, then, an apt illustration of the way in which primal motifs from many directions in myth adhere to the figure of Arthur.

Gawain's monstrous opponent and the giant Ysbaddaden whom Arthur eventually outwits have many counterparts in other Celtic stories, apart from the one in which a similar character challenges CuChulainn. Indeed, the same, or much the same, uncouth giant lumbers through the imaginations of almost every people, leaving his bootprints indelibly embedded in almost every country's early culture. Arthur's followers encounter him on several other occasions, in mountains, in castles, and in halls. He is bigger than two men, or alternatively bigger than three; sometimes he is described as black; his normal weapon is a mighty club. And it is this image that we see etched in the chalk of several of our hillsides, undoubtedly at its best in that famous figure at Cerne Abbas, in Dorset, where he strides across the slopes carrying his identifying club, an erect counterparting phallus in this case indicating a possible connection with fertility.

Once when this figure occurs, in the story of Owein (or, in Chrétien de Troyes' French version, Yvain), one of the early romances of the Arthurian collection which we shall consider in the next chapter, he seems to have the character of a supervisor of the world of nature. He is, Owein is told, the keeper of the forest. A thousand wild animals graze around him, as he sits on a mound in a clearing deep in the woods. Most significantly the animal which he uses to summon the other animals to him is a stag, and by setting it roaring he demonstrates his power over the wild creatures of the forest, which come and bow to him, as if he were their lord. The stag and the surrounding animals seem to identify at least this particular giant as a version of Cernunnos, lord of the beasts, the stag-god who lurks among the trees in the background of the whole of this mythology.

Geoffrey of Monmouth's explanation for the primal presence of the giant – the enormous adversary who has to be tackled first, in these early

Sir Gawain is secretly visited by the wife of the Green Knight

Gawain beheads the Green Knight

tales, before Arthur can settle to his more ordered role as king – is that this country was originally inhabited by giants. 'At this time the island of Britain was called Albion. It was uninhabited except for a few giants.' Brutus, the great-grandson of Aeneas, came to Britain with the survivors of the Trojan War. He found the island most attractive, decided to stay, and drove the remaining giants into the mountains to live in caves.

One of the other Trojan leaders, Corineus, settled with his men in Cornwall, which, it turned out, was where most of the giants had gone. One particularly ugly one who lived there, twelve feet tall and strong enough to pull up oak trees, was called Gogmagog, a name which, as Geoffrey of Monmouth presumably well knew, comes from the Bible and is representative of evil. This name became divided in later British lore, and the resulting schizomorphic figure is depicted, as Gog and

The traditional figures of Gog and Magog from the Guildhall, London

Magog, outside London's Guildhall. In spite of two destructions of the effigies, once in the Great Fire and once again in the blitz, this version of the tradition proved so strong that replacement figures of the divided character (perhaps at one time intended to represent Gogmagog and Corineus) still perpetuate there a custom dating back to the Middle Ages. One might say that it was Geoffrey who was in error, and the Guildhall tradition which is right, about whether the names were one or two; but there is no doubt that Geoffrey intended Gogmagog to be a single creature, albeit bearing two originally separate Biblical names in combination. At first a grandson of Noah, Magog seems to have then become a country, of which, in Ezekiel, Gog was the ruler; and they emerge as two names representing the nations of the devil in Revelation, chapter 20, where it is said that at the end of the millennium Satan would be released to 'go out to deceive the nations which are in the four quarters of the earth, Gog and Magog, to gather them together to battle'.

Corineus (to return to Cornwall) is attacked by the giants, led by Gogmagog. A battle takes place, and all except that one giant are killed. Corineus wrestles with him personally, and succeeds in throwing him out to sea. From that day this island has been quite free of giants.

The early Arthur is, in one of his aspects, related to that type of figure: one of his first roles is that of representative of the human species in its primal battles with a world of monstrous disorder. He and his associates are, in this element of their nature, the dragon-slayers, the liberators from oppression, whom we badly needed to make the world habitable. We come across the same figure in the Norse Eddas, where giants and ogres are destroyed in an early period of the world's formation; and a lingering element of this need filters through almost into historic times, with such sagas as that undertaken by Beowulf, far-famed friend of the Scyldings, who wrought feud on the grim spirit Grendel. Grendel, that almost human creature lurking in the mist on the high moors, just beyond the controlling scope of knowledge, is perhaps one of the clearest embodiments of the archetypal menace which characters like Arthur, Finn, and Beowulf are required to counter.

In this capacity Arthur gained popularity early. His name crops up in folklore in a wide spread of locations, and so too does the figure of the 'worm', the dragon, and that of the giant, in local tales throughout Britain. The 'Marvels' attributed to him in the Nennius appendix testify to something more than lore, in this connection, since they are as it were an official form of recognition; and it is interesting that the episode of the hunting of the boar should be among them. There is, moreover, similar official documentation of the spread of this popularity to Europe. A sculpture over the door of Modena Cathedral, in Italy, which dates from the early-twelfth century, depicts Arthur in a scene which we shall encounter more than once, the abduction of his queen. And another Italian example, on a mosaic in the cathedral of Otranto, bearing the words 'Rex Arturus', dates from the year 1165. In this he occurs along with other popular worthies, such as Noah and Alexander; but his primitive, non-human position is emphasized in this case by the fact that here (although as far as I am aware nowhere else) he is depicted as riding on a goat. This, according to the twelfth-century writer Walter Map, was what the king of the dwarfs did, the king of a race of little people who lived in a world underneath ours. There are, in fact, many facets to the early Arthur, and this connection preserved in an Italian cathedral is one instance of how important the primitive, extra-human associations are to the development and the fame of Arthur as a figure in myth.

Of course Arthur catches his boar, after hunting it from the coast of Dyfed through the mountains of Preseli, down through the hills and valleys of South Wales, where place-names still record the memory of both Arthur and the boar, and finally driving Twrch Trwyth into the river Severn, where, in the water, they surround him. There they succeed in taking the first part of the treasure required by the giant, but Twrch Trwyth reaches the other bank and the chase goes on into Cornwall. Somehow they manage to complete the acquisition of the treasure, and force the boar into the open sea, where apparently he drowns, since we hear no more of him. And Arthur goes to his seat in Cornwall to rest.

A few more tasks remain to be done, but the steam has run out of the story, and they are passed over quickly. The men return, like destiny, to confront the giant with their collection of marvellous objects. He no longer struggles against his inevitable death. Handing his daughter over, he says that Arthur is to be thanked for her; she would not have been given to Culhwch of his free will. Culhwch sleeps with Olwen then. 'And Arthur's men went home to their own lands.'

Opposite above: The sculpture of Arthur above the door of Modena Cathedral
Opposite below: The mosaic of Arthur riding on a goat from Otranto Cathedral

 n ceste partie
nous dist lhis
toire que apres
ce que la nuit
du tournoient
fu passee et que ce vint a len
demain matin le roy artus se
fu appareillie il oy la
nner œuurt car il e
coustumier et pour
ent tous ceuls qui le
soient a moult prud
tost que la messe fu d
tous ses barons surt

9 The court at Caerleon

Lady Charlotte Guest, in her notes to the translations she produced in 1846 of the Welsh romances of Arthur, remarked that as long as the court at Caerleon and its Round Table form an ideal world for us, then King Arthur is not dead. Looking at the early development of this phenomenon, she said that we are 'forcibly struck with the powerful influence which those legends exercised over society, and the ascendancy which their principal hero so decidedly maintained. Nor can we withhold our wonder at the singular destiny which has awaited this extraordinary being.'

It is remarkable that so much that has been said about the person of Arthur, over so long a period, could validly be said again. In the previous chapters we have reviewed some of the causes of the phenomenon, and in this one we will trace the convergence of these streams of influence – the near-religious folk-figure and the historical reality – with yet another powerful force, that of the high ideals of early medieval romance: courtliness, chivalry, knight-errantry. Arthur became a focal point for these currents too; and in the merging of these various elements there came into existence what Lady Charlotte aptly termed 'this extraordinary being', part British hero, part king of Fairyland, part ideal medieval monarch.

The early romances are best exemplified by three twelfth-century Welsh stories and the poems of Chrétien de Troyes (who wrote in Old French in the last decades of that century) which are closely related to them. In all these, and in several other romances in which Arthur occurs (such as 'Sir Gawain and the Green Knight') the king himself is a background figure, a supervising presence surrounding the deeds of the heroes, who are, or become, knights at his court. Occasionally he himself does emerge from the background, as he did in 'Culhwch', to issue instructions or go on a journey; but more often his role is to provide the circumstances in which the hero's adventures can take place. By now his sovereignty has become throughly established. From being simply 'dux bellorum', leader of the battles, he had become 'penteyrned', chief ruler, and now he is called by Chrétien 'le roi Artur', and in Welsh stories 'ameraudur', a title which is translated 'emperor'.

The relationship between the three Welsh stories and Chrétien's great poems is not precise. Each omits things which the other includes, and in some cases there are signs that matter has passed from Britain to France

Sir Gawain taking part in a tournament before Arthur and his court

and come back again. Sometimes the correspondences are very close; sometimes the authors have exercised their personal imaginations, so that the details diverge. It is now largely agreed that neither the stories nor the poems are translations of each other, and that therefore both artists were working from a common source, about which we know nothing.

A summary of one of these stories, the story of Owein, or, in Chrétien's version, Yvain, shows the new elements which went to the making of the Arthur of romance. It starts off, as most of them do, with Arthur holding court at 'Caer Llion' on Usk, a specific location which makes the subsequent conventionalized world of forests and castles seem all the more fantastic. It is time for the telling of tales, and one of the knights tells of a strange experience which he once had. In his search for adventure, he was travelling alone, armed, across the wildernesses of the world. At last he came to a castle, where he was made welcome; his host, asking at dinner what he was doing on his journey, provides him with the challenge which he seeks: that is, a suitable opponent to engage in combat. Following his directions the knight rides out next day into the forest and, as predicted, he comes to a clearing, where he finds a giant black man, one-eyed, one-footed, armed with an iron club. This is a person we have met before, surrounded by the wild animals of the woods, and so apparently related to the god Cernunnos in his role of deity of animals. I am, he announces (in Chrétien), 'the lord of my beasts', and in the British tale this is demonstrated by the animals bowing down to him. In spite of these impressive characteristics it is not this being who is to provide the necessary adventure, and he simply sends our hero on his way towards his goal.

This he eventually discovers. It is a fountain under a great tree, with a bowl tied to a marble slab; by throwing water over the slab with the bowl, a storm is raised which attracts the arrival of the knight who guards the fountain. High-flown descriptions (in both languages) attend the storm. Duly the knight arrives, unseats the Arthurian knight, and to his humiliation takes away his horse. It is not a very heroic outcome, but the body of the tale is concerned with the need for this episode to be revenged.

The hero of the main story, Owein, accordingly sets out. He travels the route described, to the edge of the world and its desolate mountains, and at last he comes to the castle, where he receives the same courteous hospitality, and in due course goes on his way to the clearing with the giant in it, who directs him towards the fountain. The storm and the knight's arrival follow, and they engage in combat.

This time the guardian of the fountain is not in luck. In his encounter with the hero of the tale he receives a mortal wound, and retreats to his city to die. Owein, pursuing him, gets trapped in the city's entrance-gate, from which he is rescued by a maiden who gives him a ring and a magic stone, which will make him invisible as long as he wears them.

Great mourning overcomes the city when the knight who guarded the fountain dies, and Owein sees from a castle window the funeral procession pass by. In doing so he falls in love with the lamenting widow, and through the intercession of the maiden who has taken up his cause he is eventually introduced to her. Now the lord is dead she needs an equivalently effective fighter to safeguard her domain. The improbability of Owein's coming to marry the widow of the man he killed suggests that this theme is a hazy reference to a succession custom which had, by the time the stories were assembled in this form, been long forgotten. The knight who wins the encounter (perhaps a regular or ritual matter) gains the kingdom, which in turn entails marrying the queen. The fountain plays some sort of symbolic part in the kingship contest. It is explained in the story that it has to be defended for the kingdom to be safe.

Thus Owein finds himself in the demanding role of defender of the magic fountain. Arthur eventually arrives there (in the French version because he appears to be at war with that domain, in the British one in search of Owein) and goes through the ritual of pouring water on the slab. He himself does not fight, and Owein defeats his representatives, Owein's own former colleagues, who joust in disguise. Much is made of the fact that a knight in full armour wearing an unfamiliar topcoat cannot be recognized, even by his closest friend.

With his new wife's permission, Owein goes off with Arthur for a time. In the course of further adventures, however, he forgets both about her and his promise to return, and in due course a recriminating messenger turns up at Arthur's court. So overcome with guilt is he that he leaves the court and lives wild in the woods, until eventually he strays into the territory of his neglected wife, where he is cared for and brought back to health, unrecognized. He finds himself once more involved in a tournament, defending the territory which was for a time his; but having successfully combated a new opponent and won the kingdom for himself again, he is not willing to stay. He travels, thoughtful, through the deep forest, wanting nothing except to travel the extremes of the world and its wilderness. Both story-tellers, Chrétien and the unknown Briton, follow this proud departure with a series of adventures, combats with giant serpents, the taming of a lion, the rescue of a maiden, a fight with a giant, and in Chrétien several more encounters at the magic fountain. After these ramblings the story ends where it started, in Arthur's court at Caer Llion.

Both versions are clearly based on ancient British material, if only through their choice of hero, whom Chrétien names as the 'fils du roi Urien', thus identifying him as Owein son of Urien, king of Rheged, a North British historical character who was transformed into the heroic protagonist of many Welsh episodes. His appearance here illustrates a point which has been with us from the beginning – that the British material became transposed from its original wider setting and isolated in the west of Britain, from where it presumably travelled to Brittany. It also links us with the characters and episodes of earlier chapters, since it was for Owein's father Urien that the sixth-century poet Taliesin wrote, himself the mythicized centre of an early tale. But many of the features which have now begun to enter the Arthurian collection are unlike these ancient elements, and differ too from the very basic ritualistic themes such as the combat at the ford (in this case a fountain or magic spring) and the winning of a kingdom through the marriage of its queen. What we see starting to influence the matter here is the distinctive attitude and body of values of the Middle Ages.

Perhaps most striking of these is the idea of the individual's quest, on which the narrative of adventures is originally based. Arthur as troop-leader, or his gang of co-operating champions, has faded into the back-ground. One man alone sets out, riding solitary through forest, mountain, and wilderness, seeking adventure. He has all-important standards to fulfil, the protection of women and the need to win ritual-ized combats on their behalf. When in the course of his travels he comes to a habitation, traditionally a rich and isolated castle, he expects, and receives, luxurious hospitality. It is, to the inhabitants of the castle, natural and commendable that a high-blooded knight should be riding by on his own in search of adventure. The concept of adventure itself as an end and an achievement, which seems so indeterminate to us, seems to them to require no further explanation.

It is the quest which takes precedence over everything. To understand much of the spirit of the later Arthurian matter we must recognize this notion in its seminal form in the twelfth century. Rather than stay with the woman in the kingdom which he has defended for her, Owein returns to the search which eternally occupies the followers of Arthur. Having for a second time rescued her from her enemies he declines her offer of the kingdom again and rides out alone in search of his further destiny. Twice in other stories of this period the quest itself overrides love and duty, overcoming even that need to protect and benefit a woman – Peredur parts from the woman who loves him to continue his search, which we shall hear about again, for the Castle of Wonders; and in another story closely paralleled by Chrétien, Gereint rejects the comfortable life available to him with his lady Enid, saying to his father, 'There is a quest I must go on; and I do not know when I shall come back.'

Indeed these other twelfth-century tales which Chrétien popularized in France, and which represented the first flowering of Arthurian Romance in Britain, make several things clear about the style and aspira-tions of the court in Caerleon. Again and again a solitary hero sets off for unpredictable adventures in a strange land. We can understand the circumstances which gave rise to this: the sense of new possibilities; the stretches of untamed land in a thinly populated Europe; the physical surroundings of the great forests with their newly-cleared enclaves and long, dark pathways; the dangerous presence of wild animals; and a scarcely-conquered background of primitive custom and belief – the god Cernunnos might be present in the forest no less than the wild animals. In face of this was the need to cling to newly-established notions of courtly civility, and to Christianity. We must also see these attitudes in

Gawain takes leave of Arthur as he sets out on his quest

the context of a highly-developed political structure precariously balanced against a harsh physical world.

A theme which runs through these Romances, and is a principal influence on the make-up of Arthur in his full form, is that of personal responsibility. It fits within the corporate idea of Arthur's followers, but he himself, and by extension all his leading knights, have in the end to make their personal and moral decisions. It is perhaps odd to find this element forming so early, considering the generally accepted view of medieval society, with its Guilds, sense of social placing, anonymous craftsmanship, and conformity of style. But again and again even the most generalized dispute is settled by representative champions in single combat, and one of the functions of Arthur's court is to provide a place from which the hero can wander away on his own. Indeed such characters as Owein son of Urien, in these early medieval forms, are as recognizable as individuated heroes as they were in the heroic tradition represented by Taliesin's eulogies, and as they will later be shown to be in the work of Malory with the approach of the Renaissance – the conventionally accepted realm of the individual.

In spite of any changes of approach such as shifts of emphasis from Arthur as troop-leader to his single knights as heroes, there is through all this an underlying continuity which identifies it as a single matter. In the late-twelfth century when these elements had come together in their perfect form, we are in the immediate shadow of Geoffrey of Monmouth. And his great work represents better than any other the pervasive eclecticism of the Arthurian material; all the traditional material from Britain's early development had gathered itself together around the nucleus of Arthur.

Geoffrey of Monmouth was an ecclesiastic, originally from Monmouth, who seems to have spent much of his life in Oxford, and to have passed his last years (by then the absentee bishop of a Welsh see) in London. He wrote in Latin, and most of his sources were in that language; some were the same as ours are – the works of Gildas, Nennius, Bede, and the Welsh church annals which give us much of our chronology. It is clear that he also understood what he terms 'the British language', and through that he probably drew on the other main stream of tradition, the folk and mythic one, which we can similarly tap: some parts of the Mabinogion, perhaps, and the poetry of Taliesin. It seems clear too that many traditions and archaic histories were available to him which are lost to us, and probably he had an ear for tales current in his time which only achieved written form through him.

'The History of the Kings of Britain' is a book of Homeric ambition, which traces the origins of the occupants of the island from the time of giants through the Roman occupation and the reign of Arthur, ending with the Saxon invasion. It is, because of this purpose, the repository for all the material which at that time constituted British myth, as well as for some (but not much) authentic history. To a large extent the structure of the mythological material imposes itself on the book – the remnants of religious cults, the coming and departing of the Romans, Merlin's prophecies, the Saxons' arrival, and in the middle, forming the bulk of the material, Arthur.

Geoffrey reveals with his first words his literary ancestry, by opening with the same passage on the beauties of the island as that used by Gildas, Nennius, and Bede. The Britons, he reveals, were descended from Brutus, the great-grandson of Aeneas, who came through Europe to this island with the descendants of the survivors of the Trojan War. Presumably this starting point was a conscious continuation of the *Aeneid,* but the doings of the Greeks after Troy soon get lost in the narrative once we come to Britain. What facts he gives of Britain's early history may be allocated to Gildas, who himself took at least some of them – for instance, the 800-mile length and 200-mile breadth of the island – from Pliny. Geoffrey's Brutus (whom he evidently heard of from the compilation of Nennius) seems to be included mainly to give Britain a name, since he called the island 'Britain' after himself. But the connection of the origins of the British with Greece and eastern Europe is, as we have seen, not altogether fanciful, since Celtic tribes with similar traditions and culture affected both extremes of Europe. Stylistic similarities in metalwork indicate too that there was contact between the Greek world and the Celtic Continental homeland in pre-Roman times. The movements of Geoffrey's Trojans through Europe in, presumably, the first millennium before Christ has probable parallels in the real movements of people, which we have seen reflected in various names and episodes of British and European myths.

From this distant beginning, in the land where Trojans wrestled with giants, Geoffrey moves confidently into the pre-Roman period, for which he has much information to offer, some of it later to prove influential. The cities of Carlisle and Bath receive their names from the respective kings Leil and Bladud, who built them. Bladud dies in an attempt at aeronautics, like Icarus, and is succeeded by his son Leir. Leir we have already met, in the form of Llŷr; later, through the works of Geoffrey's successors, he became developed as the King Lear made famous by Shakespeare. In Geoffrey he gave his name to Leicester, and although he had no male heir he had three daughters; and he gives the framework of the now familiar story.

Many others, too. But Gorboduc, Cunvallo, Gurguit Barbtruc, and Guithelin came briefly out of almost complete obscurity and retired back into it at once. In the middle of a long catalogue of civil wars and successions we do meet two more familiar figures, the brothers Belinus and Brennius, rivals for the kingship. These are none other than Beli and Bran, two of the most ancient gods of the Celtic peoples, known to the Romanized Gauls as Belenus and Brennus; in a previous chapter we have found the former mentioned as the king of Britain when the Romans came, and in a later one we shall find the latter involved with the ownership of the grail – so that once again Geoffrey is, in spite of the appearance which he gives of writing fanciful pseudo-history, deeply influenced by authentic national myth.

Just as the cults of Beli and Bran may well have competed for dominance in pagan Britain, so the brothers Belinus and Brennius in Geoffrey's 'History' at first divide the island between them and eventually decide to fight the matter out, Brennius from the north, Belinus from the centre and the west. They battle on their northern border; and Belinus wins. He then ruled the island as a whole, and under him civilization became established. Brennius returned, and peace was eventually settled between the two factions, so that they ruled together, and made Britain into an important European force. We have seen already how Belinus's name was, according to Geoffrey, preserved in his chief city, in the name of one of its great gates, the water-gate to the river, called, after him, Billingsgate.

Geoffrey's second main phase, the arrival and occupation of the Romans, contains, as one would expect, some historical factuality, though dressed up still in imaginative trappings. He relates at length Caesar's invasion, Claudius's visit, and the arrival of Christianity. Maximus, whom he calls Maximianus, rises to power, takes an army to the Continent, conquers Gaul, fails to return, and consequently leaves Britain 'denuded of all its armed soldiery', just as we have already heard Gildas describe. Picts and Huns combine with Danes and Norwegians to assault the helpless island, once the Romans have gone. And the stage is set for the story of Vortigern, which formed an important episode in chapter five.

In Geoffrey's 'History' the brothers Hengist and Horsa, named by Nennius and Bede, grow to almost mythic proportions. It is they who become Vortigern's (and Britain's) enemies, sending for troops from Germany, exploiting the king's friendship and his strategic vulnerability, and finally meeting for a treaty with their long knives concealed in their boots. All this comes from Nennius, as does the resulting flight of the king into the mountains of Wales. But at that point Geoffrey of Monmouth introduces not the Welsh prophet Emrys, but his own invention and mouthpiece, the wizard Merlin. In doing so he moves decisively, unlike his sources, into Arthurian myth.

Historically Geoffrey's story is still firmly fixed in the sub-Roman period, in which the characters of Hengist, Vortigern, and Ambrosius continue to preside over British political affairs. After Arthur we return to a world in which the kingdoms of the Dark Age kings give way to Northumbria and in due course Mercia too. The Britons embark on civil war, retreat to Brittany, and abandon Britain to the ravages of its enemies and a deadly plague. It is, in fact, a summary of the historical basis of the mythology; but in between is the long central section of the 'History' devoted to the development of the idea of Arthur.

Geoffrey's Arthur is the first great combination of those separate facets of the character which we have been reviewing. He is part supernatural being, part a figure from early history, leading his nation in defiance of its eventual fate; and he expresses the new concepts of chivalry and idealism which were to prove so fruitful as a by-product of the image of Arthur throughout the rest of that century.

The life-story of Arthur as told in the 'History' begins with his conception. Merlin arranged it, in an episode which seems to be connected with the conception of heroes in other myths: the king of Britain is disguised to be indistinguishable from the husband of the woman he loves. Arthur becomes king rather abruptly – there is no kingship test in this version, as in the later ones – and sets about his battles (from the list in Nennius) with the Saxons. His campaigns range throughout Europe, and back at home the splendour of his court at Caerleon becomes world-famous. 'If I were to describe everything, I should make this story far too long,' says Geoffrey, after several pages of recounting its riches and pageantry. The climax of success is the powerful British king's defiance of the Romans, his invasion of the Empire (during which, true to form, he finds time to rescue a maiden from a giant), and the war against the Romans, which echoes the combats of Maximus's British troops against the eastern Emperor Theodosius. With considerable losses on both sides he defeats the Roman army, and ends the claims of Rome to exact tribute from Britain.

In departing for these foreign wars Arthur had left both the kingdom and the queen in the guardianship of his nephew Mordred. As he was about to cross the mountains to advance on Rome itself, news came to him of Mordred's treachery. He had usurped the throne and (as so often happens in the mythic taking of a kingdom) married the queen. Arthur returned, Rome tantalizingly untaken, and his last campaign had started. As we have seen, this theme of Mordred's connection with his death is one of the oldest and most clearly authentic, since it occurs in the Annals, in a statement that the battle of Camlan took place in the year 537, in which battle Arthur and 'Medraut' died; and because of the way in which

The inscribed stone on the bank of the river Camel near Slaughterbridge

these year-lists were derived from contemporary Easter tables, the
original entry might have been made in the year itself. Nennius's
appendix, the 'Marvels', states that Arthur killed his own son, whom it
names as Amir – a name which somehow failed to become prominent;
and we shall see that this tradition too survived, since Mordred is later
said to be not only Arthur's nephew but his son as well.

Mordred has formed a league with Arthur's enemies the Saxons, and
the king returns to fight in a divided country. He pursues Mordred to the
'River Camblan', which Geoffrey says was in Cornwall. Traditionally
this is identified with the Camel, a river which runs through northern
Cornwall looping through the rolling land below Bodmin Moor and
skirting the coastline near Tintagel. Below Camelford it wanders through
fields, and suddenly at Wadebridge it swells into the major estuary which
issues past Padstow. Above Camelford it runs through a curving valley
towards Slaughterbridge, which is the area where the battle is often
reputed to have taken place. Here, the river becomes very small –
though the width of the valley indicates that it was once more substantial.
This cultivated and enclosed land is not battle country, at least not now,
but up above Slaughterbridge there is a banked enclosure and some
defensive works, apparently built in stone and now turfed over, overlooking the river and the alleged site of the battle; and this, together with
a very persistent tradition, makes it a suitable place to think of as the site
of Camlan.

Some supposed support is given to this theory by the discovery of an
ancient inscribed stone on the river bank below this hill, just upstream
from Slaughterbridge. One would have to stretch the evidence considerably to persuade the scarcely legible inscription to yield any connection
with Arthur – though Lewis Thorpe, in his excellent Penguin Classics
edition of Geoffrey's 'History', has done just that. One can, I think, make

Above: The earthworks near Slaughterbridge which are a possible site of Camlan
Opposite: Arthur enthroned, from a fourteenth-century French tapestry

out in the clearly cut but distorted lettering the words 'iacit' and 'filius'; but the names either side of these are indistinct. The place, Slaughterbridge, probably gets its bloodstained name from the massacre which took place when the Saxons met the Cornish there in the ninth century. Perhaps the stone too belongs to that event; yet one feels intuitively that the writing is older. In any case what we apparently have here is another example of a battle not originally Arthur's becoming allocated to him.

That one of the traditional sites of Arthur's death should be so close to the supposed place of his birth, Tintagel, emphasizes the importance of the Cornish roots of the Arthurian legend. Certainly Geoffrey seems to show an awareness of this at several points of his narrative. It was in Cornwall, then, somewhere along a river, that it is assumed the forces met and the final battle took place.

Mordred died first, Arthur being mortally wounded in the skirmish. He was, says Geoffrey, carried away then to the Isle of Avalon, for his wounds to be treated. With unusual restraint he leaves the story there, but implies elsewhere that Arthur is destined not to die but to await the right time to return. This theme – the hero's immortality – seems to have been a folk-tradition at that time, and perhaps something to that effect is recorded by the ancient collection of lore known as the 'Stanzas of the Graves', where it is implied that no-one will ever find Arthur's grave.

The Avalon theme was probably current long before the twelfth century when it entered literature, but its artistic possibilities ensured that it would then become increasingly prominent. The air of mystery was of great appeal. The Norman poet Wace, in the 1150s, leads the trend towards the unknown, the ambiguous nature of his end:

> Merlins dist d'Artus, si ot droit,
> Que sa fin dotose seroit.
> Li prophète dit verité.

'Merlin said of Arthur – if I read right – that his end should be hidden in doubt. The prophet spoke truly.' He had been taken to Avalon 'por ses plais médiciner'; he is there still, awaited by the Britons, who say he will return again. 'Men have always doubted, and – as I believe – always will doubt, whether he is alive or dead.'

Geoffrey did not dwell on the theme of Arthur's return. His focus was more towards Britain's roots and its glorious past, towards an ideal age, which must have been still suggested by the great Roman ruins in places such as Caerleon, which clearly, to Geoffrey, was a symbol of a way of life the first part of the twelfth century had not achieved. He refers to its gold-painted gables, its palaces and churches; and we have a first-hand record that these were there for him to see, since Giraldus Cambrensis, who passed through Caerleon with Bishop Baldwin in 1188, wrote down his impressions of it. 'Many vestiges of its former splendour may yet be seen; immense palaces, formerly ornamented with gilded roofs, in imitation of Roman magnificence . . . a tower of prodigious size, remarkable hot baths, relics of temples, and theatres, all enclosed within fine walls, parts of which remain standing.' Unfortunately none of this grandeur still shows, largely because the modern town of Caerleon is in the middle of the area of the great Roman camp, but one can easily imagine how it must have been, and what it must have symbolized to Geoffrey and to Gerald.

Isca (as this great camp was called in Latin, from the name of the nearby river Usk) was built in the first subduing of South Wales, in about AD 75, a central administrative fort connected to the field forts of the same period at Carmarthen, Neath, and Brecon. The Welsh name seems most likely to be derived from a phrase meaning 'fort of the legions', the exact equivalent of the Latin term 'castra legionum'. The legion in question was the Second Augustan, and its presence here makes this legionary fort equivalent in status to the other two in Britain, York and Chester. When it was in full use it had accumulated, in the space between the defences and the river, a sizeable civil settlement, inhabited by soldiers' families, traders, Roman Britons who felt more secure (or found they grew more prosperous) under the shelter of the legion. Outside the fort too, and hence (by being outside the subsequent modern town) still visible, was a substantial amphitheatre. The legion stayed at Isca until the end of the fourth century, when part of the Second Augustan was at the Saxon Shore fort of Richborough, and by which time South Wales was under the control of the new fortress at Cardiff. Little but the grass-covered amphitheatre and some box-like foundations is left to see now, in contrast with the grandiose ruins of the twelfth century.

In Geoffrey's work very little is chosen at random. Names, episodes, places, all have some significance in the context of British tradition. His choice of Caerleon as an Arthurian centre is no exception, since Caerleon was ideally representative of a distant and impressive past. It must have stood for the civilization, the urbanization of Britain, for the forces of progress and Christianity so admired by Gildas. This was not what

Opposite above: Sir Bedevere casts Excalibur back into the lake, while the wounded Arthur sits in the foreground
Opposite below: The blind goddess Fortune and her wheel. Arthur is enthroned at the top

Arthur had previously meant to the story-tellers; but it was what he was to come to mean increasingly during the later Middle Ages. In Geoffrey's eyes Arthur had clearly taken over, at Caerleon, the Roman standards of power and grandeur.

The immediate and immense success of the material which Geoffrey of Monmouth had brought together in his 'History' is due to a combination of historical factors which operated to propel Arthur into literary immortality. The work was probably finished in 1136, around the end of the reign of Henry I and the start of that of Stephen, a time of extreme uncertainty. Viewing it as an attempt to overcome such uncertainty helps us to understand both its nature and its popularity.

The troubles at this time were mainly dynastic; and at a period when kings owned their countries as if they were private estates the ruler must have formed an essential part of the nation's awareness of itself. Ever since the death of William I the succession in England had been disputed. This must inevitably have given rise to a national trauma of identity, in a country which was in any case of very mixed make-up. The situation was not helped by the general unpopularity of the Norman dynasty in England, whose chief support stemmed from the vested interests of their Norman barons. Henry I died, after a repressive reign, on 1 December 1135, in the course of a war in his home territory of Normandy against his rival and son-in-law, Geoffrey Plantagenet. Henry's daughter and only surviving heir, Matilda, had been married to this Count of Anjou in the vain hope of ending the competition between the two houses. The situation accurately reflects the state of rivalry operating throughout Europe at that time. England thus found itself in the position of being an important appendage to either the Dukedom of Normandy or the Countship of Anjou. Since the Norman barons on the whole still controlled Britain, the acceptance of a Plantagenet succession posed difficulties and Geoffrey and his royal wife Matilda continued to be unpopular in England. It was under such circumstances that Stephen of Boulogne, a powerful Norman baron himself and the grandson of William the Conqueror, more or less seized the throne.

Stephen had considerable British territories, and above all possessed the advantage of having married a woman who was a descendant of the Saxon royal house. The apparent loss of identity for Britain, as a pawn in the rivalry of the lines of Normandy and Anjou, could be resolved by seeing Stephen as a British, rather than a Continental, king. Much of the 'History' must of course have been completed before Henry's death at the end of 1135, but its publication very shortly afterwards fitted fortunately into the resulting situation. There were the effects of the desirability of finding a pre-Norman basis for Britain's identity, together with the possibility of a new order of government and a new outlook presented by the new British-based king.

The hope and the opportunity did not last, but it spanned the four years following the production of Geoffrey's 'History'. And it gave rise to the realization that the English crown might be a force of government in its own right, and a political factor in Europe distinct from the other dynastic blocks. It encouraged a common interest on the part of the various groups which would eventually make up the new British people, an interest in their country's original and natural independence. Above all at this time informed opinion in England must have desired peace and stability. The power of the Angevin factor, represented by Geoffrey Plantagenet, began to reassert itself towards the end of the 1130s, and constantly in the background were, on the one hand, the other claimants to the Norman succession, and, on the other hand, the still powerful independent Welsh and Scottish rulers.

Because of their common interest in the identity of Britain, Arthur became the common property of Norman, Saxon, and Briton. It was fortunate that he so well suited the temper and style of the time, the need for courtliness and the consciousness of a surrounding uncertainty. It is significant to the point of being symbolic that Geoffrey's two great followers, Wace and Layamon, were respectively Norman and English, presenting his successful Latin book to their own sections of the British people, the one in Norman-French, the other in Middle English. They added, as every compiler did, their own touches – Wace, for instance, initiating, and Layamon expanding, the founding of the Round Table. In their hands the elements of chivalry and nationalism combined to establish their warrior-hero as an emblem of Britishness; and by the time at which the second of them wrote, at the turn of the twelfth to thirteenth century, we find the transformation of Arthur complete.

Here once again there is a harking back, but it is to a more developed form of the British idea. Layamon's 'Arthur the king' is king of a land where Saxon as well as Celt can feel at home – a land of wishful imagination rather than of history. 'Might never any man think of bliss that were greater in any country than in this; might never man know any so much joy, as was with Arthur, and with his folk here!'. To Layamon he embodies the pre-Norman English attributes of his own ancestors, a medieval version of the warriors and heroes of Germanic saga, but firmly and essentially placed in the world of the island Saxons. He is a sort of Beowulf figure, but in an England which had successfully assimilated its Celtic culture, and which had survived beyond these latest invasions to emerge, eventually, as a real and self-identifying country. Arthur was instrumental in this process, and not surprisingly, since that had always been his role.

> Bute while was an witehe,
> Maerlin ihate,
> he bodede mid worde,
> his quithes weoren sothe,
> that an Arthur sculde yete
> cum Brutten to fulste.

'There was a wise man once called Merlin; he spoke with words – his sayings were true – that an Arthur should yet come to help the British.'

THE DEVELOPMENT OF ARTHUR

And so it forthinketh me a little, for I have loved
them as well as my life, wherefore it shall grieve me
right sore, the departition of this fellowship: for I
have had an old custom to have them in my
fellowship.

Arthur, in Malory's *Le Morte d'Arthur*, 1469

o Camelot

One of the characteristics of Arthur from an early stage had been a tendency to remain in the background; he presided, as an influence or a reference point, over the adventures of other people. He never entirely lost this characteristic and in the most imaginative sequence in his story, in which his role is that of deceived husband and betrayed friend, his main contribution to the events consists of remaining absent and unaware. But at one point this tantalizing figure does fully emerge, at last, from the background, to reveal a leader who is at the same time a strong king and a noble person. In this form he embodies the qualities which we would, perhaps eternally, regard as human, decent, and good.

Arthur as king, in the early part of the story told by Malory, is the representative of a hope for a new and better Britain. That is not a new view of him, nor is the situation in which he emerges unfamiliar. On the death of Uther Pendragon the country is 'in great jeopardy', not through foreign invasions but because of civil war. Every strong lord wanted to be king. This, from Tacitus through Gildas and into the historical context in which Geoffrey of Monmouth wrote, has been one of the conspicuous political elements in British tradition, and contributed to a large extent to Arthur's development as a popular image. A strong kingship was required both for the maintenance of internal law and order and for the resistance of outside interference, a situation which must have been general until organized central government prevailed, after the arrival of the new political ideals of the Renaissance. What may be unusual in the case of Britain is the degree of self-awareness which the mythology shows, a recognition (perhaps due to the insularity of the country) of where and what this nation was, and therefore of the extent to which it needed to retain (or achieve) cohesion. Arthur is not just a security against invasion; he is, even more, a medium of unity.

Merlin (in Malory's tale) set about providing this solution. He knew that the rightful king should be Arthur, Uther Pendragon's son, but first he had to make him acceptable to the barons. Everyone assembled to decide the matter, and on emerging from the cathedral after a service they found in the churchyard a sword stuck in an anvil on a great stone, with gold letters on it saying that whoever pulled it out was 'rightwise king born of all England'. Those ambitious for the kingship tried, and failed, to pull it out.

Arthur arrives on the scene by accident; his destiny is unavoidable and

Arthur removes the sword from the stone and is acclaimed king

therefore requires no effort on his part. He has come to the jousts with his foster-brother, Kay, with whom he has been brought up in ignorance of his true parentage. With providential carelessness Kay forgot to bring his sword, and sent his younger brother back to their lodgings for it; but there is no-one in, since they have all gone to watch the jousting, and in an empty city Arthur casually takes, instead, the sword which was sticking in the stone. Kay on recognizing it tries to claim the kingship; but when replaced in its stone the sword will yield to no-one but Arthur. His right and his blood are thus revealed, and after everyone who disputed the matter had had the chance to try the test, and backed by the people's support, he becomes king.

All this takes place in London, and Arthur has come so far from his roots that it is necessary for him at first to conquer Wales, like any other king of England. Then to achieve security he fights his first war against the kings of other parts of Britain. Great battles and sieges follow, as a result of which he wins the right to rule (as Malory points out) not through his natural inheritance, as son of the late king, but through superior strength and ability. With Merlin at his side he rides through a whole book of early adventures, in which the discovery of his parentage and the acquiring of his sword Excalibur from the mysterious Lady of the Lake, stand out as high points in his 'youthful exploits'. During this period also he unknowingly begets his future enemy, Mordred.

Everything about the story is foreknown, and foretold by Merlin to Arthur. Mordred will kill him; and when it comes to the time when he must take a wife his choice of Guenever is not a wise one – 'but there as a man's heart is set, he will be loth to return' – since she will be loved by Lancelot, and will love him in return. But foreknowledge makes no difference, in myth, to the avoiding of catastrophe. Arthur marries Guenever. With her he receives from her father the 'Table Round' (given to him by Arthur's father, Uther Pendragon), a board which seats no less than a hundred and fifty knights. From then on the greatest honour Arthur can give to a loyal supporter is to make him a knight of the Round Table, an investiture which places on its recipient the demands of extreme integrity and chivalry. The emblem itself forms the centre-piece of the court which the king then establishes at Camelot, his principal seat from the time of his marriage.

Feasts and jousts, departures and returnings, fill the long days of the high period of the court at Camelot. One senses from time to time the doom and enchantments out in the darkness beyond the reach of the court's bright lights. Characters, some slightly ludicrous, some (like the king's sister the enchantress Morgan le Faye) highly sinister, venture and scheme through a long episodic sequence, which brings us eventually to the militaristic climax of Arthur's mission, his assault on Rome. Malory's Roman war is derived from Geoffrey's (via the English metrical romance version called 'La Morte Arthure'), but this time Arthur is not interrupted in his final advance on the city. Malory treats the episode as a high point of the king's career, the successful, exuberant

Guenever in bed gives a messenger a ring for Lancelot

period before the onset of tragedy. When Mordred's treachery calls him home, he is at war not with Rome but with Lancelot, whose part in the story was an addition made after Geoffrey.

Like Maximus, and like the previous Arthurs, the English king defeats the Roman forces in France, and moves across Europe into Italy. Conquering Italy city by city he approaches Rome, and the senators and cardinals beg for mercy. In return for being spared they offer to crown him Emperor, and accepting this peace treaty he rides triumphantly into Rome, 'and was crowned Emperor by the pope's hand, with all the royalty that could be made'. The long-lasting wound left by the Roman occupation of Britain was at last requited.

It is after the return from Rome that Lancelot enters Arthur's story. He starts with heroic deeds and adventures of his own, establishing himself as a fully-formed hero, a major character in the saga in his own right. The deeds of Lancelot, which Malory takes from a French romance, occupy a whole book of his 'Morte d'Arthur'. He is the archetype of nobility, a man of 'great gentleness and courtesy'. Jousting and journeying and rescuing ladies, he and the knights of Arthur's court live a high life in a land of forests and castles. Clearly these are days they will look back on with longing and regret when times become solemn for them.

Two great sagas intervene between the adventures of Lancelot and the

culmination of his part in Arthur's story: Tristan's deeds and difficulties – themselves a miniature version of the whole saga of Arthur –
and the long, tantalizing search for the grail. Both these, again, we shall
be considering later. They transmit timeless and deep significances (from
those roots which we have identified in earlier sections of this book) into
the developed and articulate world of the very end of the Middle Ages.
But Lancelot is something different. He is human and fallible, with his
staunch medieval principles conflicting with his growing vulnerability in
the face of temptation.

Lancelot was a later addition to the story and he brought with him
fresh attitudes and ideas. He was not a complete invention, a character of
fiction or fantasy. His name, through the French version of it, Lancelin,
is ultimately derived from a character who appears marginally in the old
Welsh stories and poems, spelt variously Llenlleawc or Llwch Lleawc;
and it is cogently argued (for instance by R. S. Loomis) that this character
in turn is a variant of the Irish god Lugh, or Lug, the youthful rider who
arrives and dominates the old order of the deities at Tara. He in his turn,
as we have seen in an earlier chapter, is the European Celtic god Lugus,
eponym of Lyon and Carlisle, often equated with the Roman Mercury.
One of the very odd and interesting facts about myth is that the same
individuals are born again and again, so that the god Lug whom we met
in a previous incarnation, in a previous chapter of this book as the Welsh
hero Lleu, now turns up not (as then) as the wronged husband, deceived
by Blodeuedd, but as the essential lover, Lancelot, deceiving Arthur.

No character in mythology comes into a story without carrying with
him a cloud of associations, and these influences and ancestors form part
of what Lancelot is: like Lugh (and apparently Lugus) he is a representative of a younger generation, an arriving hero, a challenge and a warning
to the established order. That is one strand of his lineage, but a more
immediate element in it comes from the French literary convention in the
context of which he emerged. In Provence in particular a highly civilized
society had given rise, during the twelfth century, to a distinctive cultural
climate. A community of knights deprived of the stresses of war and of
its chances of military enterprise, in that particular stretch of peace and
wealth, had developed a special convention of entertainment. The courts
in which they spent their time were served by travelling troubadours,
whose task it was to develop the theme of romantic love, a complex
which owed some of its attitudes to the distant remnants of Roman
decadence, and much of them to wish-fulfilment in a rather rigid social
situation. The poet sings from the standpoint of the lover, who portrays
himself as the humble servant of the lofty lady, her feudal subject or
vassal. She can command him; he is committed to obey.

It was this literary fashion which formed the immediate background to
the work of Chrétien de Troyes, and when he first introduced the love of
Lancelot for the queen into the Arthurian matter, in his poem 'Li Romans
de la Charrette', written in about 1170, he was participating in a popular
stylistic game, rather than consciously contributing to a myth. But the

The body of the maid of Astolat, who died through unrequited love for Lancelot, is placed in a barge

idea was so appropriate (and foreshadowed, as we shall see, by the Arthurian-related tale of Tristan) that it quickly established itself as essential to Arthur's story. A large-scale prose version followed, in the early part of the next century, and much of Malory's material is drawn from that.

Malory is not primarily engaged in a literary convention, nor is he intentionally purveying myth; the story he tells is an acutely human one, depicted in realistic and often touching terms. Above all he sees it as a matter of human relationships, of people trusting, loving, failing, and hurting each other. The poignancy of the situation is increased by the fact that they are people we come to know and respect, all of them special in their way and none of them entirely in the wrong.

The queen is, from an early stage, jealous of any suggestion of an affair between Lancelot and any other lady. It is not specified that he and she are lovers; in fact Lancelot several times strongly denies it, and it is not in his nature to lie. But 'Queen Guenever had him in great favour above all other knights, and in certain he loved the queen again above all other ladies and damosels of his life, and for her he did many deeds of arms. . . .' Arthur accepts that it is Lancelot, rather than he, who will defend the queen when she is in peril. Although she is imperious and often rude in her treatment of him (an attitude to be expected in the convention of courtly love from which their story came) he turns up whenever needed with absolute reliability.

It is when they all come back from the grail search that things become more serious. Lancelot and Guenever took, it seems, to meeting for a drink. 'They loved together more hotter than they did toforehand, and had such privy draughts together, that many in the court spake of it.' They have their enemies, a faction including Mordred, who plan to make use of this affair for their own ends. With quarrels and reconciliations, the two approach the inevitable, by no means unaware of the danger, but somehow trusting in the continuation of their luck. One more threat to Guenever and one more rescue follow, and a sad little interlude in which Elaine, the maid of Astolat, who loves Lancelot obsessively, tries to seduce him, is rejected, begs him to marry her, and fails in that too. 'Fair damosel, I thank you, said Sir Launcelot, but truly, said he, I cast me never to be wedded man.' She says she will die of this unrequited love, and at once does so, causing her body to be placed in a barge with an explanatory letter, and floated down the Thames to Westminster, where Lancelot, Arthur, and Guenever then are.

Finally Guenever is abducted by a knight who loves her, and is rescued by Lancelot. This turns out to be one rescue too many. During the course of the adventure he spends a night with her, and Malory clearly implies that his later insistence that she had been bodily faithful to the king throughout is from then on something of a distortion of the truth: 'So, to pass upon this tale, Sir Launcelot went unto bed with the queen, and he took no force of his hurt hand, but took his pleasance and his liking until it was the dawning of the day.'

They are discovered, she is impeached and about to be burnt, again he rescues her, and now it is in open defiance of public knowledge and at the risk of the king's discovery. But still Arthur remains obstinately unaware. Mordred and his brothers watch and plot, telling each other self-righteously that the king should not be allowed to suffer this indignity. And so 'it befell a great anger and unhap that stinted not till the flower of chivalry of all the world was destroyed and slain.'

The end is no less impressive for being foretold and foreseen. In the manner of characters in many myths, these cannot help themselves. There is a sense too, as so often, that we have heard the story before, and that therefore they must know it too. But they go towards their end with something like sad resignation. In their final confrontation Arthur expresses to Lancelot not so much anger or accusation but the woundedness which could only be suffered by a man of noble innocence. 'Well well, Sir Launcelot, said the king, I have given thee no cause to do to me as thou hast done, for I have worshipped thee and thine more than any of all my knights.' It is all he says, and there is an implication in it that it is now too late, and they are all doomed.

When Lancelot comes back to a land now devastated by war, from which all his friends and companions have gone, and in which all the high adventures of the court at Camelot are part of a golden past, he speaks his last words in his turn to the bishop who has just buried the queen. 'Also when I remember me how by my default, mine orgulity, and my pride, that they were both laid low, that were peerless that ever was living of Christian people, wit you well, said Sir Launcelot, this remembered, of their kindness and mine unkindness, sank so to mine heart, that I might not sustain myself.'

Once again it is nostalgia which lies at the root of the idea of Camelot,

The round table of King Artus of Brittany. A nineteenth-century engraving of a fourteenth-century French miniature

and all the more poignant is its expression in Malory through our sense of his position at a turning point of Britain's development, a fact manifested in the language itself. In 'Le Morte d'Arthur' we see the emergence of what we now know as English. It is no accident, but a part of the essence of this final development of the idea of Arthur, that it is expressed in the first great work of the modern English language. Thus once again Arthur succeeds in embodying a step in our cultural development. He appears in Malory as a past ideal and at the same time as the expression of the conflict, with which the Renaissance was to be preoccupied, between the personal and the general, love and duty, the individual and his social role. All the recurrent themes of the Arthurian matter combine to effect this – the internal strife of civil war, the idea that all good things are coming to an end, the looking back at the achievement of complete success, and finally the looking forwards to a promised return. To Malory it provides the opportunity to make a statement not just about virtue, but about England. For him it is, ultimately, England which the story is about. Its instability, its independence of mind, its tendency to do damage to itself.

> Lo ye all Englishmen, see ye not what a mischief here was! for he that was the most king and knight of the world, and most loved the fellowship of noble knights, and by him they were all upholden, now might not these English-men hold them content with him. Lo thus was the old custom and usage of this land; and also men say that we of this land have not yet lost nor forgotten that custom and usage. Alas, this is a great default of us Englishmen, for there may no thing please us no term.

The idea of Camelot, like the idea of Arthur, has had its useful applications. It summarizes the 'golden-age' aspects of the imagery which surrounds Arthur. It would be an error to try to locate it, just as it would be to try to identify the places which Odysseus visited on his voyage. Camelot has had a partial manifestation in geography in many times and places, but as a whole it belongs to a Platonic ideal world, in the map of the imagination. Once again the name itself was a contribution of Chrétien's, and so belongs, like Lancelot, to the literary world of French romance. Malory made it central to our thinking about Arthur, and he located it firmly at Winchester. He did so because that city had, in ancient times, been a royal capital. It was the seat of the kings of Wessex, and after the Norman conquest it retained the status of a royal headquarters. Such a centre suited the new English Arthur better than the older tradition of a court at Caerleon, and Winchester's Arthurian connections had become thoroughly established in Malory's sources.

The 'Round Table' which still hangs in the great hall of Winchester Castle hung there then, referred to by Caxton in his preface to Malory. This table, recently dated by carpentry experts and radiocarbon tests, appears to have been made at Windsor in the mid-fourteenth century. This itself is an indication of the popularity at that time of the Arthurian cult, and we know that Edward III held jousts which he called the 'Feast of the Round Table', for which occasions this remarkable circular board might have been made. The table now at Winchester gained in popularity as its true origin became forgotten, and was apparently redecorated in the reign of Henry VII or Henry VIII (hence the centre-piece of a Tudor rose), and was proudly shown to the visiting Emperor Charles V by Henry VIII in 1522. It was repainted in the same form in 1789, and has been thoroughly cleaned and structurally repaired during 1978, as a result of all of which it now looks brand new. Startlingly large and colourful, it dominates the fairly modest Great Hall, which is the last remaining part of the thirteenth-century castle at Winchester demolished by Cromwell in 1651.

Winchester appears to have been accepted as a main seat of Arthuriana

The Winchester round table

for several centuries. But Malory's Arthur ranges widely throughout Britain, and the wars against Lancelot take place in the north, starting at Carlisle and proceeding into Northumbria, where Lancelot's castle of Joyous Gard is identified as either Bamburgh or Alnwick. Ironically this last movement of the matter to northern Britain perhaps reflects a part of its origins, in the heroic early literature of the north Britons. The princes of whom Taliesin and Aneirin sang, such as Urien king of Rheged and his son Owain, survived a long history in British tradition and are present at the end, though scarcely recognizable, as Arthurian knights: 'King Uriens' and 'Sir Uwaine'.

The locations are not provided just by chance. Carlisle (where the court is, in Malory's story, when the adultery is revealed) was important in Roman times as a centre for the defence of the Wall, and its importance seems to have continued without break into the time of Urien, whose capital it may have been. Bamburgh (traditionally Lancelot's seat), a powerfully romantic, rock-perched fortress overlooking a flat, straight sweep of shore, was also occupied continuously from Roman times and before. It seems likely that it was originally occupied by the tribe the Romans knew as the Votadini, who during Roman times served the important function of providing a friendly buffer state between the Wall and the Picts, and in that capacity, as allies and protectors of Britain, sent a colony under Cunedda, at the end of Roman control in about AD 400, to save the western coast of central Britain from the Irish. Under their British name, Gododdin, they re-emerged into our view, and into this book, when they fought a last desperate battle against the growing Angle kingdoms. By then their stronghold at Bamburgh had become the seat of the king of an incipient Northumbria, Ida, who ruled from there in the late 540s. It is therefore clear that in continuing Arthur's northern associations Malory is (perhaps accidentally) being true to the context of the myth. Arthur is still most appropriately found on the crucial frontiers of Britain's identity.

There has, perhaps for this reason, always been a tendency, in the literature, to locate Britain's national hero at Britain's most significant spots, however diverse these might have been. And so it is with Camelot. It was Leland, the sixteenth-century antiquarian, who lodged in the literature of the subject the idea that Camelot was to be equated with the hillfort of South Cadbury, which lies just off the present A303 to the east of Ilchester, in south-east Somerset, near the Dorset border. Whether the fort there known as Cadbury Castle had been traditionally connected with Camelot, or whether Leland simply made the association himself, we do not know. But in spite of the basic error in trying to pin Camelot down, there is much that is appropriate about the Camelot-Cadbury comparison.

What is interesting about Cadbury is the extent of its stratas of history, age after age of use being imposed on one another, so that it reads like a summary, itself, of all Britain's phases of origin. From the Stone Age through the Bronze Age to the Iron Age and the Roman occupation, on into the Dark Ages and the Saxon invasion and up to the late Saxon period immediately preceding the Norman conquest: every step in the genesis of the nation is represented in Cadbury's archaeology. Each new occupation of the island, and each advance in civilization, had a major instance on that large hill. It is, in the physical world, what the mythology is to the people's awareness: a succession of self-identifying layers, each one partly what it is because of the previous one, adding up to a final cumulative statement.

In Cadbury's case this process lasted some four thousand years. Excavations carried out under the direction of Professor Alcock between 1966 and 1970, on the broad top of that large round hill above South Cadbury village, revealed its earliest use to have been in the Stone Age, about 3000 BC, the time of the people who built those chambered tombs

South Cadbury hill

and long barrows. A Bronze Age farm followed, in the first millennium
BC, and occupation seems then to have been continuous into Iron Age
times. It was then (about 500 BC) that the hill first became a defensive site,
giving us the earliest sign of warfare or troubled circumstances. This Iron
Age occupation was unusually long, since it only came to an end through
what must have been a massive assault by the Romans, said by Alcock to
have taken place in the 70s. The length of Cadbury's independence, and
the manner of its fall, must both have added to its significance and
importance.

What is remarkable about it is that it was brought back into use.
Extensive refortification of pre-Roman sites after the departure is very
rare, and this alone makes Cadbury of special importance. Although its
independent Celtic use was so long-lived and so extensive that it remains
essentially an Iron Age site reoccupied, the Dark Age settlement there
(which began towards the end of the fifth century) was also fairly
substantial. As at the court of Maelgwn at Deganwy, the evidence
consists of sherds of eastern Mediterranean wine-jars, an indication of
power and wealth; and the spread of these over the site shows that the seat
of this rich ruler was a large one. Since the evidence in the form of finds
and structures lies under the later Saxon building and over the original
Iron Age defences and the signs of Roman attack, it can be dated to
precisely the period to which the historical prototype of Arthur, from
what little evidence we have for such a figure, must belong. This should
not, however, lead us to think that it could ever become sensible to say
that Arthur *was* this person, this wealthy and well-housed prince on
Cadbury. That would involve a misleading and restricting assumption
about what is entailed in the idea of Arthur. In so far, though, as Arthur is
to be regarded as the embodiment of a national idea, then Cadbury has
much in common with him.

When the great Iron Age fort was rebuilt in the Dark Ages, after the Romans had gone, the reference back to pre-Roman Britain could not have been unintended, and may even have included a long view back to the marvels of the Bronze Age. However practical the action was, it was also symbolic. Fortifying Cadbury then was a demonstration of the consciousness of the idea of an independent Britain, of which the pre-Roman Iron Age country must have constituted the ideal. It could at that moment have been reborn, and we have seen that it nearly was. Cadbury, so old and great, must have formed an appropriate focus for such thoughts.

Interestingly Alcock notes that even the building techniques used in the refortification constituted a regression to the pre-Roman age. They had forgotten the Roman use of mortar, and reverted to the dry-stone and timber construction used by their distant ancestors. Partly for that reason there is nothing left standing. Excavation has revealed the outlines of buildings of Cadbury's many periods of use, including a large hall thought to be of the post-Roman period. The outline of a gateway of that period has also been identified, but once again it was largely a timber structure, and there is nothing of it, or its surrounding defences, to be seen. The great wooden towers and palisades rotted, their bases became ploughed over and forgotten, and only the tenacity of legend has perpetuated, through the nine hundred and fifty years of neglect and agricultural peace, the real significance of this broad, scrub-fringed hill.

It is a sight made awesome by association rather than by visual impact. It does not bear the lines of its use as visibly, nor does it stand out as impressively, as for instance Ham Hill or Maiden Castle. From a distance what is most impressive about it is its long flat top; it is not as high as several neighbouring hills, nor particularly sharply set, nor is it (like Glastonbury Tor) any specially remarkable shape. Yet is has an un-doubted citadel nature.

Folklore has always surrounded it, and placed there long before the excavations one of the many sites of Arthur's long sleep. He and his knights are said to be lying waiting in a vast cave in the hill's interior, and according to one version of the story they ride out each year at mid-summer to water their horses in the river below.

South Cadbury's use in history finished in Saxon times, when the secure position provided the site for a royal mint in the reign of Ethelred, the early eleventh century. And there seems to have been no established connection between this place and Camelot in Malory's time, or he would not have said explicitly that Camelot was Winchester. Malory wrote 'Le Morte d'Arthur' around 1469, and when William Caxton produced the first printed edition of it in 1485 he says, apparently thinking of the Roman ruins at Caerleon, that 'divers now living hath seen' the ruins of the town of Camelot, with 'great stones and marvellous works of iron, lying under the ground'.

To Caxton, even more than to Malory, Arthur was real rather than symbolic: 'the most renowned Christian king, first and chief of the three best Christian and worthy, King Arthur, which ought most to be remembered among us English men tofore all other Christian kings.' Through Caxton indeed, in his ordering and editing of Malory's work and in the printing of the book itself (which fixed the myth finally in a form secure from the interpretations of copyists), Arthur enters modern times.

Malory wrote in the reign of Edward IV, and therefore in the context of the Wars of the Roses. When he finished the work in 1469 Edward's reign was eight years old, and some element of order had briefly been re-imposed on the anarchy of the previous decade. The memory of that chaos, however, in which the intermittent insanity of Henry VI had given rise to a ruthless and destructive struggle for the succession to the throne, was not easily wiped out. In 1469 things had begun to look decidedly insecure again, the king being at one point in that year taken prisoner by the man who had originally ensured his enthronement, the Earl of Warwick, known as the 'King-maker'. The next year there were two alternative kings, the insane Henry being reintroduced to the scene by Warwick, while Edward schemed against them from exile on the Continent; and at that point, when Malory finished his book, the Wars of the Roses were far from over. Once again the background of civil war which dominates the myth is a counterpart of the historical circumstances governing the time in which the myth grew.

By the time that Caxton was printing 'Le Morte d'Arthur', in 1485, things were very different. It does not matter whether his presses actually rolled after or before the month of August, that apocalyptic time when Henry Tudor and his uncle landed on the coast of Pembroke and marched to meet the king at Bosworth. Just as the product of Geoffrey of Monmouth was achieved in time to be available at the start of the reign of Stephen, so Malory's great work appeared in printed form in time for the start of a new era, though it itself was largely a literary culmination of the old one. The effect of the two events – the printing of 'Le Morte d'Arthur' and the battle of Bosworth – taking place in the same year must have made a relationship between them at least likely. On the one hand there was the re-establishment of a native British monarchy through the victory, under the symbolic and prophetic emblem of the Red Dragon, of a descendant of the ancient British house over a descendant of the Norman and Plantagenet usurpers, in almost literal fulfilment of Merlin's prophecy. And on the other hand we have the contemporary reappraisal of Geoffrey's ancient notion, the matter of Britain, expressed through the image of its mythic king and now through the physical medium of printing. A national spirit which was in a mood to welcome one event would have been disposed to accept the other.

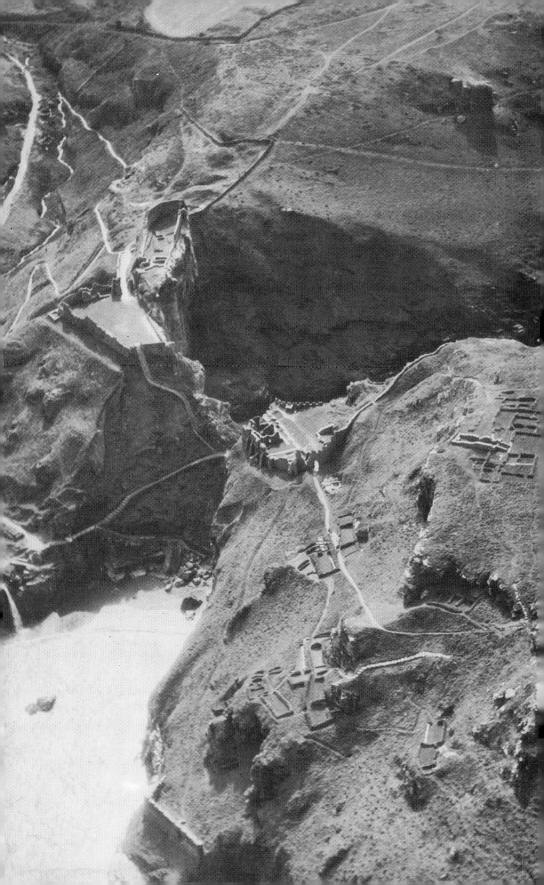

1 Tintagel

Just as a dim folk-figure lies behind Arthur the nationalistic hero, so behind the romantic ideas of chivalry and courtly love which dominate the high period of Arthurian literature lie some ancient themes of myth. It is significant that when the deepest matters of all occur in Malory's retelling of the tradition, he deserts the medieval world of Winchester and reverts to Cornwall, which, like Wales, had retained its identity as a Celtic land in spite of the power and vigour of its new neighbours. Cornwall was in many of the early stories Arthur's home. During the period of post-Roman resistance, it would have been an ideal image of an original pre-Roman Britain. In spite of their interest in the tin mines the Romans left surprisingly little impression on it, and it remained a land with attitudes and values of its own. Even today, you cross the Tamar into a different country. According to Malory, then, Arthur was born in Cornwall; and because Malory's was the final version of the myth, Cornwall is Arthur's official birthplace. The specific connection with Tintagel, as we shall see, stemmed ultimately from Geoffrey of Monmouth.

Even more than with Arthur Cornwall is connected with a hero who is at the same time one of the most distinctly British and, in other aspects, one of the most international of the Arthurian group: Tristan, or, as Malory calls him, Tristram. Tristan's story came, as if by a process of natural attraction, to be closely and prominently involved with the Arthurian matter. The Cornish bases of the two heroes give them, in the myth, a common heritage.

Arthur's father Uther Pendragon, king of all England, fell in love with the wife of a rival leader, the duke of Tintagel. Since, rather to his surprise, the duke will not allow Uther to sleep with the lady, he besieges the pair of them in their castles, she in Tintagel, he in another. The help of the wizard Merlin is sought, and at once he prophesies what will be the outcome of this affair: a child will be conceived, and when born he is to be delivered to Merlin to be reared.

Merlin achieves the adultery for Uther by what is, to myth, an old and practised trick. He makes the seducing king appear to be the lady's husband. We have seen in an early chapter of this book that Pwyll, in his exchange of kingdoms with the king of the otherworld, was afforded, but loyally resisted, the same opportunity. The Greek hero Heracles (among others) was conceived by the same trick, Zeus taking the form of

Tintagel, showing the medieval castle which spans the narrow isthmus of rock joining the 'island' to the mainland

his mother's husband, thus providing him with a suitably heroic parentage, and her with a justifiable claim to innocence.

Arthur is in due course born, by which time, following the death of the duke of Tintagel, his parents have married. The incident of the form-changing conforms with the common mythic notion that there has to be something special, usually supernatural, about the conception of the hero. In Irish stories the lover comes to the well-protected lady in spite of all efforts to prevent it; and Zeus, in Greece, again and again achieves his desires with someone else's wife by changing his shape. That Arthur should be handed over to Merlin at birth is also to be expected. The more primitive ancient British hero, Lleu, was reared not by his mother but by the wizard Gwydion, Merlin's predecessor in the role, and introduced by him to his heroic career. Pryderi too, the other young hero of Welsh myth, was removed from his parents' home at birth and brought up by a neighbouring lord. Arthur is reared in the home of a foster-father appointed by Merlin, under Merlin's supervision, and from there re-emerges on the death of his father. We have already seen what happens then.

Quite why myths frequently appear to require this fosterage it is hard to say, but it does seem to refer to a primitive and widespread custom. If so, its survival in versions of the Arthurian myths as late as that of Malory testifies to the resilience of such references. It is particularly noticeable that it happens also to both Mordred and Tristram, in 'Le Morte d'Arthur', and so seems to be an identifiable Arthurian theme. Fosterage, we are told, was an important custom among the Irish Celts, and occurs in the stories of heroes such as CuChulainn; and the practice is referred to also in the early Welsh laws. Possibly the Christian custom of bestowing godparents is a faint reflection of this old convention.

In Tristan's case such common themes are quite apparent, and are sometimes duplicated or multiplied as the result of several different versions being run together. His story is interposed into the saga of Arthur at the point when Arthur has established himself as a great European ruler, before the personal tragedies begin to take over, and it forms a prelude to the downfall of Arthur.

Tristan is, for Malory, the son of King Mark of Cornwall's sister, who dies after giving birth to him, leaving him in the hands of one of her women. Tristan survives several early attempts to destroy him, in particular by his new stepmother, who sees him as an obstruction to the inheritance of her own children. Just as in Greek myth such attempts fail and the deaths of Oedipus, Paris, Zeus, and Perseus, though all apparently certain, are all evaded. It is an indication of the status of the hero, usually in the form of the threat which his advent poses to the ruling power, and also a demonstration of the power of destiny, that he survives while others (like the innocents slain by Herod) die.

Tristan is sent at an early age, accompanied by a tutor, into France – an unconscious reference, perhaps, to the progress of his story, through Cornwall into Brittany and thence into French literature. There he remained until he was mature, and developed his lifelong interest, the sport of hunting, which Malory recognizes as the mark of good breeding. 'Thereby in a manner all men of worship may dissever a gentleman from a yeoman. . . .'

Once back in Cornwall Tristan embarks on his career. It begins with a visit to the court of King Mark, his uncle, who is under pressure from the king of Ireland. An Irish champion has landed at 'Tintagil', and because of his reputation no-one can be found to challenge him. Tristan obliges, frees Cornwall from the Irish threat, and, wounded, is established by the king in the castle of Tintagel to recover. However, only by being treated in the country from which he had received a poisoned stroke could he be cured. Tristan therefore goes to Ireland, where he meets the daughter of the king, La Beale Isoud, 'the fairest maid and lady of the world'. Their love is immediate and mutual, and destined to a tragic end.

It is in due course discovered that Tristan is the knight who defeated and killed the Irish champion, and not surprisingly he has to leave Ireland in a hurry. Promising his everlasting faithfulness to Isoud, he leaves her in a scene of great emotion; he then sails to Cornwall, and lands again at Tintagel.

Jealousy begins to spring up between King Mark and Tristan, and the king begins to think of a way to dispose of him. He had heard Tristan praise the beauty of the daughter of the king of Ireland, and on that basis decides to marry her himself. Knowing that Ireland is hostile to Tristan, he plans to send him there, with a proposal of marriage from him to Isoud. 'And all this was done to the intent to slay Sir Tristram.' The hero, however, cannot refuse, in spite of the danger.

Various adventures intervene, but in the end Tristan and Isoud find themselves again in each other's presence, and their love grips them once more. Because of events which have taken place in the meantime, Tristan is able to carry out his task of asking for the hand of Isoud, from the king of Ireland, for his uncle and master, King Mark. And although the Irish king, with some integrity, expresses his wish that Tristan should marry her himself, owing to the bonds of duty that cannot be; and he parts with his daughter to be taken to the Cornish king.

It is clear to her mother and her attendants that the match will not be one of romance and to ensure that Mark and Isoud, once wedded, will love each other, the queen sends with her a magic drink, to be drunk by them together at their wedding, the enchantment of which (unknown to Isoud) will cause them to love each other for ever.

Perhaps it requires Wagner's powers of expression to deal adequately with the idea of the overwhelming invincibility of that love by which Tristan and Isoud are to be forever governed and through which they are forced through no fault of their own to their ultimate destruction. Through Wagner, indeed, the story is well known. They found the potion in the cabin, and ignorant of its purpose took it to be some fine wine. Indeed it was, but its power made permanent and total the love which already existed between them. Tristan was now more than ever beset by the conflict of his duties, to his king and to his love. In fact the vows which he had already given to Isoud, to remain faithful to her, seemed to be in contradiction to his mission of delivering her to a man she could never love. Such paradox is a feature which lies at the core of myth. The conflict of honour and passion is also a principal part of the medieval ideas of chivalry and courtliness; and this makes the story of Tristan highly characteristic of the particular combination of ancient and contemporary themes in the Arthurian material, a combination which does much to make it so expressive and so beguiling.

After some further rescues and encounters, the lovers reach their Cornish destination, and the wedding takes place. Tristan is in many ways the shadow of Lancelot. He too stays as a slightly mournful presence in the background of the court; like Lancelot he rescues the queen from an abductor and brings her home to her husband. Malory explicitly recognizes the connection, by having his Isoud announce 'that there be within this land but four lovers, that is, Sir Lancelot du Lake and Queen Guenever, and Sir Tristram de Liones and Queen Isoud'. And like that of Lancelot and Guenever their love attracts the envy of ill-wishers, who plot to reveal it to the king. Mark is rather easier to rouse to suspicion and anger than the trusting Arthur, but for a time he finds it expedient to remain friends with Tristan. The romance, and the constant adventures of the court, go on.

Malory's story perpetuates what seems to be an obvious mistake, perhaps derived from an early compiler who has confused two different redactions: Tristan marries, in Brittany, another lady, also, however, called Isoud. Lancelot delivers what seems to us a well-deserved rebuke: 'Fie upon him, untrue knight to his lady that so noble a knight as Sir Tristram is should be found to his first lady false, La Beale Isoud, Queen of Cornwall.' Neither the traditions of loyalty of the time nor our time-free literary judgements will support this confusion, and one wonders why Malory, usually so confident of his structure, continued it. The source which he cites attempted to save Tristan's honour by claiming that he had no relations with the second Isoud more substantial than 'clipping and kissing' – an abstinence due more to ignorance on her part than to loyalty on his, since 'the French book', he says, 'maketh mention that the lady weened there had been no pleasure but kissing and clipping'.

Tristan's prowess as a fighter in tournaments and single combats increased, his reputation becoming second only to that of Lancelot. Because of the repetitions and complexity of the adventures with which he proves himself, we have the feeling of a long spread of golden days, before he once again reaches Isoud, his original love. Like Lancelot at one point in his stormy relationship with Guenever, Tristan goes mad, and runs naked and wild in the forest. King Mark unwittingly has him taken back to Tintagel, where he is recognized by the queen. When the king hears who it is, he has him banished, and with some bitterness Tristan retreats to Camelot. It is interesting that in the story of Tristram in Malory the comings and goings between King Arthur's court and 'Tintagil' are always done by sea.

Tristan and Isoud take ship during their flight

Isoud pursues Tristan with letters, but it is not until many tournaments later that they meet again. His growing fame in 'Logris' reaches the ears of King Mark, and his enormous success with Arthur becomes a further motive for envious hostility. It is in the end King Arthur who brings about a reconciliation, but in view of the increasing blackness of King Mark's character, it is unlikely to last. Rather touchingly the trio at Camelot and Tristan at Tintagel continue to correspond, and the two love-tales cross at one point, when King Mark drops Arthur a curt note warning him about Lancelot, which he soon forgets. Back at Tintagel Mark makes successive attempts to get Tristan killed, and finally the hostility is so open that Tristan and Isoud flee together to 'Logris', the land of England which, in this story, is clearly differentiated from Cornwall.

For a time they are happy. 'They made great joy daily together with all manner of mirths that they could devise.' Tristan goes hunting again, taking up his early hobby, 'for Sir Tristram was that time called the best chaser of the world'. All hunting terms, Malory says, were coined by him. Interspersed with these leisures are endless tournaments and feasts, with the four great lovers now together. In Malory's telling or in the French literature from which he drew his material, there is a feeling that such luxuries are irretrievable even for the readers of the time. The sense of life as an ornate game is strong in late medieval literature, and must have served the purpose of compensating for the ruthless reality which pervaded the period. Johan Huizinga, in *The Waning of the Middle Ages,* his sensitive analysis of the Continental literature of this age (some of which formed Malory's sources), notes the air of irony, of gentle banter, which underlies the images of romance. 'In reading this antiquated love poetry, or the clumsy descriptions of tournaments, no exact knowledge of historical details avails without the vision of the smiling eyes, long turned to dust, which at one time were infinitely more important than the written word that remains.'

Malory's version of the story is interrupted by the grail sequence, and that in turn leads to the culmination of the Lancelot-Guenever-Arthur affair, so that Tristan's love story is suspended uncharacteristically at a high point. He briefly winds up the tale later, but the basic versions of it, in the Continental poems, add a coda in which Tristan returns to his other Isoud (or Iseult, or Isolde). A final episode, clearly derived from the story of Theseus's return from Crete, tells how Tristan sent for his first Isoud and told the messenger to hoist a white sail if he succeeded in bringing her, a black one if he failed; in jealousy his wife reported to him that the sail approaching was black, and he died of a broken heart. Isoud, queen of Cornwall, like Juliet, died as well, for his unnecessary death. We feel again the force of their destiny.

There is no doubt that the story itself is extremely old, though we have it in written form only from the mid-twelfth century. Possibly a little after that a long poem on the subject was written by Chrétien de Troyes, which, though lost, can be inferred from the main French version, the prose 'Tristan' from which Malory drew. In Britain Geoffrey of Monmouth somehow missed this promising subject, but Tristan entered English literature in the metrical romances of the next centuries, and so became associated with the Arthurian material from which he was originally entirely independent.

Even older than the story is the character, since he appears in both the Triads and the Mabinogion: Drystan, son of Tallwch, or, in one case, son of March. Tallwch, apparently, is a Welsh version of Talorc, the name of a Pictish king. There are strong Tristan associations in lowland Scotland, and a tradition dating from the twelfth century holds that this hero came from Lothian. This northern origin, however, seems incompatible with the firmly-based Cornish, Irish, and Breton connections of the story. And it seems at first sight to be contradicted too by the only piece of evidence to tie this highly mythic figure to history: the 'Drustan' stone.

The Drustan stone is a slender elegant pillar beside the road leading down into the Cornish village of Fowey, a monolith on which it is now only possible to make out faint signs of lettering. Its significance lies in its inscription. It bore on one face the wording: DRUSTANUS HIC IACIT

Opposite: The crowning of Arthur
Overleaf: An aerial view of Tintagel, traditional birthplace of Arthur

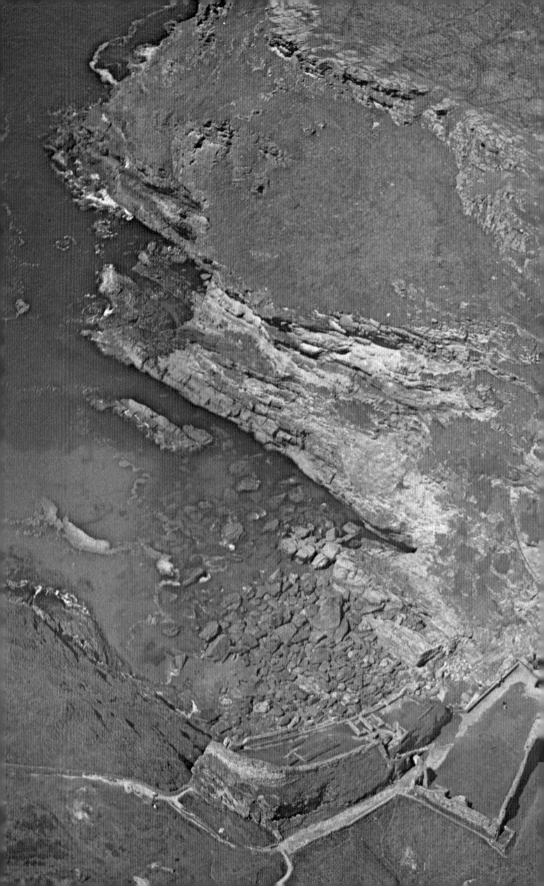

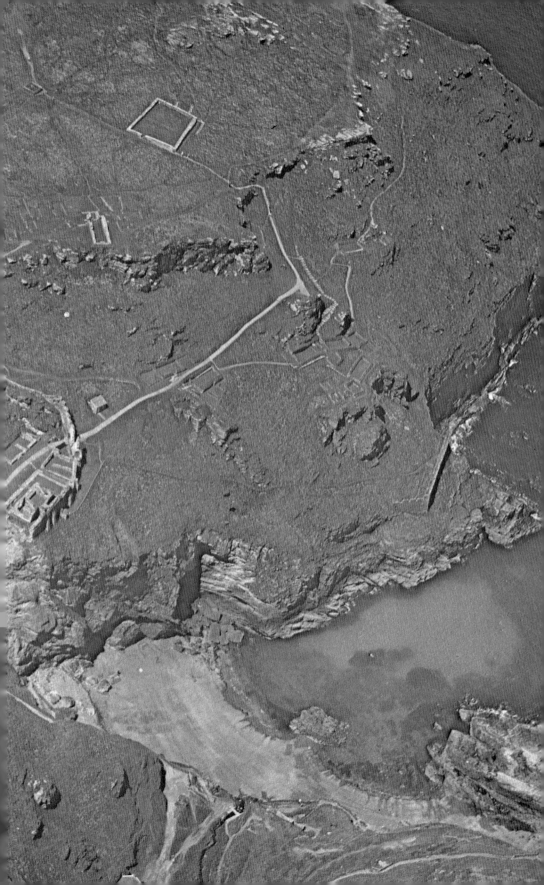

auant mei auant le
contes ia endroit a p...
Et si retorne au roi an
grant baronnie.

mei or ie tele au...
7 retorne au roi loth...
qui ses espies auoit...
par les chemins.

du
que
roi
che
uen
ma
roi
bai

se mistrent et repen...
france. 7 cheuau chief
quil uindrent au cha...
ot fet fermer seur la

neueu. que li roi...
par ses espies. 7 sin
il le sot si monta a
mes. com cil qui ses

quil aut a cheuee...

ne au roi artu 7 a ceu...

iens dece que li preud

monde. certes vous...

CUNOMORI FILIUS, or, translating the Latinized names, 'Here lies Tristan, the son of Cynfawr'. Apart from the use of his name, the Tristan connection is supported by the identity of this Cynfawr, since an early Cornish document, the Life of St Paul Aurelian, says that this sixth-century king of Dumnonia (the area which included Cornwall) was also known as Mark. We have seen that in one of the Triads, Tristan is March's son, not his nephew, and this is further evidence of the ambiguity of this relationship. 'March', in Welsh, means horse, and an old local tale in North Wales tells of King March's secret. He had (like Alexander in a Greek tale) horse's ears. Perhaps some horse-god has been involved with the story at some stage; but if so, all that is left of him now is the name, March.

The Tristan stone, commemorating a chieftain of that name who (whatever his Pictish connections may have been) evidently died in Cornwall, probably in the second half of the sixth century, was found lying a little north of its present position, which is only a mile or two

Opposite: Four medieval miniatures illustrating parts of the Arthurian tales: Arthur rides at the head of his knights (top left); Arthur ambushed by the king of Orkney (top right); Sir Gawain riding through a forest (bottom left); Guenever banishes Lancelot (bottom right)
Below left: The Drustan stone
Below right: Castle Dore from the air

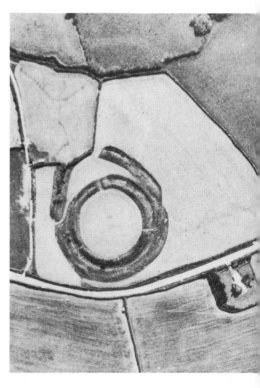

south of the area's most outstanding Iron Age fort. Castle Dore has, partly as a result of this connection, partly because the story has from a very early period been related to this area, come to be viewed traditionally as the seat of King Mark.

It is a large, banked ring-formation, an earthwork rather than a stone fortification, standing on a ridge with views out over mild, open country. It lies rather obscure and neglected on a hillside among the lanes which entangle the countryside above Fowey, just by the crossing of the Golant-to-Tywardraeth with the Fowey-to-Lostwithiel roads. Castle Dore is not easily seen from the ground, but presents a neat concentricity from the air. As ring-forts go it is modest, unspectacular, and fuzzy now with gorse and bracken. An ancient track runs down the ridge towards the sea, its line now occupied by a minor road, a route thought to have been in use since the Bronze Age.

When the earthwork was excavated in the 1930s it was discovered that it had in its history undergone a long succession of uses. Starting in the third century BC, the high time of Iron Age British independence, it remained in use until the coming of the Romans, at the turn of the era. It seems that it was then abandoned, but significantly, like Cadbury, it was reoccupied on a large scale during the post-Roman period. During those crucial centuries between the removal of the legions, at the beginning of the fifth century, and the dominance of the Saxons, at the beginning of the seventh, it was the seat of a major chieftain.

This Dark Age leader used the deserted fort built by his remote ancestors, empty by then for some four centuries, and it is this reference-back that is of such importance to our understanding of the myths. That this was Cynfawr's palace seems almost certain, and if the Tristan myth is as ancient as it seems likely to be then he, Cynfawr, probably already knew of it. Such a man might have been influential enough, in his employment of bards, to effect the transfer of the locale of the story from Pictland to Cornwall, and hence set it on its way to Brittany and France. That he might call his son Tristan, or Drustan, is equally easy to accept, and perhaps the later suggestion that he himself was also called Mark arose from his interest in this theme. We have seen already how material did travel great distances in Britain at that time, when a common language gave the country a rare unity of culture. Some such theory (and this seems the most likely) is required to explain how an ancient hero with a Pictish name came to be connected with Cornwall, and even more strangely tied to a historical Cornish dynasty.

Cynfawr's importance is attested by the archaeology at Castle Dore. He built himself a large wooden hall within the defences, aisled, porched, and flanked by buildings of lesser stature. The archaeologists deduce from the size of the post-holes that it was high and spacious, and although all one can see there now is turf, it is clear that this was of the nature of those king's halls in the courts which feature so frequently in the myths. The only note of grandeur now left lies in the approach to the entrance-way on the eastern side, where the earthworks bulk above you and provide an impression of power. The inside of the fort is like a flat round dish, with no signs of Cynfawr's great hall, entirely enclosed and screened from any outlook by its high banks.

It is Cynfawr's presence there that makes it natural that Tristan should become associated with such a place. And it is not at all hard to understand how both he and Arthur should have at least part of their stories located at Tintagel, on the north side of the same Cornish peninsula, across its neck from Castle Dore. Although twelfth- and thirteenth-century ruins are now what one sees there, the use of the site goes back to the fifth century, and one can hardly believe that such a naturally-defended headland was not in use in periods long before that. Tintagel, by its very nature, expresses antiquity. It is a place where elemental forces dominate. Physically as well as traditionally it is removed from the normal world.

The literary sources connect Tintagel with Arthur from the twelfth century onwards. Clearly what is referred to from then on is the castle there, and the later use of this site as a base for the romance of Tristan is probably also due to this visible medieval emblem. But in the beginnings of the Arthur story we are in a slightly different world, one of magic, of mysterious conception and removal at birth, a world dominated by the magician Merlin. It has the character, and possesses the identifying elements, of the world of Celtic myth.

It is interesting, in this connection, to find that the site was originally religious rather than military. Before the first castle was built there in the middle of the twelfth century, and from a very early period, there was a Celtic monastery which grew to be a religious centre of some importance. It started probably as a simple hermitage in the fifth century, perhaps the cell of the local saint, Juliot, whose lifetime spanned the turn of the fifth century to the sixth. Finds indicate that from the sixth century until perhaps the ninth it flourished as a community of considerable size, including an oratory with its tomb-shrine of a founding saint, and buildings around it which may have provided for guests as well as the resident monks. Leslie Alcock remarks that the remains at Tintagel represent 'a degree of elaboration without parallel in these islands'. Christianity evidently rooted itself here effectively at this early stage. Interestingly the finds of monastic date included imported pottery, like that found in the courts of kings, indicating that wine and oil were brought to Tintagel from the eastern Mediterranean. The religious community was therefore as well provided for as its political counterparts.

The pitch of the land, the unregulated noise and movement of the sea, the mood of elemental dominance, give Tintagel much more an atmosphere of mystery than of practical involvement. The site juts into the Atlantic, an 'island' formed of a massive hunk of rock, almost completely severed now from the craggy coastline by a fault exploited by the storms. It falls in magnificent cliffs to the surrounding ocean, and it is on this intimidating promontory that the Celtic monastery was sited, the medieval castles being partly on the headland, partly on the landward

The headland at Tintagel which forms such a natural defensive site

side of the rock neck. The humble Celtic settlement is perched on a number of ledges on the steep slopes of the 'island'. No doubt the flat grassy top of the bulk of rock enabled some rather windswept cultivation. The monastic habitations themselves are crouched on the leeward slopes. The ruins of the clearly magnificent medieval castles by contrast, tower over the crags of the rock bridge. All around the coast is black-cliffed and cave-pitted, carved into a wonderful complexity of jutting heads and sloping slabs.

When the lords of Cornwall built their castles there during the twelfth, thirteenth, and fourteenth centuries, it must have been with a consciousness of tinting military strategy with the aura of a mystic rite. To build a castle on such a headland must have involved a symbolically romantic act. The ruins which we can see there now are of two periods on two separate sites; the one which is reached first, including upper and lower wards, belongs largely to the time of Henry III. By then the second building, the inner ward (reached by a steep path down from the headland and up again onto the 'island'), was already old.

This, the first Tintagel castle, was built in the 1140s, at the beginning of the reign of Stephen, by Reginald, earl of Cornwall, who was an illegitimate son of Henry I. The date is of interest, since it means that the castle at Tintagel came after, not before, the publication of Geoffrey of Monmouth's 'History'. It is known that some changes were made to that work, however, after its first edition; and possibly the explicit reference to Tintagel – 'the castle is built high above the sea, which surrounds it on all sides, and there is no other way in except that offered by a narrow isthmus of rock' – was one of these additions made between the first publication and the version we now have. If so, then the placing of Arthur's conception at Tintagel was an invention of Geoffrey's, probably inspired by a visit to the new castle, and it came to Malory and thus into the permanent tradition from that ultimate source.

One end of Reginald's Great Hall has now fallen with the cliffs on which it was based into the widening chasm – Geoffrey's 'isthmus of rock' – between the 'island' and the mainland. But the walls of the other end have survived, though they look out rather precariously over the steep slopes. Around these are the more extensive ruins of the walling added in the next century, when Richard, earl of Cornwall, Henry III's brother, built the castle on the mainland. It is these, Richard's constructions of the mid-thirteenth century, which form the bulk of the remains to be seen there now.

While Arthur's beginning is allocated to this highly identified headland, Tristan's (though he comes to Tintagel later) is equally firmly sited in the world of myth. He is the son of the king of Lyonesse, and Lyonesse is, essentially, under the sea. The tale of its inundation depicts a vast wave sweeping over the land, ahead of which one horseman (named by tradition as Trevelyan, the founder of that famous Cornish family) rides to safety. The convention is that the lost kingdom stretched from the Cornish peninsula to the Scilly Isles, and as usual there is some substantiation for what is, at the same time, a universal mythic theme. The Anglo-Saxon Chronicle refers to an inundation, when the sea swallowed up towns and people, though it does not say that it was off Cornwall. Looking down at low tide people have thought that they could see the outlines of buildings; but most significant of all these indications is the visible outline of field patterns off the shores of the Scilly Isles themselves, showing a definite loss of inhabitable land. Of course there have always been such losses in coastal countries, and once again we have two distinct contributions of fact and fanciful imagery combining to make an effective, functioning myth.

There is hardly any mythology which does not have its own Atlantis myth. We have already seen it elsewhere in Britain, in the story of the drowning of Cardigan Bay, Gwyddno's kingdom; and further north on the same coast, just below the hill on which Taliesin, in the myth, addressed King Maelgwn, lies another sunk city on another flooded plain. Between the two is Caer Aranrhod, now a dark reef of stones, at one time, in the story, the castle of that dangerous goddess. In the factual world, we find at many places on our coastline the unmistakable signs of sunken forests, the roots of trees which once grew where the sea now is. And that tide still comes in, piling up sand over buildings, crumbling away churchyards, turning headlands into islands. In the Scilly Isles themselves there are many instances of tidal encroachment, and the land-area has clearly changed a great deal since the Roman period. But none of this makes Lyonesse, beautiful drowned country, any less of a myth.

The flood myth, so common in Europe, is at its strongest in the Middle East. The earliest traceable example (as so often) seems to occur in Mesopotamia. From there it spread, and probably encountered related stories already in existence, a common feature of which seems to be (as in the Cornish one) the motif of the single survivor. In Greek myth the story of Deucalion, who escaped from a flood sent by Zeus to punish mankind for its faults, bears close connection with the Hebrew myth of Noah. Plato's full account of the drowning of Atlantis came originally from Egypt, and is clearly structurally related to this Cornish case of Lyonesse.

Such relatedness is a distinguishing feature of myth. Myths tend to look structurally alike; but so do trees, horses, or butterflies, or, come to that, chairs, or bicycles – and for the same reason. The members of each category have in common that they function and survive in a certain type of environment. Certain things about these myths are so similar that one naturally suspects borrowings, even across centuries and oceans; but it need not necessarily be so.

An example of such a correspondence occurs in a striking form in the case of Tristan, whose situation and career bear remarkable similarities to those of the Greek hero Hippolytus. They both had stepmothers who tried to kill them. They both liked hunting. Hippolytus fell in love with his stepmother, and Tristan with his uncle's wife, or, if Mark was originally his father, with his stepmother. Both heroes then become the object of attempted destruction by the wronged husband. They both, in the end, die near the sea. Certainly the connection with horses, emphasized by the names Hippolytus and March and by the hunting habit of the heroes, and the association of horses with the sea (epitomized by the horse- and sea-god Poseidon) seem to indicate that both myths refer to the memory of a horse cult. One cannot help feeling also that something important, but unfortunately obscure, is being said about relationships and generations.

The ambiguity of the father-uncle perhaps provides a clue. It cannot be insignificant that in Malory's collection of Arthurian themes this same position occurs again. Mordred, the fatal opponent, who also in the end brings about a conflict with Arthur by trying to seduce his wife, is Arthur's nephew, his sister's son; however, because he is the product of an incestuous affair in Arthur's early career, he is also Arthur's son. The importance of the relationship of sister's son to mother's brother is well established in myth; Gwydion, for instance, was the mother's brother of the hero Lleu, whom he brought up. Moreover he himself was also sister's son to Math, the king whom he both plotted against and made demands on. In Greek myth the gods sometimes married their sisters, so that the hostility which existed between for instance Cronus and Zeus was of this uncle/father-nephew type. Similarly, Creon was the brother of Oedipus's mother, and in the myth provides the tension between the generations which, through the death of Oedipus's father, is otherwise missing. Malory makes much of the relationship between Gawain, also a sister's son to Arthur, and the king, as if it is understood (as it seems to have been) that such relations had special claims on one another.

The explanation is available, if one accepts the possibility of the long survival, through the sort of medium represented by myth, of ideas related to matrilinear inheritance. Without patrilineal descent, a man's nearest relative of the next generation would be his sister's son. He it would be, therefore, who would represent both an obligation and a threat. On the transition from one social custom to the other, what is more, a whole class of people, namely sisters' sons, would be deprived of rights to which, by ancient custom, they might have felt entitled. It is a long way from such times to Malory and the end of the Middle Ages, but the power of survival of themes in myth is well established, and when, as in this case, they refer to what is inevitably a permanent biological situation (the tension between the generations and the matter of inheritance) as well as the ordering of society, then their longevity is perhaps not so odd.

Malory was probably not aware that in the process of telling his stories he was, in a way, summarizing the thoughts and values which had governed Britain through its coming into being, through its adolescence, and which were now to form the basis of its maturity. We for our part can look forward from his standpoint, whereas he was concerned in looking back. The epitomy of what he sees as ideal resides, in the manner of the notions of the Middle Ages, in the sphere of love, the dominating influence in these old romantic stories. Courtly love was, for him, a noble custom which one could no longer even pretend was a feature of real life.

> But nowadays men can not love seven night but they must have all their desires: that love may not endure by reason; for where they be soon accorded, and hasty heat, soon it cooleth. Right so fareth love nowadays, soon hot soon cold: this is no stability. But the old love was not so; men and women could love together seven years, and no lycours lusts were between them, and then was love, truth and faithfulness: and lo, in likewise was used love in King Arthur's days.

If love was his way of contrasting the old, imagined, ideal with the new reality, the means through which he did this were his ideal lovers, Tristan, and, particularly, Lancelot, 'the truest lover of a sinful man that ever loved woman'. The conflict is always apparent: chastity and eroticism, asceticism and romance, permanently strung in delicate tension. In *The Waning of the Middle Ages* Huizinga points to this inner conflict as being the characteristic of that time, when idealized values made their last stand against encroaching reality. Love is at the same time the emblem of the unobtainable, the reason for the underlying sadness, unfulfilledness, of existence – and also the aim and motivation of much of life's activity. The Chronicles (he points out) show that chivalry was an elaborate pretence. But precisely because of that, the age of Arthur, the love of Lancelot, bear the force and attraction which have made them survive. 'That reality has constantly given the lie to these high illusions of a pure and noble social life, who would deny? But where should we be, if our thoughts had never transcended the exact limits of the feasible?'

2 Avalon

When it was all over, Lancelot came back. He searched for the queen, and found her in a nunnery. They are dismayed and overawed by the harm which their love, without their knowledge, did. She says to her ladies: 'Through this man and me hath all this war been wrought, and the death of the most noblest knights of the world; for through our love that we have loved together is my most noble lord slain.' She tells him to retire to his territory and take a wife, a suggestion which shocks his medieval sense of chivalry profoundly. 'Nay, madam, wit you well that shall I never do, for I shall never be so false to you of that I have promised.' The tense and final interview, in the presence of others, draws to an end. 'Wherefore, madam, I pray you kiss me and never no more. Nay, said the queen, that shall I never do, but abstain you from such works: and they departed.' Heartbroken, he takes horse, 'and rode all that day and all night in a forest, weeping'. Weeping, one feels, for, among other things, the wasted chances.

It is typical of Malory's approach that he should represent even the final downfall of Arthur in such personal terms: as the outcome of the romantic love between Lancelot and the queen. It was not, even on his own showing, so. The end had been foretold with the birth of Mordred, and its working out had been only a matter of time.

Arthur unwittingly slept with his sister, and of that liaison Mordred was the offspring. Merlin pronounces that through him Arthur and all his knights would be killed, and since he added that the child would be born on May Day, Arthur ordered that all male children born that day should be brought to him. Such was his power that they were brought, Mordred among them. Not knowing which was the fatal enemy, he had them all put in a ship and sent to sea, with the usual desire shown in such stories to ensure their destruction without actually having to kill them. Leaving that loophole open is the flaw in this safeguard, and Mordred, like Oedipus and Paris, avoids death. The ship was wrecked, most of the other children apparently died, but Mordred was cast up, 'and a good man found him, and nourished him till he was fourteen year afterward'. We have already seen how these themes – of attempted destruction and its avoidance – have formed part of the story of Tristan; and that of fosterage occurred in the story of Arthur.

Mordred does not appear again until towards the end of Malory's saga; fate is slow in delivering itself, but all the time we know that the last

Glastonbury Tor, the traditional site of Avalon

Above left: Mordred and Arthur in combat during the battle of Camlan
Above right: Arthur sending the boatload of babies out to sea

encounter is in preparation. He reappears in the court almost surreptitiously, and we hear of him plotting to reveal the love of Lancelot and
Guenever to Arthur, after the return from the grail search. He and other
of Arthur's nephews trap Lancelot in the queen's bedroom, and although
he fights his way out through their ranks it is clear that things are now too
serious to be ignored. Several are killed in the process. Mordred, of
course, escapes. The war which develops between Arthur and Lancelot is
not directly caused by Mordred, but by his brother Sir Gawaine, who
demands revenge for the death of other brothers in the fights surrounding the rescue of the condemned queen.

Lancelot and the queen are besieged at first in Joyous Gard, and an
inconclusive confrontation is broken by the intervention of the Pope. He
demands that Arthur should take back the queen, and Lancelot accordingly delivers her to the castle in Carlisle. Malory (in all this drawing
from the thirteenth-century French prose work) relates a tense and
moving scene, in which Lancelot's integrity is displayed against
Gawaine's vindictiveness and Arthur's wounded bitterness. Under
threat from Sir Gawaine Lancelot leaves and goes abroad, alone. 'Alas,
most noble Christian realm, whom I have loved above all other
realms . . . and now I shall depart in this wise.' He looks back with

regret at his ever having come there at all; 'but fortune is so variant, and the wheel so moveable, there nys none constant abiding.'

It is understood, in Malory, that Lancelot came from, and returned to, France, which was, as we have seen, the birthplace of his story. To pursue the war on him, therefore, Arthur and Gawaine have to take an army overseas. This, in accurate medieval terms, involves the difficulty of the security of his rule at home. On his previous expedition to Rome he had put the kingdom and, significantly, the queen, under the control of two appointed governors. Now he unwisely makes Mordred sole ruler, and puts the queen too under his guardianship. We saw in an earlier chapter that in Geoffrey of Monmouth's version, before the insertion of the story of Lancelot by the French source, this regency, and its sequel, happened during the expedition to Rome.

Mordred forges letters from France saying that Arthur has been killed. He has himself crowned king, and with the kingdom, as so often, goes the queen. She however escapes from her would-be husband, and shuts herself up in the Tower of London, where he besieges her in vain. The news reaches Arthur, and he at once raises the siege against Lancelot and leaves for home. Mordred draws supporters and awaits him at Dover; it is clear, as Arthur lands in a country now ruled by a usurping king, that his great days are over.

From Dover the war moves west. Warned in a dream by Gawaine's ghost that to fight, as appointed, would bring about his death, Arthur decides to form a treaty to delay the battle until Lancelot and his troops can arrive to support him. Gawaine, dying at Dover, has written a reconciling letter to Lancelot asking him to come to the king's aid. The two opponents then come together with a small band of retainers to endorse the treaty, but aware of Mordred's treacherous disposition Arthur gives instructions to his army that if they see a sword drawn they are to attack. Mordred, on his side, equally trusting, has given the same instructions. The treaty is agreed, however, and they drink to it, and it seems as if Arthur's life is to be saved. But fate then pulls its characteristic trick. An adder comes out of a little heath bush, and bites a knight on the foot. He draws his sword, unthinking, to kill it; 'and when the host on both parties saw that sword drawn, then they blew beamous, trumpets, and horns, and shouted grimly.' There is no stopping the battle then.

It is an old tradition that the battle of Camlan began by mistake. When the story is told in the twelfth-century Welsh tale, 'The Dream of Rhonabwy', it is due to the mischievous intriguing of an envoy. And in one of the Welsh Triads, Camlan, 'between Arthur and Medrod', is cited as one of three battles with 'frivolous causes'. The tradition that both Arthur and Mordred fell in that battle is, also, extremely old. We have mentioned it before as being one of the earliest of all references to Arthur – 'Gueith cam lann in qua Arthur et Medraut corruerunt' –given by the Annals as in the year 537.

That Camlan should be represented as a battle in a civil war between rival kings, is, as we have noted, also a significant tradition. In view of the part played by internal strife in early British history it is highly appropriate that the mythology should represent the end of the Round Table, and the death of Arthur with all its consequences, as being brought about by the disagreement of its own members. In Malory this point is duplicated, since it is firstly the quarrel of Arthur and Lancelot and secondly the quarrel of Arthur and Mordred which lead to the destruction of them all.

Arthur's death had been most thoroughly prophesied. He could not have thought, in view of Merlin's original warning of Mordred's role, that he would be able to avoid it by anything as superficial as a treaty, still less once Gawaine's ghost had threatened it for the next day. The adder was sure, from the start, to come out of the bush. Warned again in the battle that he should leave it before too late, he nevertheless cannot resist a last attempt to kill Mordred himself. Dying, Mordred deals Arthur a mortal wound on the head. Just before the final departure, Malory's version (following his French source) inserts that magical sequence in which Sir Bedevere is three times commanded, and twice fails, to return the sword Excalibur to the lake from which it came. The knight, his last companion, carries him then to the water-side, where a boat draws up to take him; women in black hoods, three queens among them, weeping, receive him on board.

> Ah my lord Arthur, what shall become of me, now ye go from me and leave me here alone among mine enemies? Comfort thyself, said the king, and do as well as thou mayest, for in me is no trust to trust in; for I will into the vale of Avilion to heal me of my grievous wound: and if thou hear never more of me, pray for my soul.

Geoffrey of Monmouth evidently found the name Avalon in a French source. It appears in the earliest of the 'chansons de geste', the 'Couronnement Louis', in about 1130. He it was who set in motion the theme of Arthur's departure there to be healed: 'mortally wounded' he 'was carried off to the Isle of Avalon, so that his wounds might be attended to'. Wace, translating Geoffrey back into French, adds that 'he is yet in Avalon, awaited of the Britons' –

> Encor i est, Breton l'atandent,
> Si com il dient et entandent;
> De la vandra, encor puet vivre.

And Layamon, translating Wace into robust Middle English, adds the mystical and unforgettable boat:

> floating with the waves; and two women in it, wondrously shaped; and they took Arthur anon, and bare him quickly, and laid him softly down, and forth they gan depart. . . . The Britons believe yet that he is alive, and dwelleth in Avalun with the fairest of all elves; and the Britons ever yet expect when Arthur shall return.

Malory is more ambiguous. He tempers the superstition with a new realism, qualifying it without destroying it. He tells of Sir Bedevere the next day coming to a chapel and a hermitage 'betwixt two holts hoar', where he found that the hermit, a former bishop of Canterbury, had recently buried a man brought to him in the night by a number of ladies. In the French version from which he was working this corpse is explicitly Arthur's; but Malory, preserving the native tradition, leaves the matter open. 'Thus of Arthur I find never more written in books that be authorised, nor more of the very certainty of his death heard I never read, but thus was he led away in a ship wherein were three queens.' The hermit, he says, did not know for certain that it was King Arthur's body. And he records with accurate perception the folklore which, then and now, may be found in places around the country:

> Yet some men say in many parts of England that King Arthur is not dead, but had by the will of our Lord Jesu into another place; and men say that he shall come again, and he shall win the holy cross. I will not say it shall be so, but rather I will say, here in this world he changed his life. But many men say that there is written upon this tomb this verse: HIC JACET ARTHURUS REX, QUONDAM REX QUE FUTURUS. [Here lies King Arthur, one-time and future king.]

Malory's immediate source for this seems to have been a west-country poem, written earlier in his century, which explicitly locates 'Artourez toumbe' at Glastonbury with a 'latyn verse' written on it: 'Hic jacet Arthurus, rex quondam, rexque futurus.'

It is, as we have seen, an old idea; and no doubt it embodies an even older one that we shall all return, death being not an end but a transformation. Since the Celts believed in reincarnation, there must have been, in their thinking, the notion of an otherworld where, at death, one went to pass through the transition between departure and return. MacCana, with whom it would surely be foolish to disagree, writes in his book *Celtic Mythology*: 'Nothing about the Celts is more certain than that they believed in life after death.' We know from the Irish stories in particular that they envisaged the dead as living on a distant island, and the Welsh poem 'The Spoils of Annwn' suggests a series of worlds, known by different names, through which the soul must pass. One of these, called Caer Wydyr, Glass Castle, has the support of other sources in suggesting a tower of glass, surrounded by water; and the recurrence of this idea makes it appear to be of special significance.

The idea of water as an insulating medium against the harmful influences of the spirits of the dead seems to be common to many mythologies; and probably this idea contributed to the habit of burying the dead on islands, which seems to be indicated by cases such as Bardsey, off the north Welsh coast, with its legend of graves of twenty thousand saints. If this were indeed the custom, then it is a natural consequence that islands should be equated with the otherworld, the place where the dead wait for their return. In mythology the journey to the 'beyond' being across water is a familiar notion, as in the case of the passage of the Styx.

Procopius (a clerk at Byzantium in the reign of the Emperor Justinian) gives a very striking version of this idea applied, presumably by mistake, to the whole island of Britain. To that island, he says, the dead are conveyed from the land of the Franks. The voyage of death was as firmly established as the notion of the country of the dead itself. Certainly in the early sources (although Malory calls it a 'vale') Avalon was always considered to be an island.

The name, Avalon, is supposed to be originally Celtic, although its derivation as usually given appears to be fanciful: 'Afallen' is the Welsh for apple-trees, and the idea of a vale of apple-orchards has seemed to many to be a suitable form for an elysium. On the other hand it is said to derive not from the Welsh for apples but from the name of a mythical king, Afallach, who (whether or not because of this connection) was regarded as a king of an afterworld, like Pluto. He, however, is shadowy in more senses than one. It seems always to have been assumed that Avalon was one of the names of the British version of the realm of the dead, and, from its confident use when it appears in its first recorded form, and the ease with which it was generally assimilated, this seems likely to be right.

In connection with Avalon as afterworld we find the goddess or enchantress Morgain, or Morgen, frequently mentioned, Avalon being sometimes considered her home. And she in her turn is commonly connected with healing. She appears in Geoffrey of Monmouth's 'Life of Merlin', written in about 1150, as the leader of nine similar enchantresses, carrying Arthur away to be healed after the battle of Camlan. The work known as the 'Vulgate Lancelot', a large prose work written in France in the thirteenth century from which Malory drew much of his material, propelled her as a major figure into Arthurian literature. In Malory's version she becomes King Arthur's sister, Morgain le Fay, and he adds as an afterthought that it was she who led the veiled women in the boat which took him away to Avalon. Originally a Celtic goddess, Morgain appears in more basic form in Irish myths as the Morrigan, a battle-goddess who aids, or threatens, CuChulain and the other Irish heroes. Clearly, however, it is a different aspect of her which we meet as Morgain the healer, queen of the land of Avalon.

Whatever Avalon may have been originally, there is no doubt that from the twelfth century onwards it has been identified as Glastonbury. That what is being reported then was an old tradition seems almost certain. It might well be objected by anyone coming to Glastonbury through the well-established Somerset countryside today that the place is not an island. But in ancient times it was; the surrounding marshlands are so low in relation to sea-level that they were, even so far inland, at one time occupied by sea. From Roman times the marshes around Glastonbury have been best characterized as floodland; and in the sub-Roman period it seems likely that the Tor, together with the Abbey site and Wearyall Hill, was almost completely surrounded by water, connected to the neighbouring land by a ridge to the east. During the high monastic

Wearyall Hill seen from Glastonbury Tor, the area which was once an island

period strenuous attempts were made, by the building of sea walls, to prevent the general flooding which had been notorious in Somerset. Perhaps then Glastonbury ceased to be obviously an island, and if Malory had this place in mind when referring to Avalon he might have had reason to call it a vale instead of an isle, in spite of the departure from convention which this represented. Floods continued into the succeeding centuries, indeed Glastonbury found itself surrounded by sea again as late as 1811, but now the sea can no longer penetrate into this area, and what flooding there is comes from the nearby river Brue and its offshoots.

Certainly from up on the Tor itself one is struck by the flatness and extent of the plain surounding it and its associated group of hills. When that wide plain was covered in water, this prominent hill-group, seen for instance from the distance of the Mendips to the north, must have appeared peculiarly isolated.

That Glastonbury was originally regarded as an island is evident from its pre-Saxon name: Ynys Witrin, Glass Island. It seems to have been known as this in the seventh century, and presumably, unrecorded, before that. The Saxon name by which it is known now seems more likely, etymologically, to have come from the name of a tribe than to be a sort of translation, even though one is tempted to see in it a continuation of the original idea. Glass was made in the Middle East and Egypt from at least as early as the third millennium BC, and was in common use throughout the Roman Empire. Presumably the name used in the various languages to describe it pre-existed it, referring to natural properties or effects. The Old English word 'glass' may well have come from an earlier term meaning 'shine'. There also exists in Welsh a word which is the same as the Teutonic one, 'glas', which means both blue and green, terms which very accurately describe the evasive colour of Roman bottle-glass.

Nobody has satisfactorily explained why a grassy island in a tidal inlet, dominated by a conical, smooth-sided hill, should be called Glass Island, nor has anybody explained why one of the names of the country of the dead seems to have been Glass Castle. Some clue may, I think, be gathered from the Irish burial mounds, where, particularly at New Grange, one can see that the huge tomb was, originally, covered over with lumps of white quartz. These, perhaps with the chipped faces set on the outside to reveal the sparkle of their crystals, must have glittered like the substance to which the name glass was given. Around the edges of the similar but small mounds of the burial chambers in Wales large numbers of white quartz pebbles have been found; and it seems perverse of archaeology to attribute to the quartz of these mounds some sort of ritual significance, rather than to conclude that they were intended to decorate the tomb's outer face. If I am right, then Glass Castle was a good description for the place you went to when you died. And Glass Island would well describe a collection of such sites.

That Glastonbury had been a religious centre for some time seems probable from the archaeology, and this aspect will be discussed again later in connection with the grail story. On the secular side we have conclusive evidence of Glastonbury's early habitation, since towards the end of the last century two lake villages were found in the area, dating from the third century BC, that is, from the pre-Roman, Iron Age Celtic period, a period of high artistic culture and some degree of civilization. This can easily be seen from the artefacts which the surrounding peat has so well preserved. They indicate a wide range of activities – reaping hooks and querns, for instance, showing that the waterside people culti-vated the nearby dry land – and the distinctive hatching and patterning on their pottery relates them to Celtic people elsewhere.

All that can now be seen at Glastonbury of a lake village, which would have been a collection of huts based on platforms raised above marshland at the edges of water, is a series of low humps in a field. Once the eye picks them out it is at once impressive how numerous and densely packed they are. Presumably the people fished, as people living in such condi-tions naturally do elsewhere; a dugout canoe, hollowed from a single tree, was found nearby. Though there are distinct signs that protection was one of the villagers' main requirements, this first settlement at Glastonbury remained isolated from history and the international world. Before it could have been disrupted by the coming of the Romans, with their inevitable introduction of trade, politics, and coinage, it had (for some undetermined reason) come to an end. Perhaps the water level rose inconveniently, and the inhabitants moved elsewhere.

At about the time that the lake villagers moved, and the Romans approached from the Channel ports, Christianity came into existence. It is a persistent and very ancient belief that it reached Glastonbury unex-pectedly early. When the Saxons came they found already there a curious structure known as the 'Old Church', around which legends of some potency had accumulated. It was a wattle and daub construction, said, in spite of its simplicity, to have been built by God himself, or at the very least by one of Christ's disciples. It is noteworthy that the local legend has always assumed that religion and Glastonbury are inseparable.

It is one of the saints' 'Lives' which indicates that this had been so even in pre-Christian times. The 'Life of Saint Collen', purporting to describe the foundation of a monastery at Glastonbury in the sixth century, provides a strangely disturbing instance of the conjunction of two religions, which hints at the existence of a religious cult at Glastonbury before the coming of Christianity. St Collen was approached by one of British myth's otherworld kings, Gwyn ap Nudd, whom we have met before as one of the combatants in an annually-repeated contest. Nudd, his patronymic, is none other than the god known in the Romano-Celtic world as Nodens, whose late shrine at Lydney, the other side of the Severn, indicates at least his long survival in the south-west. Collen the Christian encountered Gwyn the Celtic god on the Tor, on the summit of which Gwyn's castle appeared to him. Since this particular god is also, in his capacity as leader of the Wild Hunt, the collector and conveyor of souls to his own afterworld kingdom, the association of the island of Avalon with the world of the dead is given some substantiation by this odd legend.

It was Giraldus Cambrensis, writing in the 1190s, who first recorded the belief that Glastonbury and 'insula Avallonia', the resting place of Arthur, were one and the same. We must suppose him to have been reporting an existing piece of lore, but the circumstances under which he did so inevitably throw some doubt on the authenticity of the tradition, since other motives can, as we shall see, be found in its background.

By that time, the period of the twelfth-century Arthurian revival, Glastonbury's importance as a monastic centre and place of pilgrimage had become considerable, and there is some reason to suppose that it had been a place of such influence rather longer than any other spot in Britain. The legendary material which is the nearest we have to early history associates the first monastic settlement there with St Patrick, and although this is probably a mistake it does seem likely to reflect a genuine connection with both early saints and Irish monks. William of Malmesbury, who took a keen interest in Glastonbury, wrote in the early-twelfth century that pilgrims came there to visit the relics of Irish saints. There is, however, no archaeological evidence for a settlement on the Abbey site during the sub-Roman period, although a pre-Saxon grave-yard has been identified on the site of the medieval church.

There is, however, evidence of a settlement on the Tor, which (to-gether with the area of the Abbey and that of the Chalice Well) formed the original island. This steep-sided, 500-foot-high cone rises very improbably from the plains of Somerset, a country so generally flat that the towers of its churches act as navigational marks for the traveller. If church towers were, in the past, conspicuous features above the frequent floods, how much more must the Tor have been. By its nature it could have been either a defensive position or a place of hermitage, but the evidence of sub-Roman period habitation of the Tor, in the form of pottery, signs of metal working, and a small, hollow, Celtic-featured bronze head, which defiantly resists explanation, does not show whether it was secular or ecclesiastical.

We do know that when the Saxons came they found on the later Abbey site the small wattle building which has always been known as the Old Church. It also seems clear that it was already old in 633, when it was restored by Paulinus, Bishop of York. Around this church, and because of it, the later monastic buildings grew up. The first historical fact about the place is that it rose to prominence in British affairs under the shadow of St Dunstan, a person of almost legendary strength of character who became its abbot in about 936, and at the same time became a powerful political influence at the English court. Under Dunstan Glastonbury adopted the Benedictine discipline, with its emphasis on learning and labour.

After the troubled times of the Danish wars, when England became united again for a time under the Danish King Canute, he signalled his intention of living in peace with his country's past by coming to Glastonbury to worship. He gave the Old Church a charter, in 1030. Not long after this trouble erupted again, and in the early Norman period there was considerable bitterness between the conquerors and the old order. Glastonbury was still important; Henry I's nephew, Henry de Blois, who was a brother of King Stephen, became abbot here in 1126 and it was he who initiated the main building programme.

That it is not the results of Abbot Henry's work which we see there now is due to one of Glastonbury's most traumatic events. The whole place burnt down, newly built, in 1184. The old wattle church, built by God or Christ's disciples, which had made the place so holy, was completely destroyed. It stood in the middle of what is now St Mary's Chapel, the previous version of which had been carefully built around it. What was evidently almost as tragic for the monks was the loss of all their treasure and relics, which both gave the place its status and assured its continuing prosperity.

It is a measure of the Abbey's central importance to English political life that the king, Henry II, treated this as a national emergency. He personally undertook to ensure that it would be rebuilt, and set about raising funds. A massive rebuilding programme was instituted almost at once, and it is the ruins of this work of the late-twelfth century which we can see there now. Henry II died in July 1189, after which the funds which the monks relied on started to dry up. The new king, Richard I, Coeur de Lion, was committed to a grand and extravagant gesture, the Second Crusade. Jerusalem had been lost in 1187, and the Pope had called for a crusade for its recovery. Frederick Barbarossa, the Holy Roman Emperor, set out in 1189, and the king of France and Richard joined him the next year. This quite clearly meant that the new king had no time or money to spare for Glastonbury.

Henry II (who was the grandson of Henry I and son of Geoffrey

The ruins of the Abbey at Glastonbury

Plantagenet, count of Anjou) had led two expeditions against the Welsh princes, in 1158 and 1165, neither of which had been totally successful. Wales remained unconquered, and lived alongside its neighbour in a state of uneasy alliance. According to Giraldus Cambrensis, Henry had been told by a bard during one of his Welsh expeditions that King Arthur was

Rossetti's romantic nineteenth-century impression of Arthur's tomb

not, after all, alive, but had been buried, and that, moreover, the exact site of his grave was known. It was at Glastonbury, and its location was described precisely by the bard to the king. Whether this story is retrospective or not, the discovery of Arthur's body would have done much to counteract the persistent belief in his Welsh revival. Geoffrey of Monmouth had boosted the reputation of the prophecy that Arthur would return, which itself was based on a much older and less personal prophecy that the British people, 'the native dragon', would one day recover and drive out the invaders.

That being so it is likely, and is so reported by Giraldus, that Henry encouraged the idea that the monks of Glastonbury should find Arthur's grave. Since it was not until 1190, or perhaps 1191, that they complied, the discovery itself cannot have been at Henry's direct instigation. They did, however, have an even more plausible motive. It was clearly stated that the monks had lost their relics in the fire, and relics were of crucial importance to a monastery. No doubt it was too much to hope that some further saints might be discovered, but they did know that they were reliably said to possess the remains of Britain's most eminent ancient hero, then at the height of his popularity following the immense success of Geoffrey's book.

Scholars still argue about whether it was really Arthur that they found, and so seriously is this debate conducted that we cannot dismiss it. It seems very probable that they did find the grave of a sixth-century chieftain, and that it was of an unusually important and impressive form. Excavations in 1962 revealed the hole from which they drew the coffin, and the date of the disinterment is unusually certain, since the grave contained chippings made by masons engaged on the rebuilding programme. We have the records of three independent chroniclers for the discovery, two of them, one being Giraldus, writing at the time.

The grave was found at a considerable depth, they tell us. A lead cross was found first, identifying the site, fixed to a slab with (so Giraldus adds) the inscribed face inwards. The two contemporaries differ about whether the body was in a sarcophagus or a wooden coffin; and neither of them was actually there at the time. They differ too about what was said on the lead cross, but in this case Giraldus had actually seen it. He visited Glastonbury in 1192 and 1193, and wrote about it in his 'De Principis Instructione'.

The authenticity of the discovery does to a certain extent depend on the authenticity of the cross, since this is the only evidence for the claim that the person buried there was Arthur. The chieftain was accompanied in his grave, we are told, by his wife. The two skeletons remained on display for some time, and a tomb for them was built in about 1192 inside the new church; in 1278 it was opened to be inspected by King Edward I and his wife Eleanor. Significantly Edward had just returned from his first major campaign in Wales, resulting in an ill-fated treaty with Llewelyn ap Gruffydd, which left the Welsh prince independent in the west, though theoretically subject to Edward in territories nearer the border. It must have been some relief to Edward to see the proof that Arthur was not going to come back.

After inspection by the king and queen, the older king and queen were re-interred. They were then placed in an elaborate tomb in front of the high altar, the site of which was discovered in 1931, though the structure had been destroyed and the bones dispersed in the Reformation. The lead cross, however, survived. It was seen by Leland in the 1540s, and its inscription reported. Most importantly it was included by Camden in the 1607 edition of his 'Britannia', which for the first time presented an illustration of it.

From this we can see what, in the seventeenth century, was believed to be the form of the identification found in the twelfth of a burial made in the sixth. Certain things about the cross (specifically the shape of some of the letters) make it seem unlikely to be a forgery undertaken in the twelfth century. Leslie Alcock argues for the possibility that it was made in the tenth century, when Dunstan raised the level of the graveyard and thus obscured Arthur's original memorial. If that were so, however, it is hard to see why Dunstan should have buried a cross with the now obscured grave, rather than leaving a surface memorial above it. And it seems unlikely too that no memory of its being there should have survived at Glastonbury, where knowledge of its existence apparently had to be reintroduced by Henry II from an equally inexplicable survival in Wales. On the face of it the matter is not susceptible to proof, but any theory about it has to deal with some remarkable inconsistencies in the evidence.

Perhaps most notable among these discrepancies is the inscription on the lead cross itself. The cross exhibited by Camden says, quite legibly in its antique script, 'Hic iacet sepultus inclitus rex Arturius in insula Avalonia'. However, the wording given by Giraldus – and he, alone

among our sources, had seen the cross at the time when it was dis-
covered – is so strikingly different that we must suspect the Leland-
Camden one of being inaccurate. 'HIC JACET SEPULTUS INCLITUS REX
ARTHURUS CUM WENNEVERIA UXORE SUA SECUNDA IN INSULA AVALLONIA.'
('Here lies buried King Arthur, with Guenever his second wife, in the
island of Avalon.')

The authorities tend to dismiss Giraldus as unreliable, and in doing so
they evade an awkward question. Why should he, however fanciful and
gullible, have claimed that the words he saw gave Guenever as Arthur's
second wife? Since no tradition exists that Guenever was Arthur's second
wife, it is most unlikely that such a detail would have been added to a
forgery, and this point alone, for all its inconvenient obscurity, seems to
indicate a factual, rather than a fictional, inscription.

It is true that one of the Welsh Triads states, very oddly, that Arthur
had three wives; but since it also says that they were all called
Gwenhwyfar the explanation would seem to be that there were discrepant versions of Gwenhwyfar's ancestry. A tradition that he had three
wives, in any case, is by no means a reason for having him buried with his
second.

The puzzle remains, at present, unsolved. If Camden's engraver took
such meticulous care over the lettering that he managed to reproduce a
genuinely ancient form, how could he have been completely wrong
about the wording? If he was right then how or why would Giraldus
have made such an odd mistake? The cross itself unfortunately disappeared, although it can be traced as far as the eighteenth century. And the
question of the grave of Arthur, said by an early Welsh verse in the
'Stanzas of the Graves' to be a mystery, remains a mystery still.

Just as Guenever's inclusion in the burial adds a tantalizing hint of the
possibility of a mortal Arthur, so the occurrence of her name here also
strengthens the case for the Arthurian relations of Glastonbury. In myth
she was indeed connected with this place. One of the most persistent
elements in her story is her abduction – in Geoffrey of Monmouth (as in
later versions) by Mordred, but in other tales (evidently well enough
known to be depicted in a twelfth-century sculpture in Modena
Cathedral) by some other figure. This story, which finds its way into
Malory's 'Le Morte d'Arthur', appears to be derived from the theme of
the battle of the seasons, since it takes place on May Day, like the annual
contest over the abduction of Creiddylad, daughter of Lludd, by Gwyn
son of Nudd.

The best version of this apparently ancient sequence occurs – as,
ironically, do many of the prime instances of mythic themes – in one of
the twelfth-century saints' 'Lives'. In this case it is the life of none other
than Gildas himself, now transformed into an impeccable St Gildas. And
this too, such is the circularity of our material, tells us several things of
interest both about Glastonbury and about Arthur. It was written by
somebody called Caradoc of Llancarvan in about 1150.

St Gildas, it says, was the contemporary and friend of Arthur, king of

The ruins of the Lady Chapel

Britain, but hostility developed between them after Arthur had killed one of Gildas's unruly brothers. Gildas, when they meet, is forgiving, and they again become friends. The saint eventually comes to Glastonbury, 'at the time when King Melwas was reigning in the Summer Country' – quite clearly (and conventionally) an interpretation of Somerset, but also possible evidence of Melwas's original nature as a king of Summer. Caradoc refers to Glastonbury's British name: 'Glastonia, id est Urbs Vitrea . . . that is, the glassy city, which took its name from "glass", so named originally in the British tongue.' Later he (or someone adding a note) explains that this original name was 'Ynisgutrin', island of glass, and that the English version 'Glastigberi' is a translation of it.

Glastonbury was at the time, he says, 'besieged by the tyrant Arthur, with an innumerable host, on account of his wife Guennuvar' whom 'the wicked king' (presumably Melwas) had violated and abducted. Arthur had searched for her for a year – again some seasonal reference – until he found her taken by Melwas to the security of the natural defences of 'thickets of reed, river and marsh' which Glastonbury offered. Caradoc displays the characteristic attitude of the medieval church to Arthur, calling him 'tyrannus' and 'rex rebellus', and he shows Gildas and the abbot of Glastonbury to be nervously eager to patch up the trouble before it caused more damage.

Clearly Caradoc is dealing with old material of various different sorts, but he does give us evidence of a connection of Glastonbury with Arthur preceding the discovery of the grave. He also provides a description – though we must remember he is talking of the past – of an untamed, undeveloped area, a view of the wilderness still surrounding, perhaps, the magnificent new buildings risen there in his own time.

After the fire the rebuilding continued slowly, and it was not completed by the time of the re-dedication in 1303. An earthquake in the meantime, in 1275, had destroyed the older church on the Tor, leaving only the tower, which stands there still. The medieval monastic world came to a conclusive end with the Dissolution of the Monasteries in 1539, when Glastonbury's abbot was hanged and the Abbey's possessions given to the duke of Somerset. Enormous and eloquent ruins now mourn this brutal termination.

Still standing are parts of the Lady Chapel – though not the whole of that structure which originally enclosed the wattle church – and one wall of the main church, with part of its western entrance. The decorated upper portions of this, with columns and broken arches, indicate the quiet harmony between elegance and grandeur which that twelfth-century building must clearly have achieved. The Abbey ruins still manage to dominate the town and can be glimpsed in the background of Glastonbury's humble provinciality.

From the area of the Abbey the Tor rises in the distance above the other slopes of the one-time island, though it lacks from here the startling prominence which distinguishes it in its longer views. It is undoubtedly the Tor which gives to the Glastonbury area its special identity. The Tor's visual quality seems to insist that it bears significance, and within its shelter, on the site of the old island itself, one has a feeling of Avalonian calm. Avalon – if it extended from Wearyall Hill, included the Abbey site, and ended the other side of the Tor – was no slight island. And still it offers seclusion and the feeling of surrounding shelter, a peacefulness induced by protection without enclosure. Seen, for instance, from the calm of the Chalice Well gardens, in a cut between the slopes of the Tor and those of Chalice Hill, Avalon's three hills group themselves in an easy relationship, which itself induces a mood of harmony.

If myth occurs when the facts of historical events converge in people's minds with the fancies of their imaginations, places like Cadbury and Glastonbury have a lot in common with myth. Camelot from fantasy and Cadbury Castle from history make a combination, in which a real place counterparts a mythic one: and Avalon and Glastonbury are such a pair, twinned concepts so related that it might be better to think of each of them as another aspect of the other. 'Le Morte d'Arthur' ends with Lancelot bringing the body of the queen to lie beside her lord, coming on foot 'from Almesbury unto Glastonbury'. No doubt Malory is bearing in mind the legend of the discovered grave when he thus states more or less explicitly that Arthur was buried at Glastonbury; but he is also recognizing Glastonbury's unique position in British religious thought, its possession of mystical charisma on a national scale.

MERLIN

I have been in many shapes
Before achieving this convenient form. . . .
I have been a drop in the air,
I have been a shining star,
I have been a word in a book. . . .
I have the knowledge of the stars,
Of stars which pre-exist the earth.
I know where I have come from,
And the number of the worlds. . . .
I have slept in a hundred islands,
I have lived in a hundred cities.
Learned Druids, do you prophesy of Arthur?
Or is it of something older:
Is it of me you sing?'

Taliesin, in 'The Battle of the Trees';
a poem in the 'Red Book of Hergest',
MS *c*. 1400.

Sedentis est deliberare. Sedente itaqȝ eo .i. delibante ⁊ disponente
de edificanda turre quȝ magis ꝯsulerint in psidium sibi ꝯstruere:
egressi sūt duo dracones. ¶ Coniunctio annectit narracōem
⁊ ordinat ut sit ꝯtinuatio ad hystoriam. ¶ Interfecto cōstantino
rege ⁊ filio eius constante: vortegirⁱⁿs surripuit regnū cuⁱ ꝓ.

3 Out of the mist

By now we could hardly be surprised to find that the myth of Merlin stems from two different roots. On the one hand there is a possibly historical character of the heroic age, who had become developed and distorted by the influence of legend, and on the other hand there is a primitive folk-figure, the product of superstition, fantasy and decayed religion.

Myrddin ap Morfryn was said to be a British poet writing in North Britain during the sixth century. We have a few of what some take to be his authentic poems, though others think they belong more probably to the heroic literature of the ninth and tenth centuries. Unfortunately they do not tell us much about the man, as opposed to the embryo legend. This legend has clearly affected some of the poems, which exist only in medieval manuscripts – the late-twelfth-century Black Book of Carmarthen and the Red Book of Hergest of about 1400 – and so are probably influenced by a retrospective view in which the two Merlin figures have already merged.

It is implied that Myrddin, like Aneirin and perhaps Taliesin, his supposed contemporaries, fought personally in those bitter battles in the area of the Wall, during the second half of the sixth century. Because of the slightness of the evidence for this, however, it is possible to argue that there was no historical Myrddin at all, and that he is a result of the attribution of a popular legend to a figure who was given that name. But at least some of the battles which the poems mention do appear to have taken place, and the question of whether or not he was there is now a matter of taste.

What confuses this issue in particular is the very early date of the start of the legend, the attribution of clearly non-factual elements to the figure named Myrddin. At an early age he became identified with the mythic character of the Mad Prophet. What is more interesting is that even before that he exemplified a theme so recurrent and widespread that it has been given a name – the Wild Man theme.

This is the real legend of Myrddin, and it lies behind much of the saga of the developed character. In Myrddin's particular story, as told in the poems attributed to him, this theme occurs when, as a result of the battle of 'Arfderydd', he goes mad. The battle appears to be that mentioned by the Annales Cambriae as having taken place at Arthuret, near Carlisle, in 573. The madness results in Myrddin living wild in the forest. No doubt

The youthful and precocious Merlin reads his prophecies to Vortigern

with poetic licence he says at one point that he has been living with the wild men of the woods for fifty years. He wears no clothes, lives in the trees, and consorts with the wild animals.

It is this sudden madness and the living like an animal in the woods that mark Myrddin as being the vehicle of that mythic theme of the Wild Man. One of his immediate relatives is the Irish hero Suibne, who also went mad during a battle, and then runs wild in the woods; he too is gifted, like Myrddin, with poetic inspiration. There was an old belief in both Ireland and Wales that such things did happen: both that men lost their senses at some point of crisis and fled into the woods, and that there were people who became prophetically or poetically inspired. Giraldus Cambrensis records this in the same passage as the one in which he mentions Merlin, whom he calls Merlinus Caledonius, in his 'Description of Wales', written in 1194: 'There are certain persons in Cambria, whom you will find nowhere else, called Awenddyon, or people inspired; when consulted upon any doubtful event, they roar out violently, are rendered beside themselves, and become, as it were, possessed by a spirit.' It seems likely that this was the mode of prophecy undertaken by Taliesin, whose obscure pronouncements and spell-binding effect we have come across in chapter six. In this, as in several other features, Myrddin is Taliesin's shadow.

We have already encountered, too, several cases of the first aspect of this madness. In the romance of Owein, or Chrétien's Yvain, the hero takes to the wilds in remorse at the realization that he has abandoned his lady; he wears no clothes, long hair grows on his body, and he lives and eats with wild beasts. Tristan, in the course of his anguished affair with King Mark's wife, becomes for a period insane, lives in the woods naked, fed by herdsmen and shepherds. And Lancelot at one point, rejected by Guenever, jumped out of a window in sudden madness and ran wild in the woods for two years, eating fruits and drinking (Malory says) nothing but water. The eventual recovery of all three of these British heroes is so similar that we cannot avoid the conclusion that they are acting out three versions of the same story. They are in each case found at or brought to the place from which they ran, and come under the care of the woman through love of whom they had gone mad.

There does not appear to be this love-element in the madness of Myrddin. But his running wild in the woods is obviously an instance of the same idea. Heracles too had bouts of madness; and Professor Jarman, whose work on the legend of Merlin must constitute the main authority for this subject, cites the biblical case of Nebuchadnezzar. He ate grass, grew hair on his body, and lived away from the company of men. It is, Jarman says, a theme which results from the fear, later turning to fascination, of what lies outside the clearing in the universal forest in which primitive man inevitably lived. Hence the special interest in the image of the outcast; hence, among other things, Robin Hood.

The Green Man (at one time represented in May Day customs, as Jack-in-the-green, by someone dressed up in a wicker framework covered all over with greenery) is perhaps related to this concept. The name 'Robin', so commonly applied to some sort of elf, together with Robin Hood and his friends' habit of always dressing in forest green, seem rather to suggest that our supposedly historical national outlaw owes not a little of his enduring success to his descent from a long line of wood-spirits and tree-gods. He took the form in which we know him comparatively late for such a figure, being mentioned by Langland in 'Piers Plowman' in the fourteenth century, at which time popular ballads telling his story came into existence. These cohered into a full narrative form in a work known as the 'Gest' of Robin Hood, which tells the basic story made so familiar by later plays, pantomimes, and films. The 'Gest' depicts an apparently historical figure, and from the mid-nineteenth century there has been no shortage of antiquarian proofs of his historicity.

Whether the story of the man who lives in the forest has attached itself to Robertus Hood of Wakefield, who may or may not be the same person as Edward II's valet Robyn Hode, or alternatively whether the person concerned was a fugitive mentioned in the Rolls of Henry III, does not affect the authenticity of the greenwood theme. It is accepted even by those who want a historical Robin that he and his henchmen became, or perhaps originally were, popularly associated with the May Day dances, which does much to draw out his family resemblance to the other forms of the Green Man. It would unfortunately take us too far from Merlin to consider the whole question of the May Day festivals and the rites of summer and fecundity which they involved. But once again there is no doubt that history and the remnants of religion merge at this intriguing point.

It seems inevitable that in the series of invasions which make up the early history of this island, displaced populations would have, from time to time, been forced away from the settled areas to live as best they could in the wilds. Like the giants whom Brutus and Corineus banished to live in caves in the mountains, who turn up again whenever a hero has to stray from civilization into wild country, these people may well have lingered, being occasionally accidentally re-encountered, in remote places: and lingered further in the memory as a vaguely remembered threat.

In any case increasing urbanism must have brought with it the awareness of the contrast with a type of life which, far from being urban, was not even domestic. Foresters, charcoal-burners, shepherds, continued to represent pre-urban, or extra-urban man into the Middle Ages; as did the hermit – a frequent figure encountered by lost or wandering knights in the romances and in Malory. And with the more effective imposition of law these exceptions came to be joined by outlaws.

Probably a wide variety of ideas go to make up the Wild Man theme, and if so its ability to span them would account for its persistence. One aspect of that theme forms a main strand in the myth of Merlin.

From his supposed origin in the north Myrddin seems to have migrated, in story, at an early stage, and come to settle in Carmarthen. Almost certainly his connection with that place arose from a phonetic confusion. The name of the town was derived from that of the Roman camp there, Maridunum, hence something like Caer Mardin, and in due course Caer Myrddin. Since the first word meant 'fort' and the second appeared to have no meaning, the 'Myrddin' would be naturally assumed, as in similar cases elsewhere, to be a personal name. If a northern poet of that name already existed in history or legend, he became transferred. Geoffrey of Monmouth seems to have been responsible (as for so much) for giving this identification official status. His source, Nennius, located Myrddin's discovery in Glamorgan; Geoffrey moved it to Carmarthen. 'They came to a town which was afterwards called Kaermerdin. . . .' The link between Carmarthen and Merlin is, for all its popularity and staying power, extremely tentative.

Carmarthen is still called in Welsh Caer Fyrddin, 'Myrddin's fort', and still known as 'Merlin's Town'. The modern town's predecessors of various ages have borne similar names, and the association with the wizard Myrddin, which is so well-established as to remain unshakable, may well have pre-existed Goeffrey's decisive statement of it. 'Maridunum' or, as it is sometimes spelt, 'Moridunum' appears to be a Romanization of a British name meaning sea-fort. Excavation has revealed that the Roman presence at Maridunum consisted not just of the garrisoned field fort, one of the most westerly outposts of the colonization of South Wales, but also of a civil settlement. The Romans reached here probably about AD 75, and built their fort very close to the previous 'caer' – a ring-fort thought to have occupied the hill on which County Hall now stands, overlooking the bridge and the river Tywi. This, which the Romans presumably assaulted and weakened, is said to have been the capital of the tribe of the Demetae, who gave their name to Demetia, or western South Wales.

Carmarthen in due course became a Norman seat, a castle being built there in the early-eleventh century, and a stronger one (of which hardly anything now remains) being erected on that same hill above the river during the reign of Henry I. It was at the end of that reign that Geoffrey of Monmouth wrote, and at the time the place was a flourishing Norman walled town surrounded by a contrasting, and rather hostile, Welsh world. During the twelfth century too an Augustinian Priory was established, and it was there, in that same century which saw so much of our early literature produced, that the earliest of the manuscripts to preserve pieces of the collection later known as the Mabinogion was transcribed.

The Black Book of Carmarthen – now in the National Library of Wales at Aberystwyth – though it is far from being as complete a collection as the Red Book of Hergest, has the advantage of superior age. It contains, among other things, the 'Stanzas of the Graves', and some clearly ancient heroic poetry, both of which, by mentioning Arthur, establish a connection of this west-Welsh country town with the survival of Britain's national tradition. Moreover one of the poems in this early collection, 'The Dialogue of Myrddin and Taliesin', is one of the sources for the subject of Myrddin. The Priory where this valuable work took place was at the north-east end of the site of the Roman town, just below the junction of Priory Street with Oak Lane. Nothing of it now remains, except the name.

The older part of the town now occupies the area of the Roman settlement, the civil element of which apparently lay to the north of St Peter's church. The form of the present old town seems to reflect the inevitable squareness of the Roman layout. Long, straight rows of little Victorian cottages give a formality of structure which old Welsh towns do not normally have. They face outwards at right-angles from a largely empty square area in the middle, in which, presumably, much of Maridunum awaits rediscovery. At one end of this is the old church, and at the other until fairly recently was the stump of a tree known as 'Merlin's Oak'. Past this the line of this section of town runs down to the looping Tywi, which was in earlier times navigable at this point. Buildings of the first and fourth centuries AD have been found, and excavations in recent years at the back of now derelict cottages in Church Street have revealed much more of the nature of the Roman town than was previously known. Outside it, as at Caerleon, lay the amphitheatre, the shape and size of which can clearly be seen.

'Merlin's Oak', of which it was said that when it should fall so would Carmarthen, is no longer there. Legend says that it was not Merlin's but was planted in 1659 to commemorate the proclamation of Charles II. It was deliberately poisoned by a bad-tempered tradesman in the early-nineteenth century, and until the late 1970s the fragments of its stump were kept, stuck together with concrete and held up with iron. The authorities have now rather rashly removed these sad remains, and sure enough Carmarthen is falling down. The new oak planted in the Roman amphitheatre is supposed to be a substitute, and no doubt it is also intended to build a new Carmarthen to replace the crumbling areas of the town.

The church, the town's oldest building, which as it stands is mainly thirteenth century, was first built in that same period in which Geoffrey wrote, the first few decades of the twelfth century. It too bears a connection with British history, though of a later date, since it is the burial place of Sir Rhys ap Thomas, lord of South Wales, who made a significant contribution to the course of national events by supplying the support of his troops to Henry Tudor (as he moved through this part of Wales between his landing at Milford Haven and his eventual victory at Bosworth) in the summer of 1485.

What Geoffrey made of the story of Myrddin we have already discussed in chapter five. Briefly, he grafted the character of the North-British prophetic bard onto that of a different figure, the prodigious child. He took from Nennius a tale concerning a boy called Emrys, who can be identified as the mythicized form of the historical character Ambrosius; and he used Nennius's story of Vortigern's flight into the mountains of Wales as a platform on which to base the entry of his new and major character, the prophet Merlin. Because the correct Latin translation of the British name Myrddin would be 'Merdinus', a derivative of 'merdus', meaning dung, the 'd' was arbitrarily changed to 'l', and the prophet named as 'Merlinus'. Thus 'Merlin' was born.

Through the amalgamation with the Emrys legend a confusion of two apparently different Merlins entered literature: Giraldus recorded the opinion that there was both an Ambrosius-Merlin and a 'Merlinus Sylvester' or 'Celidonius', the wild wood-living northern prophet – one being the eponym of Carmarthen of the time of Vortigern, the other a northern poet of the time of Arthur. Prophecies, however, were attributed to both. It was with that function that Geoffrey put him in the centre of his story, and it was in that capacity that Merlin has thrived ever since.

As so often the foundation of this success is firmly based on myth. The precocious and prophetic child who answered Vortigern's magicians on the summit of Dinas Emrys is one of a large family of such beings. His taking over Vortigern's castle mirrors the arrival and dominance of other characters in myth, the new hero ousting the old. Geoffrey himself seems to have been surprised at the success of his partial creation, which was due, no doubt, to his having once again tapped a deep spring.

He decided to draw on it more abundantly, and after the publication of the 'History' researched the lore of Merlin much more fully. The result, towards the end of the 1140s, was a second work, but this time in verse, the 'Life of Merlin'. Interestingly this reverts much more directly to the ancient source of the character, the legend of the 'Wild Man' Myrddin, and deals with his madness and his life in the woods. Jarman surmises very credibly that Geoffrey had read the Welsh poems in the meantime, although it is sometimes argued that the two discrepant Merlins indicate that the 'Vita Merlini' is only mistakenly attributed to Geoffrey.

There is an unavoidable inconsistency about Geoffrey's two versions of Merlin's story, which he himself tried with some difficulty to explain. Hence the lingering belief in two Merlins which Giraldus recorded, a belief which was unknowingly nearer to the truth than was Geoffrey's own amalgam. There *were* two Merlins: one derived from the northern prophetic poet who went mad and lived in the wilds; and one derived from the precocious child found in Carmarthen and brought to Vortigern at Dinas Emrys.

Geoffrey's Merlin, once the striking story of his arrival is over, does little except prophesy. His mother, it is said in the 'History', was the daughter of the King of Demetia who had become a nun; and it is as King of Demetia that Merlin reappears in the 'Life', before going mad. His father (in spite of the fact that it was an essential part of his nature, for Vortigern's purpose, that he did not have one) was said by his mother to be an incubus, who came to visit her in the nunnery in the form, conveniently, of a handsome young man. Merlin's conception, like that of so many other heroes, had been supernatural, and his mother, like the mothers of other heroes, was supposed to be a virgin.

Two major events, in Geoffrey's narrative, distinguish Merlin's career after the prophecies. Aurelius Ambrosius is king of Britain at the time – an ironic confusion with one of the prototypes of Merlin himself,

Ambrosius, or Emrys – and after defeating and executing Hengist, the Saxon leader who had deceitfully tricked Vortigern, he set about restoring the kingdom which the Saxons had damaged. He wishes to erect a memorial on Salisbury Plain over the spot where the Britons had been slaughtered by Hengist's treachery on the occasion of the 'Night of the Long Knives'. Merlin is consulted as to the form the memorial should take, and he at once settles on the 'Giants' Ring', in Ireland. The stones are so enormous, he said, that if they were placed in a ring around the site they would stand for ever. But no man of this period, he went on, without the use of special skill, could erect them; they were so big that there was no-one strong enough to move them.

We have seen in an earlier chapter that Geoffrey seems to have made contact with an enormously ancient tradition, in suggesting that the stones of Stonehenge came from some other place and were originally part of some even more ancient monument. It is because of such references that his work must be taken seriously, rather than dismissed as the product of a strong imagination influenced by the conventions of the medieval church. Some of the stones of Stonehenge did indeed come from elsewhere – not, it is thought, from Ireland, but from the Preseli Hills in South Wales – and the only comprehensible reason for this removal is that they already formed a monument of special sacredness. 'These stones', says Merlin, 'are connected with certain secret religious rites.' The Giants, he says, brought them from Africa, and set them up in Ireland.

To obtain them, it is first necessary to make war against the Irish, which was successfully done. The men then tried every way they could think of to move the Ring, but in the end it took Merlin's special art to get the stones down. They were shipped to Britain and duly erected on Salisbury Plain. And of course they are still there.

Ambrosius dies shortly afterwards, and is succeeded, in Geoffrey's story, by his brother, Uther Pendragon. There then follows Merlin's second major act, the achievement of the adultery of Uther with the wife of the duke of Cornwall, and the consequent conception of Arthur. But this too, like much of this part of the story, we have come across before, since it took place at Tintagel.

The story as purveyed by Geoffrey was taken up and exported, in 1155, by Wace. It was through the use made of Wace's French verse rendering of the 'Matter of Britain' that Merlin, along with several other British characters, emerged as a central theme in medieval French literature. He entered that corpus slightly after the time of the first works of Chrétien de Troyes, and appears in his full form in the early-thirteenth-century group of texts known as the Vulgate Cycle. This series of long prose stories formed Malory's main source, and the second of them in sequence, 'L'Estoire de Merlin', which was based on a poem by Robert de Boron, enlarges and highlights the features derived from Geoffrey, and propels Merlin as an important character and an intriguing idea into our own culture.

fif com li contei uof
aul fen   a ufqua
de rome 7 orf gita for

14 Prophet of Britain

Merlin opened his prophecies with the story of the dragons, explaining to the king at the edge of the pool on the summit of Dinas Emrys the meaning of the fight between those red and white monsters; and then, in Geoffrey of Monmouth's version, he proceeded to issue numerous further prophecies.

It is easy to foretell history in retrospect, and probably rather easier if one does so in code, so that any meaning can be read into it. Geoffrey's 'Prophecies of Merlin', which he says were translated from a book in the 'British tongue', were intended as a separate work, and were published as such a few years before the completion of the 'History'. Their popularity no doubt encouraged him to include them in his new work. What people liked about them, it seems, was the scope they gave for interpretation. It became a sort of literary game.

'The Lion's cubs shall be transformed into salt water fishes and the Eagle of Mount Aravia shall nest upon its summit. . . . Next after the Boar shall come the Ram of the Castle of Venus, with golden horns and a beard of silver. . . . The Ass of Wickedness will come next, swift against the gold-smiths, but slow against the wolves' ravenous appetite.' And so on. In spite of the cryptic religiosity conveyed by the use of quasi-astrological language, one suspects mainly dynastic and heraldic references.

Overtly it is British history that is being summarized, and it has not been difficult to relate events to many of the these animal metaphors – events rather closer to Geoffrey's time than to Merlin's. 'A Lion of Justice will make the towers of Gaul shake and the island's dragons tremble': Henry I's strong-armed policies; 'Wild animals shall enjoy peace, but men will bemoan their punishments': Henry's avid protection of his game, and ruthless treatment of crime; 'The measure of trade shall be divided': Henry's meddling with the currency. It seems that what Merlin was doing was telling people what they already knew. King Lear's Fool comments on this idea of writing prophecy after the event with a multiple joke which is, even by Shakespeare's standards, of miraculous density: 'This prophecy shall Merlin make; for I live before his time.'

Although one cannot help being cynical about the prognostic element of these pages of opaque ramblings, the crypticism itself occasionally seems to put the material on a different level. The style of metaphor is curiously reminiscent of Taliesin's prophetic riddles, as Geoffrey prob-

Merlin disguised as a stag – a possible link with Cernunnos

ably well knew. And the animal images remind one too of oriental formulas, such as the Tantras of Mahayana Buddhism, where things of cosmic significance are said in terms of vipers, tortoises, and dogs. All these are intended to be baffling to the uninitiated, to require the effort of interpretation, as indeed were the prophecies issued by the Delphic priestess – as, presumably, prophecy always needs to be.

It is not, however, in this role that he seems to have inherited from Taliesin that Merlin figures prominently in the works of Geoffrey's successors. In Wace and Layamon he is rather more the Gwydion-figure, the shape-changer, the wizard always ready to provide his favoured protégés with suitable disguises. And he entered medieval French literature (from which he came back to Malory, and to us) as a sort of supervising mentor who, by supernatural powers, both knows the future and is able to change the present.

As was mentioned at the end of the last chapter, the figure of Merlin reached its peak of development in that long series of early-thirteenth-century works of unknown authorship generally known as the Vulgate Cycle. This includes the grail quest and the story of Lancelot, and ends with the death of Arthur. The second part, 'L'Estoire de Merlin', thought to have been an addition to an original Lancelot-based cycle, is itself derived from a poem, of which we have only a fragment, written by Robert de Boron in about 1190. De Boron was thus a contemporary of Chrétien's, and since Chrétien did not concern himself with Merlin it is to him that we owe Merlin's survival.

In this story, as in Geoffrey's, Merlin is supernaturally conceived. But now the reason becomes more explicit. He is sired by a devil on a maiden, as part of a plot devised in Hell to bring into the world an Antichrist. This powerful idea inevitably adds another dimension to the person of Merlin, and when he early reveals his supernatural knowledge it is his father's inheritance which he displays. Moreover the story adds that it was as a result of his descent from a devil that he was born covered in hair, an inheritance which we can see is owed rather to his distant origins as a wild man of the woods.

Much of the story is as we have seen it – the Vortigern episode, the setting up of the Round Table, the conception and rearing of Arthur – but the presence of the Devil in the background cannot be quite forgotten. Merlin does not, in Robert's story and its 'Vulgate' development, fulfil the Satanic plot by acting as Antichrist; he inherited too his mother's goodness, and turns the Devil's powers against him. But what has been introduced, or rediscovered, is the strong non-Christian element in all this wizardry.

We feel a little of this remaining in the otherwise tamed world of Malory. We have already seen Merlin displaying the role of Gwydion in connection with Arthur's origins; in the youthful adventures too he appears and vanishes at moments of crisis with pantomimic convenience. He warns Arthur against marrying Guenever, but, as if his human part is beginning by then to take over, resigns himself to the marriage as inevitable. And like any other mortal he himself then falls helplessly, and tragically, in love.

This is an element of the Merlin story which we have not so far encountered: but it is one which we might have anticipated, since in the original roots of the character there is a madness theme, and in Malory and his immediate sources madness is caused, again and again, by love. The theme seems to have crept back in through the work of someone who added a continuation to the prose work based on de Boron's poem. It was one of the 'maidens of the lake' whom he loved, evidently a water-nymph of sorts, whose name, in the French source, is Viviane. Malory (or Caxton?) called her 'Nimue', which seems to be an example of somebody's failure to read somebody else's writing. Vivien, as she is later known, is the arch enticer. She does not want Merlin's love, but she gains his knowledge. And the means she uses takes us back once again to our roots.

He is besotted with her, a predicament which she coolly puts to her own use. He tells Arthur, foreseeing as ever the future, that his own time is almost over. 'Also he told King Arthur that he should miss him.' But, said the king, since you know of your fate, why not use your crafts to avoid it? 'Nay, said Merlin, it will not be so.'

Merlin hangs about Vivien, Malory tells us, wanting 'to have her maidenhood'. Yet even that seems to be no excuse for what she does. Having learnt from him his magic arts, she makes him swear not to use them against her. While walking in Cornwall he shows her a wonder: it is (in Malory) a hollow under a great stone – in the French source an enchanted tower in a forest. He is persuaded to enter it, and using his crafts to overpower him she imprisons him there. For ever. We are aware that there is less magic and wizardry in the world from that moment on. Arthur is on his own now, having to fight his mortal battles without the benefit of spells.

The enchanted tower in the forest seems to be related to that in which Rhiannon and Pryderi were imprisoned; the 'rock under a great stone, wrought by enchantement', is inevitably reminiscent of one of the great megalithic cromlechs – their use, perhaps, guessed at or remembered by the story. But most of all it is the enticement, and betrayal, which takes us back, since Vivien's prizing out of Merlin the secret by which he could be destroyed is the same means as that used by Blodeuedd in her removal of Lleu Llaw Gyffes, and both are reminiscent of the trick played on Samson by Delilah.

Merlin ends, then, as he began, alone in the wilderness. There is something primitively ritualistic about this aspect of Merlin which does not fit comfortably into the Arthurian stories. Geoffrey of Monmouth, in the 'Vita Merlini', portrays him, as the early legend had done, living alone in the forest, and observing the stars in order to foretell the future. But this – as Emma Jung and Marie-Louise von Franz point out in their book *The Grail Legend* – is exactly what the classical authors had said that the Druids did: lived in oak woods, and practised astrology. An interest-

Above left: An alchemical representation of the ventricular system with Mercury between two swordsmen
Above right: The 'Senex Mercurius' (Merlin) appears as mediator between a king and his son

ing comparison is made in the same book between the role played by Merlin in medieval myth and that played in the alchemical philosophy of the Middle Ages and Renaissance by the god Mercury, or 'Mercurius'. Carl Jung makes much, in his book *Psychology and Alchemy,* of the function of Mercury as a psychological equivalent of the spirit of revelation. We have seen that Merlin's forerunner in British myth, the magician Gwydion, possessed, as inspirer, trickster, shape-shifter, guide, and mentor, many plainly Mercurial qualities. Several of the other parallels we drew in chapter two apply to Merlin as well as to Gwydion.

It may be going too far to suggest a Woden or Odin connection, though some have done this through the comparison of the 'wild man of the woods' with Odin in his role both as tree-god and as leader of the Wild Hunt. But Merlin has also (as Frau Jung and Dr von Franz point out), in at least two stories, a definite connection with stags. In one he rides on a stag, in the other he actually appears as one. His Irish counterpart Suibne, reinforcing this link, is associated with stags as well. And Carl Jung gives examples of the Mercury of alchemy being known as the 'fugitive stag'. Hence Merlin, like Gwydion, may not be unconnected to the horned stag-god Cernunnos, who has at least this syllogistic tie both to Woden and to the Romano-Gaulish Mercury. Caesar said that Mercury was the god the Celts respected most, and if the Merlin figure constantly recurs in our myths it might be the result of the same forces of interest, the same imaginative affinity which generated that respect.

THE GRAIL

If anyone asks me why errant knights did not go straight to Corbenic when they knew that the Holy Grail was there, I would answer him as the ancient history testifies. The castle of Corbenic surely does not move, but Tanaburs, an enchanter who lived before Uther Pendragon, and who was the wisest man in necromancy except Merlin only, so bewitched the castle that no stranger knight who sought it would find it unless chance led him.

'The Prose Tristan', 13th century.

5 Mystic vessel

In the museum at Glastonbury there is a small bronze bowl. It is an attractive and delicate object, neatly decorated with a circle of studs, the single file of which is punctuated by clusters of three. Its fine quality at once suggests that its significance is not only at the practical, domestic level: that the Iron Age 'lake villagers' to whom it belonged had some special use for it. Its good condition shows that it was not much used, perhaps even that it was disposed of almost new. Votive offerings have been found elsewhere, and that the Celts threw things into lakes for sacrificial reasons is indicated by a large collection of artefacts found in a lake in Anglesey in 1943.

Bowls, cauldrons, and vessels of such kinds haunt both mythology and archaeology. As well as the Glastonbury bowl, in the National Museum in Copenhagen there is a similar but much more impressive instance of such an object. This famous cauldron was found (again well-preserved in a peat bog) at Gundestrup, in the area of northern Denmark called Himmerland, towards the end of the last century. It had been dismantled and placed in the marsh, and was in remarkably good condition. Thought to date from the first century BC, the Gundestrup bowl clearly proclaims its non-secular quality, since it portrays what are recognizably deities (including, as we have seen, the antlered god 'Cernunnos') on the outside, and what are evidently mythological scenes on the inside. Although we cannot identify these figures precisely, they bear affinities, in style and detail, with other Celtic iconography, and the spirit in which they are presented – with a clearly non-factual quality and yet with a stark reality about the beings and scenes – finds a close counterpart in the mythology.

One of the earliest examples of the special importance attributed to a cauldron in British myth occurs in a poem of probably pre-Norman date in the collection known as the 'Book of Taliesin', and therefore ostensibly by that sixth-century poet. It is called 'The Spoils of Annwfn', and Annwfn, or Annwn, was, as we saw in an early chapter, one of the names for the otherworld of the Celts, the world existing beside or behind this material one. A number of different names are given for this place, and it is in this poem that we find the term 'Caer Wydr', Castle of Glass.

In the poem Arthur and his followers go to Annwn in order to carry off the magic otherworld cauldron. Other old friends, such as Pwyll and

The portico of a third- or fourth-century BC Celtic temple from Roguertuse in France. The niches are for human skulls, one of which can be seen

The Gundestrup bowl with what may be a scene of reincarnation or rejuvenation on the inside. A figure can be seen plunging a warrior into a receptacle

Pryderi, whom we have met as visitors to otherworlds before, are mentioned as perhaps going there too. Significantly they went by sea: Annwn, it seems, was across water. The expedition was an almost total failure; we are not told whether or not they got the cauldron, but only seven of them, out of three shiploads, returned. Arthur and the poet (who speaks as if present on that occasion) were among them.

The cauldron in the poem had the property that it would not boil the food of a coward. Both this special connection with food and this selectivity are important factors in the development of the idea of the mystic vessel.

Otherworld journeys, and otherworld talismans which heroes attempt to remove, are not exclusively concerned with magic cauldrons. Arthur, on one other occasion, goes cauldron-hunting, when in the story 'Culhwch and Olwen' he is obliged to obtain the cauldron of Diwrnach the Irishman, to boil the food for Culhwch's wedding. Since the circumstances of the raid are similar to those in the poem (though in this case Arthur carries away his trophy) we guess that it is the same expedition told of in a different form, Ireland here acting as Annwn; and elsewhere we find that the cauldron of 'Tyrnoc the Giant' had the same selective ability to distinguish cowards.

There was, in fact, a traditional list of 'Royal Treasures of Britain', of which the selective cauldron was one. The list occurs in clearest form in a fifteenth-century manuscript, and includes such things as a sword which cannot safely be drawn except by the owner, a basket which provides food for unexpectedly large numbers, a drinking horn belonging to someone called 'Bran Galed' which pours whatever drink the recipient desires, and a dish which achieves the same result. We shall come across many of these attributes again, since the functions of the various wonderful vessels and talismans gradually attached themselves to the single summarizing symbol of the Grail.

Throughout Celtic mythology several related themes occur: vessels provide unlimited food, such as the wonderful cauldron of the Dagda, a god of Ireland; or they serve different provender to different people, as Cormac's cauldron at Tara which served food appropriate to each person's rank. Some vessels are, like those mentioned above, most concerned with distinguishing cowards from brave men. The Irish sea-god Manannan possessed a cup which could reveal the telling of a lie. In the presence of a liar it broke into three pieces, and could only be restored by the pronouncement of three truths.

No less common is the theme of a journey of search. Perhaps the distant model for Arthur's expedition in the poem and the story is again Irish: the trip made by Conn to the castle of the god Lugh, the 'hidden house' which appears (as the castle of Gwyn ap Nudd did on top of Glastonbury Tor, in the tale of St Collen) only when the deity himself decides it will. There Conn is served, at Lugh's instruction, with wine out of a golden bowl by a maiden, who, Lugh says, represents the sovereignty of Ireland. The theme of sovereignty in the British stories is complicated and obscure, but certainly the maiden occurs again and again in relation to the Grail.

Vessels, a quest, a visit to an otherworld castle. These seem familiar, and indeed in chapter three we had the story of Pryderi and his mother Rhiannon who became trapped in a castle which had suddenly appeared in a land which had strangely become desolate, their hands fixed to a mysterious golden bowl. They lost the power of speech, disappeared with the castle and the bowl into another dimension, and eventually re-emerged, with the breaking of the spell, bringing with them the renewal of life in the waste land.

The search for the Grail, however, by no means ends there. Predictably, several different tributaries converge in this current, as in so many of the thematic streams of myth. The bowl in the otherworld castle, clasped by Pryderi and Rhiannon, is one; the Dagda's cauldron of plenty is another. Yet another is Ceridwen's cauldron, which appeared in the story of the origins of Taliesin, who in his former incarnation was set by the witch Ceridwen to stir the cauldron of knowledge, or inspiration, from which he learnt by accident all things past and future. Ceridwen is the prototype of the muse-goddess, the one who inspires the poets and prophets of later ages. It is those fatal drops from her cauldron which lie behind the ravings of the Taliesin of early literature, and hence, through his colleague the prophet Myrddin, indirectly behind Merlin's pronouncements too. And Ceridwen's cauldron has survived in the stereotyped image of the witch throughout the ages, those cauldron-stirring, prophesying, spell-binding old hags. They are seen as evil now, dominated by their horned god, himself perhaps exiled into this outlawry from our established religion.

There is yet another ingredient in the idea of the Grail, perhaps the most important of all, but before we can reach that point there is the journey of Peredur to the Castle of Wonders to be made.

In that group of stories of the twelfth century which occur both in the works of Chrétien de Troyes and (in later form) in the Welsh collections, there is one which Chrétien called 'Perceval, ou li contes del graal', of which the Welsh version, 'Peredur son of Efrawg', seems to represent a more primitive form. As has been said above it is likely that both sets of stories ultimately stem from a common lost original. The interesting

Perceval receives a sword from the Fisher King while the Grail is carried to table

point is that in the 'contes del graal' Chrétien shows an awareness of the Grail as an idea; indeed he mentions it for the first time in extant literature. In the Welsh story, however, there are only mysterious vessels and ritualistic situations, which seem rather to be a part of a whole world of such things than a single important example. Through Chrétien the Grail became a single object. In 'Peredur' (though in the form in which we have it this is later than Chrétien's work) we can see something of the context from which it came.

Both stories concern the adventures of an inexperienced youth who sets out from his remote home to become one of Arthur's knights. He received advice and training at Arthur's court, then went off on his own adventures. In the course of his travels he came to a river (or a lake), where he found a man fishing. The fisherman turns out to be the owner of a fine castle near the water, to which he takes the hero. In both stories the rich fisher is lame, and in the Welsh one he identifies himself as Peredur's uncle, his mother's brother. There is then some confusion and repetition, in which it appears that there are several castles and uncles involved; but putting the two versions together and shaking them out a little, it appears that Perceval/Peredur is invited to sit and eat, and while the castle's owner talks to him a number of strange things take place.

First a spear or lance is carried through the hall, blood running from its point. The youth, though puzzled, remains silent, as he had earlier been told by an instructor that he should. Then a maiden enters carrying (in the Welsh version) a great salver with a man's head on it, or (in Chrétien) a golden 'graal'. This was an unusual word even at the time, and has been generally misunderstood from the start. But it is clear that it meant a broad and capacious dish, the same type of vessel as the 'great salver' in the Welsh story, which bore a man's head. Chrétien clearly implies that it was the sort of container that might have held a salmon.

The appearance of the dish and its contents is greeted with lamentation in 'Peredur'. In both stories, however, it is noted that the youth did not ask any questions about what he saw. This silence is of importance, since the appropriate question, he is later told, would have cured the lame king of his disability.

In Chrétien's poem when Perceval wakes the castle is deserted. In both tellings the hero then undergoes various other adventures before returning to Arthur's court; these involve the familiar 'worm', or dragon, guarding a magic stone, and a one-eyed giant. Manifesting their common heritage both the tales include a powerful and unusual image which is drawn, ultimately, from an Irish story. Peredur/Perceval has spent the night in a hermit's cell, and during the night it snows. In the morning he finds that a wild bird had been killed by a hawk outside the door, leaving a splash of blood on the white snow. The contrast of the colours reminds him of the red cheeks and white skin of a woman with whom he has recently fallen in love, and he sinks into a reverie, from which he cannot be roused even by Athur's knights, his companions, who see him there while passing. Again and again in the narrative such intriguing images and their ramifying associations threaten to lead us off the trail.

Travelling then through a wilderness, in which he meets no-one, and sees no sign of dwelling, he gets back at last to his destination, the court at Caerleon. While they are feasting there a visitor arrives, a woman of great ugliness riding on a mule. Her message is for Perceval, she says, and she proceeds to scold him. When in the castle of the Fisher King, or the Lame King, he possessed, but neglected, the opportunity to cure the king of his lameness and restore to his land the fertility which it will now continue to lack. We have come across such a confrontation before, when a maiden arrived unexpectedly in Arthur's court to confront Owein, who had deserted his wife. Comparison, again, with Irish examples, shows that the beautiful damsel bearing the Grail, a counterpart of Lugh's cup-bearer, and the ugly maiden on the mule, are two aspects of the personification of sovereignty, since the 'Sovereignty of Ireland' several times takes this double form. Perhaps, then, there is a subdued theme involved in this episode, by which the Grail-hero, Perceval/Peredur, was destined to become king.

The Fisher King, we are told, has been wounded through the thighs, and it is made clear by later stories that this means that he is impotent. There is plenty of evidence that the potency of the ruler was believed by many early societies to be magically related to the fertility of his land. And Jung gives instances in *Psychology and Alchemy* where the image of the 'sick king' seems to have a psychological meaning as well: that a state of stagnation has come about through a failure of the consciousness to relate to the unconscious. 'When we are told that the King is exanimis, inanimate, or that his land is unfruitful, it is equivalent to saying that the hidden state is one of latency and potentiality. . . . The conscious mind should respond to his call. . . . A modern psychologist would therefore have advised the king to remember the existence of his unconscious and so put an end to his stagnation.' The process of re-integration is required, he says, before the sterility can be overcome, a process symbolized by the king recovering from his impotence and the land getting back its fertility. Certainly it is puzzling that Perceval's fault was his failure to ask a question. The question he should have asked, according to the ugly maiden, was 'Who is it who is served with the Grail?', or, in 'Peredur', to the effect of 'What is the meaning and the cause of these marvels?' In other words he needed to make the king reveal what it was that was hidden. The matter is so obscure that a psychological explanation seems the most credible. The subconscious, after all, does not display the characteristics of rationality.

In apparent confirmation of such an approach, moreover, it is explained to Perceval by a hermit (whom Chrétien in turn specifies as his uncle, his mother's brother) that the cause of his inability to ask the all-important question was that he unfeelingly left his mother, who has since died of grief. The hermit-uncle then reveals what he would have discovered had he asked: the Grail sustains the father of the Fisher King, to whom it bears a single Mass wafer; and this has sufficed to keep him alive for fifteen years.

Both versions, again indicating their common origin, break off the story of Perceval to deal with a similar set of adventures undertaken by Gawain. These are developed to such an extent that it seems as if there is a genuine ambiguity, at this stage, as to who the Grail hero is. This ambiguity arises again later, since Perceval (or, as he becomes, Parzival) is himself replaced by Galahad as the Grail-achiever. There is some possibility that the name Galahad is partly derived from that of Gawain. Peredur, in his turn – and 'Perceval', it is thought, is simply an attempt to render 'Peredur' into French – is perhaps etymologically descended from Pryderi, with whom, as we have seen, he has one or two things in common.

Though the duplication of the elements of the Grail search indicates that the same story has become attached to different characters, the changes of name do relate to a change in the figure of the Grail seeker himself. There is a steady progression which seems to run from the rather worldly figure of Gawain (which is how he is consistently portrayed) through the innocent and pure, yet fallible, character of Perceval, towards the idealized perfection of Galahad. Gawain, present at the beginning, remains present at the end, and forms something of a contrast, with his clumsy humanity, to Galahad's purity. This continuous progression is towards greater spirituality, a move away from humanity and materialism towards idealism and asceticism.

After the ugly maiden's denunciation Perceval is determined to get back to the 'Castle of Wonders'. The matter is left, in these early versions, uncompleted and unexplained. What took place in the Castle was of the nature of a mystery, and like such mysteries elsewhere it was apparently susceptible to explanation only under certain conditions. One cannot but be reminded of the Orphic and Mithraic cults, or particularly perhaps of those at Eleusis, where the cult of Demeter was celebrated, which also involved the myth of a land becoming waste, infertile, and eventually recovering. The nature of the rites there remained essentially secret, but it is known that they involved the revealing of certain symbolic objects and some sort of verbal formula. The words which the 'Hierophant' spoke, at Eleusis, were the real key to initiation. The occasion was accompanied (as is the Grail's appearance in Chrétien and in later versions) by a dazzling light. And it seems likely, from what slight reports we have, that the business of initiation was concerned with death and rebirth, or with survival after death.

In one of the episodes in Peredur's long journey there occurs an incident which seems even stranger and more mystical than the rest. He comes to a court full of women, whose business, it quickly becomes apparent, is restoring life to dead warriors. The healer-goddess, Morgain le Faye, and her band of enchantresses, whose home was the island of Avalon, were presumably engaged in the same sort of pursuit. Here we are told how it is done. The women take the corpse of the warrior from his horse, place it in a tub full of warm water, and add to the water a precious ointment. The man then gets out of the tub alive.

Nothing more is said of this process, but it leads us, as do several of the items in 'Peredur' and Chrétien's 'conte', to another story, in which we find a partial explanation for a great deal of this mysterious material. This is the Mabinogion tale of 'Branwen, daughter of Llŷr', which in particular concerns her brother Bran. Both Llŷr and Bran we have come across before, and evidently they were deities of some antiquity and importance in pre-Roman Britain.

The story, which takes place in North Wales and Ireland, concerns the marriage of Branwen to the king of Ireland. Bran, king of the Island of Britain, is sitting with his brother Manawydan on the rock of Harlech, looking over the sea. The ships of the king of Ireland come towards them, and on enquiring they discover his mission. He has come to ask for the hand of Bran's sister. A marriage is arranged to take place at the court of Aberffraw, in Anglesey (in historical times one of the seats of the kings of Gwynedd). Some trouble ensues, and it becomes necessary to placate the Irish king. For this purpose Bran decides to present him with the most precious thing he has, which is a cauldron with a magic property of some worth. It will restore the dead to life.

Branwen's is not a happy story, and trouble continues between the two kingdoms, in spite of the gift of the cauldron. Humiliated by her husband, she sends a message secretly to Bran, training a starling for the purpose, since all communication between Britain and Ireland is by then cut off. The starling found him at 'Caer Seint in Arfon', in other words at Segontium, now Caernarfon; and Bran accordingly gathers his men and sets off for Ireland. In those days, we are told, the channel was not so wide – no doubt a reference to the inundations of the kingdoms of Llys Helig and Cantref Gwaelod – and he himself, evidently of gigantic size, went across by wading. He was too big, the tale adds, to be contained in a ship.

After some parleying and some trickery, a battle ensues. The Irish make good use of their secret weapon. All the dead warriors are put each night to boil in the cauldron of rebirth, and in the morning they are back on the job.

The idea is, as one would expect, not new. Something of the sort seems to be indicated by the Greek story of Medea, another enchantress who possessed a cauldron, who promised the daughters of Peleus renewed youth for their father, and with that ostensible aim got them to cook him. In her case it was a means of murder; her cauldron worked well enough – she demonstrated on a ram – but when it came to the cooking of Peleus Medea omitted to utter the necessary spell. But in Irish myth a much clearer comparison is available, since at the battle of Mag Tuireadh the side led by Lugh possessed the secret of a magic well, over which spells were sung by their magicians, and into which herbs were cast. When their dead were put into the well they emerged again alive, and even fitter than before.

Is there perhaps a reference to a real hope for renewal of life? If so, is the vessel in which the dead are rejuvenated remotely related to the hollow dish-like troughs in which they were placed in the chambers of the burial mounds – one may be seen still in place at New Grange – or to those urns in which the succeeding age, the Bronze Age, placed the cremated remains of their dead, buried in their cysts or round barrows? A scene which appears to be related to these episodes of immersion in a vessel and consequent restoration appears on the Gundestrup cauldron itself, and so may well represent a mythological fable or a belief. A figure who (by his relative size) is evidently a god is plunging a warrior head down into a large receptacle, while a line of other warriors, on foot, apparently await their turn, and, moving away from him again, a line of mounted warriors seems to represent the result. Near the god and the large bowl, greeting the approaching figures (whom we might guess to be those who have died in battle) is a dog, an emblem found both at the shrine of the healer-god Nodens at Lydney and at that of his Greek counterpart Asclepius at Epidauros.

Bran's gift of the cauldron of rebirth works, in the story of 'Branwen', to his own destruction. He is wounded in the foot by a poisoned spear, and, dying, commands that his head should be cut off and taken to 'the White Mount' in London. There it must be buried with its face towards France; and we learn later that the effect of this will be that as long as it remains buried no harm will come to the country from across the sea.

The seven survivors of the battle set out. They cannot be unrelated to the seven who came back from the looting expedition to Annwn, and among them we find not only Manawydan, Bran's brother, but Pryderi and Taliesin, both in their way returners from death. The head they bear with them acts as a rejuvenating, or suspending, spell itself; and they stop and feast in Harlech for seven years without noticing that time is passing. But that is nothing. A little later in the journey they stop on the island of Grassholm for eighty years, forgetting all that they had suffered, and feasting in the company of the head.

Opposite: The ruins of Glastonbury Abbey
Overleaf: The grail legend has exercised considerable fascination over many generations. In this fifteenth-century French manuscript (below) the grail is being carried into a hall. The William Morris tapestry from a Burne-Jones painting (above) shows three knights reaching their quest's end

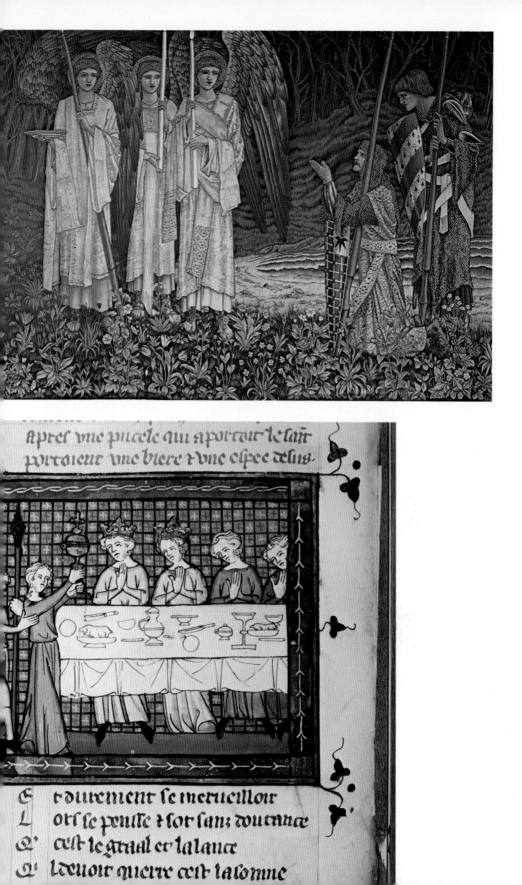

Apres vne pucele qui aportoit le saint
portoient vne biere ⁊ vne espee delus.

Et durement se merueilloit
Lors se pense ⁊ sor sanz doutance
Que cest le graal et lalance
Que deuoit querre cest la somme

Opposite: Dinas Bran, a possible site of Grail Castle
Above: A Celtic pillar decorated with human skulls

Poor Branwen had set out with them, but had not got far. Both Ireland and Britain have been laid waste by the war, and she feels the blame of it. When they land in Anglesey, near the mouth of the river Alaw, she looks back to Ireland, and with the sadness of it all her heart breaks. 'And a four-sided grave was made, and they buried her on the bank of the Alaw.' The spot had for some time been known as 'Branwen's island' by the time, in 1813, when a tumulus was found there containing an urn with the cremated remains of a simple Bronze Age burial. And indeed that low-lying west coast of Anglesey does look towards Ireland, and sometimes just after the sun has set one can see the Wicklow Hills beyond the hump of Holyhead from the tops of rises near the Alaw. The river meanders now, small and dirty, through an unremarkable countryside, and little of the burial mound is visible.

The head and its companions, in the timeless progress of the story, make their way to London. They duly bury the head on the White Mount, where it served its defensive purpose for some time. It reappears again in one of the Triads, where it is said that the digging up again of this prophylactic talisman was one of Britain's three unhappy disclosures – another was the digging up of the dragons in the Vortigern episode, which also permitted an invasion.

Ironically it was Arthur who dug up the head of Bran. The reason which the Triad gives for this rash behaviour, which, it says, led to the successful invasion of Britain, was that Arthur was too proud to consider that the island should be safeguarded by anything except his own might.

The business of the head has caused considerable discussion; R. S. Loomis thinks it is an error arising from the ambiguity (which exists in Welsh as well as in English) of the word for 'head' also meaning 'leader'. But there is no doubt, from archaeological finds, in particular the countless stone heads which are so characteristic of Celtic sculpture, that the early Celts were a head-reverencing people. At one stage they were said by the Romans to be head-hunters, keeping as trophies the heads of their enemies. And a rack in which human skulls were kept, from the third or fourth century BC, was found at a Celtic temple in Provence. Even in later times the custom of putting a head on a wall or building as a sort of protective device survived, and the sight of a stone head in an unexpected place is a sure sign of the survival of Celtic influence.

The 'White Hill' of the story is normally taken to be Tower Hill, the hill of the 'White Tower'. And some substantiation of this identification is provided, whether intentionally or by the strange process of survival which tradition shows, by the fact that Bran's cult still seems to be maintained there. The name 'Bran' means 'crow' or 'raven', and the raven is therefore the god's representative. It is said of the ravens which are kept by old custom in the area of the White Tower that their presence ensures (like Gibraltar's apes) that the country will be safe from invasion.

Bran's connection with the Grail might seem, on the evidence so far, a little tenuous. But one of the early Grail stories, a version known as the 'Didot' Perceval from its manuscript's provenance, names the Fisher King as Bron. This, as we shall see, is the naming then followed by others. And Bran has other connections with the Grail-keeper as well as this coincidence. There is some suggestion, in 'Branwen', that Bran was a river-god, or perhaps a god of river crossings, and the Fisher King is encountered by the hero when he reaches a river which he wishes to cross. Bran, like the Fisher King, was wounded by a spear, and the land, we are told, became an uninhabited wilderness after his wounding. He had, like the Grail-owner, the power of feasting his supporters indefinitely. And he owned a wonderful vessel.

If the connection is agreed – and it has been very powerfully argued by Loomis – then a great deal falls into place. Among other things it becomes apparent that 'Branwen' is in some measure an explanation of the mysteries of 'Peredur'. A spear with blood on the tip is carried ahead of a severed head on a platter. If the all-important question is 'Who is the person to whom these things refer?' then the answer is clearly 'Bran'. We have seen in earlier chapters that Bran, later Brennus, was a major Celtic god. Possibly some elements of the Grail theme are derived from the cult connected with him.

The Grail-searcher, in the stories, comes to a river, finds a man fishing, and is invited to a castle. Such a castle occurs also in an apparently unrelated story, part of a set of tales about a Norman outlaw (in many ways a relative of Robin Hood) called Fulk Fitz Warine. A mid-thirteenth-century French romance tells of his visit to a Castle of Wonders, where things took place which no-one returned to tell of, except a lone survivor. It names the castle as 'Chastiel Bran', and since the story is set on the Welsh Marches we are left in no doubt that the castle referred to is the one on a hill above Llangollen which is still known as 'Dinas Bran', Bran's stronghold.

The name of Grail Castle in almost all the most important sources is given as 'Corbenic'. This has been variously explained, for instance as coming from the roots 'cor' and 'benoit', meaning perhaps 'holy vessel', or 'holy horn', from the legendary drinking horn (again the possession of someone called Bran) which was one of the 'Treasures of Britain'. But in one instance there occurs another, and unexplained, version of this name. When Malory mentions it first, at the start of the Grail sequence, he calls it 'Corbin'. 'And so he departed, and rode till he came to the castle of

Corbin.' For several chapters before the start of the search, he names consistently as 'Corbin' the castle where the Grail was kept. The anomaly can be explained: Malory was translating in these passages from a version of the French 'Prose Lancelot', and as one would expect, the otherwise unexplained word 'Corbin' is an old French word, meaning crow or raven. Thus we are back to Dinas Bran.

These ruins on the hill above the river Dee at Llangollen more than amply suit the descriptions in the early Grail stories. Peredur and Perceval came to a river, with a castle above it; the man who owned it was fishing, and there are few better rivers in which to do that than the Dee. 'One might search,' says Chrétien, 'as far as Beirut, without finding a castle so noble or so well situated.'

Dinas Bran has about it an air of emotive suggestion, very much in the way that Glastonbury Tor stands out as a physical manifestation of undefined significance. One cannot avoid the feeling of wonder when one sees it, just as one reacts with both surprise and recognition at every sight of Glastonbury Tor. Some almost overt message is conveyed by the crumbling crags of Dinas Bran's walls, in that superbly dominant position on its high, round hill. The view from it over the valley and towards the surrounding uplands also carries an otherworld aura and even the history of the place contains the right sort of elusiveness, since it has been a ruin since about 1282. It was evidently built around 1270, on the probable site of an older fortified town. When the story of 'Fouke Fitz Warin' was written it had already, we are told, been set on fire and destroyed.

Insulated from the world by its height and dominance, and well protected by a massive system of ditches and ramparts, the ruined castle stands absorbed in its own air of antiquity just as it has done since the thirteenth century. Part of the wall of the Great Hall still stands, with two tall windows looking out over the Dee, and best-preserved is the passageway which originally formed the entrance. The base of a tower is identifiable mid-way down the southern wall. The size and ambition of style are still apparent. Nobody could ever have failed to be impressed.

This contact with Bran, then, through the name and the 'Fulk' statement that this was a castle of wonders, merges with his possession of both a magic, resurrecting vessel and a wish-fulfilling drinking horn, and with the various links, through 'Branwen' and 'Peredur', with Chrétien's 'contes del graal', to give us some insight into the sources of the Grail themes. Vessels of plenty, such as the Dagda's, and vessels of knowledge like Ceridwen's cauldron, contribute their share of elements, but it is perhaps Bran's cauldron of rebirth that lies at the root of the main stream of the mystic vessel's development. Grail Castle, in principle, cannot be found. In its origins it is the Celtic otherworld, and in its later development it is a mystical, spiritual experience and therefore located within oneself. But if it had a physical representative, then it must be Dinas Bran that has the most convincing claim to it.

The Holy Grail appearing in a vision before Arthur and his knights

16 Holy chalice

A myth has a long, slow build-up, and it cannot be explained on one level or by one analogy. Like an evolving species and like a rock structure it contains both a surface form and underlying, buried features which are not in its manifest form its own, but rather belong to its predecessors in the causal chain. The geology of a myth might reveal strata which do not show on the surface, but which form supporting layers explaining the outer shape and structure. On the other hand in unexpected outcrops some of the deep structure may almost be visible under the smooth exterior. And manifest features which seem like obsolete evolutionary residues do obtrude anomalously through the otherwise comprehensible form of myth's geomorphology.

Anyone brought up on the Tennysonian concept of the Grail, its communion-chalice form, might have wondered how a giant cauldron, let alone a dish, could possibly have developed into such a concept, and in this chapter we shall consider how the end product developed out of these remote beginnings.

We saw before how a Welsh and a French version of what became the Grail story came into existence in the twelfth and thirteenth centuries. The Grail was not at that point a Christian emblem, although in Chrétien's version it is said to carry to the ailing king his only sustenance, a single communion wafer. That, as the means of achieving everlasting life, perhaps represents the first step in the Christianization of the Grail's original significance. The sacramental vessel itself, whatever its precise nature was said to be, was a pre-Christian form. In fact the Christianizing of the Grail leaves much the same religious idea, but it goes now by a different name.

Writing a little after Chrétien, probably during the first decade of the thirteenth century, another French poet, Robert de Boron, produced another Grail story. It is he who introduces into the sequence a particular sort of Christianity; and in the style of this some have seen the influences of Gnosticism. The Gnostics were a world-renouncing, enlightenment-seeking cult among the early Christians, and their main contribution to the Grail material, if any, would seem to be a certain sort of mystical symbolism.

Robert de Boron worked from sources different to those used by Chrétien, and in doing so introduced a new theme and a new figure. From Apocryphal writings he drew a story about Joseph of Arimathea, the rich Jew who acquired Christ's body after the crucifixion and buried it. He was also said to acquire the cup used at the Last Supper, in which he collected some drops of blood from the dead body of Christ. The symbolism, in relation to the sacrament and the promise of everlasting life, is impressive; and clearly such a cup would become of high mystical importance.

After a long period of struggle in the Holy Land Joseph set off with a number of followers to seek a more peaceful spot. One of his companions, who eventually becomes the Grail-keeper, Robert names as Bron. He identifies this figure with the one whom we have already met by giving him the title of the Rich Fisher. Bron gains this in the story, somewhat improbably, by catching a fish to be placed on the Grail table. The fish was for the early Christians a symbol for Christ, who is also depicted in the Gospels as concerning himself with fishing, so that Bron is in effect including Christ's presence in the ritual meal which the Grail serves.

The title Fisher King or Rich Fisher, by which the Grail-keeper is consistently known throughout the stories, has not been satisfactorily explained. But it is interesting that at least one Celtic mystical figure –the Irish hero Finn – was visualized as being concerned with fishing, and specifically with one fish, the Salmon of Knowledge, from which he gained the same sort of all-inclusive knowledge as Taliesin drew from the cauldron of Ceridwen. And Arthur himself, Finn's British counterpart in certain roles, had to consult a wise salmon in the tale 'Culhwch and Olwen'. It is interesting that Chrétien should comment that the Grail did not contain a salmon, or other fish, as if it might have done, and as one might well have expected it to in the castle of the Fisher King. It appears too that the Romano-Celtic god Nodens, in his shrine at Lydney, was worshipped at least partly in connection with fishing. And if Bran was (as some suggest) a river-god, then it would be natural for him to develop the role of patron and exemplar of fishermen.

Again in this story of de Boron's there are signs of the early Celtic sources, since the Grail has not only the capacity to provide food in abundance, like the Dagda's cauldron and Bran's miraculous head, but it is able to distinguish between the good and the bad by failing to provide for sinners, like the cauldron mentioned in the list of the 'Treasures of Britain', and like Manannan's cup.

Because de Boron's poem leaves the Grail party moving westward to settle in a distant land, later traditions have used this as a basis for bringing the Grail to Britain. Whereas in the truly original versions the Grail-seeker and the Grail-keeper were both located in Britain, Robert's Joseph sets out with the vessel from the Holy Land; and this origin of the Grail became from then on part of its nature. It has moved a long way, as if by its own accord.

While this progression was taking place in French literature, a similar thing was happening in German. During the early years of the thirteenth century a German poet, Wolfram von Eschenbach, wrote one of the most influential of the Grail works (largely owing to its later influence on Wagner), a long poem which he called, after its protagonist, 'Parzival'. It is probable that his main source (though he seems to have denied it) was Chrétien's 'Perceval', but in the process of translating he made several interesting changes. The Grail is here not a vessel at all. Wolfram states emphatically that it is a stone.

This magic stone possesses the familiar Grail properties. It is able to provide food, for instance, and in this case clothes as well, for a large amount of people. Wolfram's story explains its origin: it comes from the Garden of Eden, and is known as 'lapis exilis'. His source, it appears, was a story about Alexander the Great, in which such a stone appeared. But we cannot avoid being reminded of the 'Black Stone' in the Ka'ba, the central shrine in Mecca, which is still the focal point of the Muslim pilgrimage, the 'Hajj', and which was the object of pilgrimage long before the time of Muhammed. Of this stone too it was said that it came from the earthly Paradise, being brought by Adam on the occasion of the expulsion.

There are magical stones in some abundance in the mythology. Peredur himself makes use of one in that Mabinogion story which contains so many of the later Grail motifs. He combats a monster by holding in his hand a stone which makes him invisible, and which he had been given by a mysterious woman. Owein too, in a story which seems at several points to be related to that of Peredur, holds a stone in his hand and becomes invisible.

One cannot ignore, either, the apparent reference in the Wolfram story to that other magically-providing stone, the 'philosopher's stone' of alchemy, particularly as the German poet uses the Latin word 'lapis' to describe it. This somewhat strengthens the case made by Jung for connecting the Grail themes in general with medieval and Renaissance alchemy, and through alchemical symbolism with psychology. He points, for instance, to what he terms a 'Christ-lapis parallel' in the literature of alchemy, and argues that the symbolism relates to the integration of the self, the unifying of 'that bundle of odds and ends which also calls itself "man" '.

In Wolfram's work Christianity itself has become a major theme: Parzival is engaged in a spiritual as well as a terrestrial expedition. There is nothing really new in this trend; it is based on the idea of the quest, and its symbolic possibilities, and it is in such a context that the Grail stories grew up. In much of Arthurian literature the quest itself is a primary motive, involving the individual's need to prove himself, as we have seen in the case of Owein. The need to prove oneself physically, in combat with giants and monsters and other knights, easily develops into the need to prove oneself morally or spiritually; and that is the true motive force of the Grail search. The Grail story is the Quest of quests.

Some of the basic themes which seem to have lain dormant in de Boron and von Eschenbach are made more explicit in another important – though, from its date in the second half of the thirteenth century, slightly later – French poem, called (after its hero) 'Sone de Nansai'. It is important for its stress on some of the themes which come directly from the original sources: the impotence, through wounding, of the Fisher King, and the barrenness of his realm which resulted from that wounding. No crops are sown, no children born, no animals produce young. And this, the idea of the waste land, is not only one of the earliest of the Grail themes but one which has shown the greatest power of survival into modern times.

It was Jessie L. Weston, in her two books on the Grail legends (*Quest of the Holy Grail* and *From Ritual to Romance*), who set out the theory of the ritualistic origins of some of these themes. Although this cultic theory is now discountenanced – rather, it would seem, because modern thinking finds it somehow distasteful, than because it can be disproved from the evidence – there is one feature of the Weston argument which is of undoubted importance. The belief in the connection of the potency of the king with the kingdom's fertility, which 'Sone de Nansai' makes explicit, finds ample corroboration in Frazer's eclectic accumulation of evidence in *The Golden Bough*; and its symbolic role in psychology is amply demonstrated by Jung. Anthropology and psychology are not the only fields to share an interest in this idea: T. S. Eliot drew the title and many of the themes of his poem 'The Waste Land', as he makes explicit in his notes, directly from Jessie Weston's books.

In between the Perceval-based works and the rather peripheral 'Sone de Nansai', a major development had taken place in the Grail story. The 'Queste del Saint Graal' is the fourth part of the so called 'Vulgate Cycle', which includes the 'Prose Lancelot' and 'La Mort le Roi Artu', and which, as has been mentioned, is the main source for Malory's work and hence for our modern understanding of the Arthurian myths. It is in the 'Queste' that the ultimate Christianization and spiritualization of the Grail themes take place. And it is there that Galahad, the perfect Christian knight, comes into being.

R. S. Loomis has argued for the possibility of deriving the name Galahad, through a series of transcriptions, from an earlier form of the name Gawain: from Galvagin, to Galaain, or thereabouts, and it seems likely that the character was not simply invented, but rather borrowed and adapted from previous mythic figures. Yet Gawain remains present in the stories, and in the 'Queste', in his own right. And (as Loomis recognized) the name 'Galahad' could arise from various biblical instances, one being 'Gilead', which occurs in the Song of Solomon as the name of a mountain, and another being a cairn of stones mentioned in Genesis, chapter 31, which 'Jacob called Galeed'. That a biblical reference is intended by the author of the 'Queste', who apparently invented Galahad, seems almost certain. He is introduced as a descendant (like Christ) of King David, as well as of the Grail-keeper, and throughout his story in the 'Queste' his attributes and emblems mark him as being himself a Christ-figure, a redeemer, playing the same role of saviour in relation to the mysterious enchantment of Britain which Christ played for the whole doomed human race.

Although much about this thinking is once again reminiscent of

Gnosticism, a clearer parallel has been found with Cistercian theology and symbolism, a movement which was powerful at the time of the story's development, following the influence on late-twelfth-century religious thought of St Bernard of Clairvaux, who died in 1153. The movement which St Bernard and his followers set off within the existing Cistercian order favoured a type of asceticism and achievement of salvation through grace which certainly has an affinity with the moral framework and the overt teaching of the 'Queste'.

The 'Queste del Saint Graal' is something of a moral fable. It also contains a great wealth of imagery, much of it suggesting the existence of lost or subconscious explanations. Transformed by Malory, the same story lacks the strong religious current, but it retains the elements of weirdness, of being slightly beyond comprehension.

Malory's great saga of the Grail has a complexity which reflects its multiple origins. By now there are not one or two but a whole set of Grail-seekers – though their adventures show the sort of duplication which arises when the same story becomes attached to different heroes. Many of the themes which have been with us from the start – for instance, the ability of the Grail to serve to everyone the food they most desire, and its dazzling light – remain strong elements in Malory. Some are heightened by the effect of his own distance from their meanings, and images such as the several night sea-journeys undertaken by the seekers, and the death-like comas which the unfitted go through in the presence of the Grail, have all the appearance of having been devised by Jung himself. There is also a robust atmosphere of courtliness and chivalry (though these were certainly in the background in the 'Queste') and great emphasis on the Round Table itself as the context of the beginning of the search.

In a sort of pre-Grail sequence we follow the events leading to the conception of Galahad. Lancelot has come, in the course of his travels, to the castle of King Pelles, where the daughter of the house, Elaine, falls in love with him. The king encourages this, since he has foreknowledge that the result will be Galahad, and that Galahad will 'achieve the Holy Greal'. The consummation of Elaine's infatuation takes place by a trick: Lancelot is led to think, in a shuttered bedroom in the dark, that it is Guenever with whom he is sleeping. The improbability of this episode somehow does not detract from its appeal. Elaine is revealed helpless and naked in the dawn light as he wrenches the window open, and her fear and his moral chagrin for a moment isolate them in timelessness. She 'skipped out of her bed all naked', and begged for mercy. He is moved by her beauty to forgive her, and 'therewith he took her up in his arms, and kissed her, for she was a fair lady'.

It is some time after, but in the same castle, that the Grail makes its appearance. It does so in the presence of the infant Galahad, and appears in much its usual form: carried by a maiden, it brings with it 'all manner of meats and drinks'. Clearly in some way it belongs to the castle, and therefore to King Pelles. And he in his turn is not a newcomer, since he is

Galahad removes the sword from the stone in the river

none other, in origin, than the old British god Beli. Beli, or as the Romanized Celts called him, Belenus, was from the beginning an alternative to Bran. 'Brennius' and 'Belinus' are shown by Geoffrey of Monmouth to be warring rivals, and it is yet another instance of the staying-power of themes that we find him here, as late as Malory, acting as Grail-keeper in place of Bran.

While Galahad grows up Malory turns his attention to Lancelot and to Tristan. The Grail story then begins in earnest, with the feeling of the start of a fresh work. The court is assembled at Camelot when the first of a series of unexpected visitors, a maiden on horseback, comes to demand on behalf of King Pelles that Lancelot should go with her to an abbey in the forest. There they find Galahad, now grown to young manhood, and Lancelot is asked to knight him. A few days later the new knight arrives at Camelot.

The theme of the empty seat had been in the Grail series for some centuries. It occurs at the same time as the special table, as a seat which is awaiting the arrival of the knight who will fulfil the Grail task, in which it is mortally dangerous for anyone but him to sit; a testing seat in accordance with the Grail theme's discriminatory concerns. When the knights sit down at the Round Table to celebrate Pentecost there is, as always, this seat empty: the 'Siege Perilous', Malory calls it, the Seat of Danger. Galahad is brought into the hall by an old man, who sits him in that place of destiny.

This is enough of a test in itself, since he alone survives that audacity. But there is another. A sword stuck in a stone has appeared floating down the river below Camelot – surprising enough in itself – with, on the handle, the instructions that only the best knight in the world, for whom it is destined, can pull it out. When several of them try it and fail, they know that the person referred to must be a newcomer; and Galahad is brought down to the river to try. Like Arthur in the earlier sword test he easily succeeds, proving the sword to be his.

That night the Grail appears in Arthur's hall; a bright light, an atmosphere of favour. They all lose the power of speech in its presence, and are dumb till it has gone. It comes covered with a white cloth: it is not known even now what exactly it is, nor can they see who bears it. 'And there was all the hall fulfilled with good odours, and every knight had such meats and drinks as he loved in this world.'

It is this event that sets off the quest, the last and greatest of the great searches which the Grail, in its long history, has inspired. The knights rise one after another and vow that they will go in search of the Holy Vessel. Arthur himself does not join the company, but all his knights in turn take such a vow. And Arthur foresees that he will from then on be deprived of the glamour of the company of the Round Table at Camelot, bereft, as he says, of 'the fairest fellowship and the truest of knighthood that ever were seen together in any realm of the world'.

The motives of the expedition are at first obscure. It is known that it is Galahad alone who will 'achieve' the Grail. The others set out deliberately on a mission doomed to partial or total failure. Yet they must go. It is as if they find their failure, their imperfection, impossible to believe, or to accept.

We follow them one by one on a course which seems chaotic and endless, and which involves a whole catalogue of bizarre adventures collected from the rich field of British and European story. Gradually the meaning and purpose of the quest is made clear, as the Grail's physical origin – the story of Joseph of Arimathea – is told again by various hermits, and as the symbolic failure of most of the Grail-seekers, and their mysterious setbacks, is shown to be the spiritual function of the search, the testing of sinners and distinguishing of the pure and good which has always been one of the functions of the mystic vessel.

Lancelot in his turn rides into a 'waste land'; and to him (as if out of compassion for his destined failure and forgiveness of the moral weakness which caused it) is given a rare glimpse of the Grail. He had seen it before, we are reminded, in the house of someone who is now (revealing old links) referred to as 'King Pescheour', the Fisher King. It now comes to him in a half-dreaming state, and he sees it heal a sick knight. Because of his sin he is unable to respond to its presence, and remains in a semi-conscious and silent state while the vessel is there. The message is rubbed home: he hears a voice which accuses him of being harder than stone, bitterer than wood. And the words went to his heart, we are told, 'till that he knew wherefore he was called so'.

The failure to make the connection is once again represented as a sort of dumbness, an inability to make the right response when presented with the salience of the Grail: 'And now I see and understand that mine old sin hindereth me and shameth me, so that I had no power to stir nor speak when the holy blood appeared afore me. So thus he sorrowed till it was day, and heard the fowls sing: then somewhat he was comforted.'

The process of self-discovery is still very much at the root of the otherwise mysterious and motiveless search. With yet another fresh beginning Malory shows us Percival undergoing it too. In his case it is perhaps initially (as it was in Chrétien's first version of Percival's story) his failure to react to his mother's plight which inhibits him; but Malory, following the trend of his sources, in the end cites Percival's carnal weakness as his disability. He takes a journey in a mysterious ship, dreams, has his dream explained to him by an old man, and finally, narrowly avoiding seduction, wounds himself symbolically in the thigh.

Returning to Lancelot we find dreams prominently featuring again, and hermits interpreting them, so that the narrative seems almost like the transcript of a course of psychoanalysis. After two dream-tellings by Lancelot we switch to Gawain, only to find him dreaming too. He has not been granted even the test of an adventure, and he realizes that something is operating against him. Another knight with whom he travels, Sir Ector, has also had a dream, and together they come to yet

'The Quest for the Holy Grail', a tapestry based on a painting by Burne-Jones

another hermitage. Sir Ector had dreamt about Sir Lancelot: he was trying to drink at a well, but whenever he stooped towards the water it sank away from him. The two knights, heavy with their ominous dreams, know that the success of the search is not for them. 'And one said to the other: Go we seek that we shall not find.' The next dream-interpreting hermit confirms this. Yet stubbornly they search on.

The Grail does not appear to sinners. The attempt to prove that you are not a sinner is forlorn. Yet human nature refuses to admit even a moral defeat. That is the theme as it is finally set out in Malory. The mystic vessel has preserved to the end its ability to make important personal discriminations. For this purpose the contrast of Galahad is necessary, and however many mysterious sea-journeys Gawain, Bors, Lionel, Lancelot, and Percival go on (and a whole series of them follows the series of dreams), we know that we are ultimately heading for Galahad's goal of Grail Castle.

In the end the sinner-father and the sinless son, Lancelot and Galahad, find themselves alone together in the last of the succession of ships. On reaching land they part, Galahad riding into a forest, while Lancelot gets blown to sea on one more journey. As from the start, this last stage in the development of the idea of the otherworld has, it seems, to be approached across water. Lancelot lands at the back of a castle and comes in due course to a locked room. He knows what is inside, and prays to be allowed to glimpse it again. The door flies open, and though a voice forbids him to enter he sees inside a dazzling light, and the holy vessel on a table. A priest is performing the Mass, but instead of the symbol of Christ's body he has in his hands the body itself. Lancelot is moved to go to him, and enters the chamber. But as he approaches the Grail he is immobilized, and falls down in a coma. He lies between life and death for twenty-four days, and when he wakes he is told that he is in the Castle of Corbenic. That, they tell him, is as near as he will get to finding the Grail. Once more, though, it appears to them at dinner, as it did in the same hall when Lancelot was first there.

Galahad in the meantime rides to Corbenic. King Pelles greets him, knowing the quest is nearly completed. How, we must wonder, can it have taken him so long and given him so many difficulties to come home? A home-coming, though, it clearly is, since the air of resolution is powerfully present in all the subsequent events. Malory winds up the Grail quest with presumably unconscious appropriateness, by reintroducing the symbols which were central to it at its start, in 'Peredur' and in Chrétien's 'conte', and by including with them others which have become added on the journey.

A sick king is brought into their presence. Joseph of Arimathea himself appears to them. A bleeding spear is brought into the hall of the Grail, and with the blood from it Galahad cures the maimed king. They are fed from the Grail with a sacrament 'so sweet that it was marvellous to tell' by Christ himself, who appears out of the vessel in demonstration of the significance of its contents. Galahad is promised the gift of spiritual, in place of bodily, life; and he takes the Grail away from Britain then for ever. In a sort of reversal of de Boron's story he takes it back to the Holy Land, and the vessel and the spear are drawn up to heaven along with Galahad's soul, when he dies there. 'Sithen was there never man so hardy to say that he had seen the Sangreal.'

There is no suggestion in Malory that Joseph brought the Grail at any point to Glastonbury. This persistent and explicit legend stems from a different source, evidently by-passed by Malory. It was mentioned in Robert de Boron's story that the Grail-bearers were going to a distant westward land, which was referred to more specifically at one point as the 'Vaus d'Avaron'. Avalon, we have seen, was a Celtic otherworld which became identified at a certain time with Glastonbury. A more direct connection between the place that Joseph went to and that religious centre is given in another version of the story, a French prose work known as 'Perlesvaus'.

Since 'Perlesvaus' refers to Arthur's burial at Avalon it is concluded that it must have been written after the discovery of the grave, in 1191. The dates attributed to it lie variously between then and 1225. Towards the end of the work what is evidently Glastonbury is mentioned again, with a description of the Tor ('la montaigne de la valee'). This, coupled with the phrase in de Boron's poem, is all the basis there is for a Glastonbury Grail legend. But these hints were later combined with the long-established legend that early Christian missionaries, perhaps some of the disciples of Christ, had built the first church there. Somebody at some point in the early-thirteenth century added the information that one of these disciples was Joseph of Arimathea. The two streams thus converge. A hundred years later it was taken as an established fact that Joseph founded Glastonbury, bringing with him two cruets containing the blood and sweat of Christ; and accordingly his body was then found to be buried at the Abbey site.

R. S. Loomis, who has done a great deal of work on this subject, suggests that Joseph of Arimathea became involved in the whole matter by mistake. The sacred vessel, in his theory, was originally a magic drinking horn, such as that horn of plenty said to belong to Bran in the list of treasures. It is interesting that a magic horn, this time with the Grail's other main property, the ability to distinguish right from wrong, survived even into Malory, where at one point Arthur is sent by his sister Morgan le Faye a horn which will spill the drink of a lady who is not true to her husband, the intention being to reveal the adultery of Guenever and Lancelot. Loomis's argument is that the phrase 'cors benoit' in 'Castle of the sacred horn' came to be understood as 'holy body', which it could also mean. Thus it was taken to refer to the body of Christ, and it was Joseph who owned that. The theory is ingenious and attractive, and certainly some explanation is needed as to why such an unlikely saint should occur in the old myth-cycle of the Grail. For one reason or another, however, it is staunchly held by the tradition and the local lore that Joseph came to Glastonbury.

The version of the legend which might be regarded as the official Glastonbury one is derived from the Abbey records (which admittedly include forgeries), in which the disciples sent by St Philip from Gaul to convert the British are said to be led by St Joseph. He and twelve followers landed in Wales, and (apparently not finding much support) took refuge on the island of 'Ynyswitrin' in Somerset, on 'twelve hides' of land granted by the local king. He there built the original wattle church.

Joseph brought with him, according to some versions, the cup used at the Last Supper, with which Robert de Boron had him moving westwards. But the Abbey records seem to have preferred the two cruets, perhaps because they had to a lesser extent the look of paganism about them. Local lore adds that on their way they rested, once within sight of their destination, on the westerly spur of the Avalonian island. Below

The Holy Thorn in Glastonbury Abbey

was what was to become the sacred ground. Ahead was the emblematic Tor. As a sign and an encouragement to his followers, after their long journey, Joseph stuck into that hillside the staff which he had brought with him from the Holy Land. It sprouted and took root, and from then on blossomed at Christmas in celebration of Christ's birth.

'Crataegus oxyacantha praecox' is, it is thought, rather an illustration of the horticultural abilities of the medieval monks, than the result of a miracle which occurred more than a thousand years ago. It tends to blossom over a period of the winter months, rather than specifically at Christmas. Knowledge of it is recorded only since the sixteenth century, and its veneration as something holy seems to have flourished in the Puritan period. Then the great tree on Wearyall Hill was apparently treated as if it, and the people's attitude to it, represented a lingering cult of tree-worship. As a result the Puritans cut it down, but fortunately this was badly done, and a bit of it lived on.

It was discovered then (perhaps after a lapse of memory from monastic times) that the freak winter-flowering thorn would propagate from cuttings. Indeed it is now obvious that, as a hybrid, it would propagate no other way. Its seeds produce only a common thorn. The origin of it from St Joseph's staff is an embellishment which cannot be traced back beyond the eighteenth century, though it seems likely to have been current locally long before that, but it is far from inconceivable that the first Glastonbury specimen was imported from elsewhere, and took the form of a stick stuck in the ground.

It is suggested by some that a tree-worshipping religious cult lies at the far end of the history of the thorn-tree's fame. If it were so, then it would be consistent that the Abbey's monks should have adapted the pagan cult to a Christian form, as the most effective way of disarming it. In any case the cult, whatever its origins, lingers on. Specimens of Holy Thorn, believed to come into bloom on old Christmas Eve, 5 January, were flourishing in various parts of Britain by the end of the nineteenth century. It has been the custom for some generations now (echoing a gift to the queen of James I) to send the royal family sprays from Glastonbury at Christmas time. And up on Wearyall Hill, beside the spot, marked by a stone slab, where the original tree stood, a suitably wind-contorted successor survives still, dutifully flowering at roughly the right time. Other specimens may be seen in the area of the Abbey ruins and in the garden of the Chalice Well.

Presumably nobody would be more surprised than Joseph of Arimathea to find that he was supposed to have stood at one point of his career on Wearyall Hill. The long process of tradition, with its errors, its assumptions, and its hidden motives, produces some strange results. But from Wearyall Hill, beside the Holy Thorn, one can come to understand the way significance can override contingent fact to become an independent force. St Joseph is a late-arriving, but nevertheless welcome, guest, in this assembly of representatives of a certain set of ideas.

When legend asserts that Glastonbury was a very early seat of Christianity it is almost certainly recognizing something, though only a limited section, of the truth. Glastonbury was sacred early; but probably long before Christian times. Perhaps it was connected, like the Christian religion, with the problem of survival of death. The progress from the mythical cauldron of rebirth, through the rituals of the Castle of Wonders, to the Mass wafer and communion chalice and the resurrected Christ, and the resurrecting powers of his body and blood, is, after all, not a discrete but a continuous succession.

From Wearyall Hill, beside the thorn, one gets a view of the whole of Avalon, and a chance too to consider its implications. There is the visual experience of the Tor, which never fails to give an aesthetic satisfaction not normally obtainable from physical features. It seems indeed to be a natural instance of the effect provided by constructed mounds elsewhere, by, for instance, Silbury Hill, near Avebury, and by the massive pyramids of Mexico and of Egypt: the quality of possessing apparent, but unspecified, significance. The view of the Tor, and the whole field of Avalon below, provides an experience which operates on several plains; the knowledge of the Bronze Age finds under the peat of the surrounding Somerset Levels, the nearby Iron Age villages of the pre-Roman community, the site of the Old Church, and around it the majestic medieval ruins, bringing the whole matter into history.

Selected further reading

There are a great many learned and specialized books on small sections of the large subject of British mythology. For the benefit of anyone wishing to follow up aspects of the matter in a more general way, however, I give below what is far from being a comprehensive bibliography. It is also not just a dutiful recognition of source-works which have been useful to me, but rather more a personal recommendation of books which I have greatly enjoyed.

Firstly, there are three general works each dealing in some detail with one of the main subjects touched on by this book.

On the roots of the traditional material: *Celtic Heritage,* Alwyn and Brinley Rees (Thames & Hudson)
On the archaeology and early history: *Arthur's Britain,* Leslie Alcock (Pelican).
On the literary development of the themes: *Arthurian Literature in the Middle Ages,* ed. R. S. Loomis (Oxford)

The broad subjects dealt with by these three are further subdivided in the literature, and a host of careful and fascinating examinations of the subdivisions support them. The following are among the more accessible:

British myth and early literature
Celtic Mythology, Proinsias Mac Cana (Hamlyn)
Rhiannon, W. J. Gruffydd (University of Wales Press)
The International Popular Tale and Early Welsh Tradition, Kenneth Jackson (University of Wales Press)
Wales and the Arthurian Legend, R. S. Loomis (Hodder & Stoughton)
The Grail, from Celtic Myth to Christian Symbol, R. S. Loomis (University of Wales Press)
The Grail Legend, Emma Jung and Marie-Louise von Franz (Hodder & Stoughton)
The Legend of Merlin, A. O. H. Jarman (University of Wales Press)
The Burning Tree – Poems from the first thousand years of Welsh verse, trans. Gwyn Williams (Faber)
The White Goddess, Robert Graves (Faber)

British pre-history and early history
The Megalith Builders of Western Europe, Glyn Daniel (Pelican)
The Celts, T. G. E. Powell (Thames & Hudson)
The Druids, Nora K. Chadwick (University of Wales Press)
The British Heroic Age, Nora K. Chadwick (University of Wales Press)
From Caesar to Arthur, Geoffrey Ashe (Collins)
The Quest for Arthur's Britain, Geoffrey Ashe (Pall Mall)
King Arthur's Avalon, Geoffrey Ashe (Collins)

The texts

The relevant works of Caesar, Tacitus, Bede and Geoffrey of Monmouth are available in Penguin Classics, as are translations of some of the works of the Arthurian 'Vulgate Cycle', 'The Quest of the Holy Grail' and 'The Death of King Arthur' – and also translations of the Middle English poem 'Sir Gawain and the Green Knight' and of the chronicles of Giraldus Cambrensis. Malory's 'Le Morte d'Arthur' is also now available in this invaluable series. The 'Arthurian Chronicles' of Wace and Layamon are published, in translation, by J. M. Dent. There are several translations of the Mabinogion now available, including again a Penguin Classics one and the highly-respected version by Gwyn Jones and Thomas Jones in the Everyman series.

Unfortunately some of the most important sources, such as the works of Gildas and Nennius, have become extremely rare.

Acknowledgments

Quotations from Welsh poetry in Chapter Six are reprinted by permission of Faber and Faber Ltd from *The Burning Tree: Poems from the First Thousand Years of Welsh Verse* translated by Gwyn Williams.

The Publishers wish to thank the following for their kind permission to use their illustrations.
Aerofilms: pp. 40, 59, 80, 84, 95, 103, 110, 154, 162–3, 165 (right). Barnaby's Picture Library: frontispiece. Bodleian Library, Oxford: pp. 1, 21, 164 (all), 198. Janet and Colin Bord: pp. 8, 12, 16, 20, 26, 36, 44, 46, 61, 151, 165 (left), 172, 179, 183, 187, 216, 231. British Library: p. 71. Peter Clayton: p. 66. Cooper-Bridgeman/Birmingham City Art Gallery: pp. 214–15 (top), 228. Danish National Museum, Copenhagen: p. 206. Giraudon: p. 159. Guildhall Library: p. 121. Robert Harding/Bibliothèque Nationale: pp. 140, 208, 226. Robert Harding/Bodleian Library: pp. 129, 143. Robert Harding/British Library: pp. 98, 174 (right), 190. Robert Harding/British Museum: pp. 112, 120, 136 (both), 145. Robert Harding/Koninklijke Nederlandse Akademie van Wettenschappen, Amsterdam: pp. 104, 105. Robert Harding/Orlandini, Modena: p. 123 (top). Lambeth Palace Library: pp. 68, 161, 174 (left). Mansell Collection: pp. 123 (bottom), 147, 184, 220. National Museum of Wales: pp. 51, 62. Photo Franceschi-Zodiaque/Hamlyn: p. 204. Photoresources: pp. 24, 31, 33, 39, 82, 115. Picturepoint, London: pp. 118, 124, 135, 214–15 (bottom). Radio Times Hulton Picture Library: pp. 76, 77, 202 (left). Jean Roubier/Hamlyn: p. 217. Michael Senior: pp. 19 (both), 54, 73, 93, 101, 117, 133, 134, 168, 213. Edwin Smith: p. 65. Winchester City Council: p. 149.

Chronological tables

Almost all the dates given here are approximate; many are debated. All these tables can do, therefore, is indicate the relative positions of the events.

I The British Heroic Period

AD 350 –

       Saxon invasion of Britain started

375 –

       Magnus Maximus withdrew Roman troops from Britain
400 – Cunedda moved from North Britain to North Wales
       Roman withdrawal completed

425 –

450 – Vortigern permitted Saxon settlements

475 – British defeats
       Campaign of Ambrosius
       Arrival of Cerdic
500 – Battle of Mount Badon
       Check to further Saxon advances

525 – Angles reported to be emigrating from Britain
       Death of Arthur, according to Annales Cambriae

550 – Gildas writing. Kingdoms of Bernicia and Deira founded
       Major British defeats

575 –

       Defeat at Dyrham isolated Wales from south-west Britain

600 – Defeat at Catterick enabled expansion of Northumbria
       Defeat at Chester isolated Wales from North Britain

625 – 'Old Church' at Glastonbury restored by Paulinus

650 –

II Sources and Manuscripts

800 – Nennius

———

950 – Annales Cambriae completed (MS 1100)

——·——

1125 – William of Malmesbury writing

1150 – Geoffrey of Monmouth writing
'Dream of Rhonabwy' compiled. Wace's Arthurian Chronicle
1175 – Caradoc of Llancarvan's 'Life of Gildas'
Chrétien de Troyes writing
1200 – Robert de Boron writing. 'Black Book of Carmarthen'
Layamon's Arthurian Chronicle
Giraldus Cambrensis writing. 'Vulgate Cycle'
1225 – 'Prose Tristan'

1250 –

1275 –

1300 –

1325 – MS of part of Mabinogion

1350 –

1375 –

1400 – First complete MS of Mabinogion

1425 –

1450 –

Malory writing
1475 –

Caxton's printing of Malory
1500 –

Index

mile comment emuuun ctole
on pur deuant la lance qui laigue · ʒ
raal. Et apref renoient hômeo qui

e nule riens nef arefnoient
ne al qui not ne lor fonnoient
aun durement fe muelle
nt ot ueu cele meruelle
a gût talent telenqueire